Round Table

Round Table

The Search for Fellowship
1927-1977

Hugh Barty-King

HEINEMANN: LONDON

William Heinemann Ltd
15 Queen Street, Mayfair, London W1X 8BE

LONDON MELBOURNE TORONTO
JOHANNESBURG AUCKLAND

First published in 1977

SBN 434 04901 8

Photoset, printed and bound
in Great Britain by
REDWOOD BURN LIMITED
Trowbridge & Esher

There can be no question that almost the whole range of voluntary social services, like most of those in local government (but excluding Trade Union activities) are manned and operated for the community as a whole by middle class people, who have both the necessary training in organisation and the requisite sense of responsibility to give up the time and energy to them . . . In short voluntary effort is not only the stuff of self-government but the true social laboratory of the country.

Roy Lewis and Angus Maude,
The English Middle Classes,
London: Phoenix House, 1949

There is no doubt that our prime purpose is the developing of acquaintance. Round Table is the universal introduction overcoming immediately the tedious barriers of formality and convention. But to hold and deepen this acquaintance there must be something more.

Rodney Huggins, President,
National Association of Round Tables
of Great Britain and Ireland, 1975/6

Contents

Illustrations

To Develop Myself

The humble may say 'To respect myself, to develop myself
– this is my true duty in life. An integral and responsible
part of the great system of society, I owe it to society and
to its Author not to degrade or destroy either my body,
mind or instincts. On the contrary I am bound to the best
of my power to give to those parts of my constitution the
highest degree of perfection possible. I am not only to
suppress the evil, but to evoke the good elements in my
nature. And as I respect myself so am I equally bound to
respect others, as they on their part are bound to respect
me.' Hence mutual respect, justice and order, of which
law becomes the written record and guarantee. Self-
respect is the noblest garment with which a man may
clothe himself – the most elevating feeling with which the
mind can be inspired.

Samuel Smiles, *Self-Help*,
London: John Murray, 1859
(Sphere Books, 1968)

Foreword

by HRH The Prince Philip, Duke of Edinburgh, KG, KT, Patron, National Association of Round Tables of Great Britain and Ireland.

There are associations of like-minded people and there are associations of people with a common purpose. Round Table seems to fall between the two. Louis Marchesi's 'Aims' were quite clear, but he did not propose a programme for achieving them. On the other hand Round Table is more than a social club because the 'Aims' demand positive action of some kind. It is this betwixt and between situation which seems to account for the tremendous success of Round Table in terms of membership and comradeship and the often disappointing response to highly ambitious plans of action and involvement.

The difficulty is the criterion of achievement. Is it more meritorious that people should be impressed by some grand achievement by Round Table as a whole, as if it were an army winning a great battle? Or is it more significant that each individual member should have become just that much better as a civilised human being through his contact with Round Table? Corporate service is one thing, individual standards, involvement and behaviour is quite something else and, as far as the community is concerned, even more important in the long run.

This book does more than relate the bare details of the history of Round Table. Running through it is the recurring clash between corporate ambitions and individual performance.

As a history it is full of interest for those who want to know how it all came about. As a commentary it should prove most valuable to those who are looking to the future of Round Table.

Philip

Acknowledgements

The author takes this opportunity of thanking the very large number of people who took the time and trouble to talk or write to him about the aspect of Round Table of which they had special knowledge, starting with present and past Tablers at Norwich: Bernard Durrant, Arthur Colman, E. G. Cooper, John Watson, James Hanly, Walter Clabburn, Tom Tillett, Tony Sims, Nick Butcher, Robin Pett, Barry Leveton; A. P. Cooper, one time Norwich Publicity Officer; Eric Fowler; Mr Laird, manager of Moss Bros which now occupies Langford's Restaurant site; A. B. Atherton of the *Eastern Daily Press* library; Philip Hepworth, Divisional Librarian; F. D. Sayer, County Local Studies Librarian. At Portsmouth: James Kenroy, Bryan Buswell, Keith Buswell, A. E. Hooper, John Freeston, Leslie Palmer, Eric Ward. Others who responded with written information: W. A. Johnson, Wolverhampton Table no. 17; Michael Arthur and James Bennett, Doncaster Table no. 7; M. J. D. Drake, Bournemouth Table no. 5; David Adams, City of London Table no. 13; J. S. Pike, Liverpool Table no. 8; D. J. Kirkham, Scarborough Table no. 88; Richard Austen, Area 35, Forest of Arden; David Lawson, Orkney Table no. 1125; Philip Pomeroy, Kingston Table no. 19; Derek Hirst, Halifax Table no. 14; Bruce Rees, Cardiff Table no. 26 – and particularly John Addyman, Weald of Kent Table no. 583, Michael Hancock, Hastings Table no. 21 and William Martin, Royal Tunbridge Wells Table no. 195 who gave him hospitality. He is grateful for the written information from T. J. Marchesi of

Southampton, Mark's nephew; Brian Whiteaker, one time editor of *News & Views*; Keith Pascall in Nairobi; Bryan Coker, General Secretary Wo-Co; E. H. Dale, Rotary Club of Halifax; Roger Levy, ex-editor of *The Rotary Wheel*; and to those he was able to talk to at length – Vic Collins, General Secretary of Round Table from 1951 to 1969; Cyril Marsh; Peter Marchesi, Mark's son; John Jackson, Secretary, Rotary International in Great Britain and Ireland; Mrs Pinder, RIBI Records; Mrs Marjorie Ogilby-Webb, Head of Intelligence Department, National Council of Social Service.

Outside Rotary/Round Table he acknowledges the information received from Group Captain G. C. Brunner, Executive Officer, British Junior Chamber; G. S. Ecclestone, Secretary, General Synod, Board for Social Responsibility; Miss Barbara Ferryman, South-East Regional Office, Toc H; Vice-Admiral D. H. Mason, Warden, St George's House, Windsor Castle.

Above all he gratefully acknowledges the help and co-operation throughout the whole exercise of Denis Tizard, General Secretary, and Rodney Huggins, President 1975/6.

Acknowledgement of permission to reproduce illustration material is made to the following: Peter Marchesi, A. P. Cooper, John Seymour Photography, D. G. Dine, Derek Hirst, Eastern Evening News, G. F. Shiffner, David Ian, Studio D (Blackpool), Berrow's Newspapers Ltd. Worcester.

The author would also like to thank Kenneth Adams for permission to quote from *Exploring the Business Ethic* and Messrs. Constable & Co. Ltd. for permission to quote from *Middletown* by Robert S. Lynd and Helen Merrell.

Introduction

It was Emerson who said that the 'use of history is to give value to the present hour and its duty'.

The most frequent question posed by outsiders to members of our movement must be 'What is Round Table?' It is very difficult to answer adequately.

For that reason alone, quite apart from its fascinating content, this excellent history book is a boon, for it acquaints the reader with all that has gone before; and for those involved in Tabling it will imbue them with a greater understanding of the standards set by their predecessors.

A Golden Jubilee is a landmark in the affairs of any organisation. The only previous official history book of Round Table was written by John Creasey in 1953 for the twenty-fifth anniversary. He was a member of Bournemouth Table for many years and a Rotarian. He was also a world-renowned author of crime stories.

The author of this book is Hugh Barty-King who, unlike his predecessor, had no inside knowledge of Round Table, Rotary or any other similar organisation before commencing his work. After considerable experience in all aspects of Press and Public Relations with various Government Information Services, London Transport and a commercial post, in 1970 he became a full-time industrial and social historian undertaking various commissions for individual bodies.

We are truly indebted to Mr Barty-King for the preparation of this book over a period of some eighteen months. It has involved untold labour and research. But this is no 'normal' history. He could have merely recorded events and ideas chronologically without comment. Fortunately and without any previous brief from those who liaised with him, Mr Barty-King has pulled no punches. He has been truthful and challenging.

Those who are involved with Round Table share a common experience through personal contact. This has been denied the author, and for that reason he has not moderated his criticism where he thinks it is appropriate.

There will be those who disagree with the author's views, but the essential ingredient of Round Table is the discussion of provocative ideals. Since all members must retire at forty, the movement is a 'living' and ever-changing body but still depends upon the traditions built up over fifty years to formulate policies at local, Area, and National levels.

The reader will learn how Table was conceived, developed and changed over the years and how it has grown. Further changes are certain in the future, but since the movement's foundation there has always been a determination to achieve and maintain its Aims and Objects.

Round Table must never become a job of work, but a pastime to be enjoyed in hours of relaxation as a relief from the daily toil. If it imposes too great demands and interferes with work and home, it exceeds its basic functions.

The vast amount of energy, enterprise and ingenuity shown by Tablers generally are qualities admired by outsiders. This History does not illustrate this aspect, probably through lack of available space.

Those who are or have been members must feel that the final justification of Round Table is the firm friendships it produces founded on community involvement and happy fellowship. Long may it prosper.

Roderick Burtt, President RTBI 1976/7
Rodney Huggins, President RTBI 1975/6

Meeting a Need

I

The Twenty Year Prologue
1907-1927

Out of Rotary, into Round Table

To create a setting in which good-fellowship can flourish and lead perchance to friendship has been a human activity since the beginning of time. In the days when a community twenty miles from home was foreign territory, the forester who journeyed to it to axe the nearby wood found a home from home in the local branch of his Friendly Society which dispensed friendliness in surroundings which quickly lost their strangeness, and he found himself no more a stranger. Participation in familiar rituals, recognition of known regalia, at once made him feel 'one of the family'. These Ancient Orders – not in fact of any great antiquity (the Foresters were founded in 1843 and the Buffaloes some years earlier) – were a 19th-century manifestation of man's desire for association which is what this story is about, to relieve the anxiety of loneliness, to counterbalance the strain of isolated concentration on business and domestic responsibilities, or positively pursued for its own peculiar pleasures.

A situation like war threw people together into trenches, submarines and bombers and, from an unwanted association and the ordeal of shared dangers, emerged a comradeship which few of them would have sought but all came to cherish. Relationships thus forged were the most lasting of all. Camaraderie such as this needed no entrepreneur, but its perpetuation in changed circumstances required a certain degree of stage management, of the kind provided for instance by Toc H. But it could be kindled artificially among a like-minded section of the community with a potential for Comradeship waiting to be stimulated by Acquaintanceship. Britain has never lacked clubs, societies, brotherhoods, associations and unions where this all-important first step can be taken.

Societies formed as pressure groups to promote causes like Temperance, Automobilism or the abolition of slavery had head offices and often regional branches, but the latter were hardly 'clubs' in the proper sense of the word. It was the groups who met for the pleasure of each other's company – for companionship in other words – who are the ancestors of the subject of this story.

Proprietors of London coffee-houses in the seventeenth and eighteenth centuries offered people an opportunity of walking into their premises, surrendering to the spirit of goodwill to be found inside and leaving his cares behind him. He had but to climb the stair, pay his penny to the woman on the landing and become a member of a 'club' for that day. The other members were those who had entered before him and those who were to follow. Behind the door of Hain's and Waghorn's, Jonathan's and Monger's lay instant belonging. Everybody was a nobody of unknown quantity meeting on the level of common membership of the human race, each electing to come from the dark of the street into the light and warmth and hum of the room whose occupants took no notice of his entrance but within minutes absorbed him so he became part of it.

> Now being enter'd, there's no needing
> Of complements or gentile breeding,
> For you may seat you anywhere,
> There's no respect of persons there;

The Twenty Year Prologue

Then comes the Coffee Man to greet you,
With welcome Sir, let me entreat you
To tell you what you'll please to have,
For I'm your humble, humble slave.

'I was yesterday in a coffee house not far from the Royal Exchange', wrote Joseph Addison in *The Spectator* (no. 568) fifty years after An Eye and Ear Witness wrote the lines quoted above from *The Character of a Coffee-House* in 1665, 'There I observed three persons in close conference over a pipe of tobacco; upon which, having filled one for my own use, I lighted it at the little wax-candle that stood before them; and after having thrown in two or three whiffs amongst them, sat down and made one of the company. I need not tell my reader that lighting a man's pipe at the same candle is looked upon among other brother-smokers as an overture to conversation and friendship.' Addison spent most of his life trying to demonstrate the futility of bitterness in political wrangling and persuading his contemporaries to co-exist with 'good nature, compassion and humanity'. In his *Spectator* pieces he tried to show how arguments which a generation earlier had been resolved by sword and cudgel need 'proceed no further than to an agreeable raillery' between friends. It was the coffee-house which provided the ideal setting for good-humoured controversy in which opponents could differ and yet remain friends, where the other person's point of view could be heard, understood, supported or tolerated without rancour. No 'Coffee House Movement' was needed to promote the coffee-drinking habit in England, no administrative organisation to maintain the chain of houses in which were cultivated the arts of toleration and moderation which had such a civilising effect on the social and political scene. There were no rules, no ritual, for these casual entrants from the street; but as their visits changed from casual to regular – because of nearness to their counting house, the number of people they met in the same line of business, the type of bulletins and newsheets kept – they tended to form a clique

who no longer wished to extend the range of their acquaintanceship, and persuaded the proprietor to hire them a
room of their own to which was admitted only those who had
subscribed – a Subscription Room. At this point the regulars-
turned-subscribers would draw up rules defining the type of
person they wished to associate with at the coffee-house, state
the qualifications of membership and the circumstances which
would move them to admonish, and then expel, existing subscribers.

Members of a Subscription Room had no corporate axe to
grind, and would not seek to express a corporate opinion on any
question of the day. In the City of London commanders of East
India Company ships tended to gather in the Jerusalem Coffee
House, stock jobbers in Jonathan's, insurance brokers in
Lloyd's. In fashionable Westminster in the 1760s those who supported the Government led by the Duke of Newcastle but
inspired by Chatham, which favoured the prosecution of the
Seven Years War against France, joined White's; those who
opposed Chatham and the war joined Boodle's. The clubs
which grew from the coffee-house Subscription Rooms and the
West End societies began by attracting people with a common interest, but as time went on the latter was forgotten and
their *raison d'être* became purely social, the meeting place of a
group of people with no common bond other than vaguely
Left or Right and an ability to pay the high subscription, with
no 'message', no outward looking activity of any kind. They
provided amenities for gambling, gossiping, eating and drinking in the company of other men, away from the womenfolk
and the responsibilities of home and business.

A main satisfaction of belonging to one of these West End
clubs or a similar patrician establishment in Edinburgh, Manchester, Bristol and other big cities, was its exclusivity, the
fact that there was only one Carlton Club, one Devonshire
Club. A gentleman did not relish having to wear an emblem
in his buttonhole which proclaimed his membership of a
movement, on the sight of which strangers could accost him

and claim acquaintance. But the middle class had no such inhibitions; by their reckoning membership of a publicly recognised movement conferred a status on them which lifted them above the working class and were proud that everyone should know it.

In the United States of America, with a mainly immigrant population of mixed nationalities who had left home on the other side of the Atlantic, class divisions were less defined, and the compulsion to demonstrate one's worthiness in voluntary exile was very strong — wanting to be recognised as part of the best element in society, financially stable and educated. Thrift and self-improvement prompted many an association, as much in the United States as in Britain. At the end of the 19th century America was dotted with 'study clubs' with objects like 'mutual mental improvement', achieved by listening to talks. From 1878 onwards bankers, lawyers, doctors, merchants, wrote and discussed papers on subjects like 'What is Mind?', 'Patriotism versus Dishonesty', 'The Relation of Science to Morality'. A group calling themselves The Ethical Society began with twenty-nine members of all denominations and political creeds who met every week in the 1890s to discuss Questions of the Day. 'Any plan the purpose of which is to benefit our city morally or humanity collectively may be placed before the society. It is hoped that public sentiment will be aroused so that any and all palpable evils with which we are afflicted may be eradicated, because the best element in society demands it.'

Clubs such as these had begun to lose some of their initial impetus when in 1905 an attorney called Paul Harris formed a club in Chicago in which he hoped members might not only become acquainted with each other as individuals but as followers of their various professions or callings. So that it should be representative of all classes and types of business men, its membership was limited to one representative of a given classification. The original meetings were held in rotation at the different places of business of the members. At the third meeting of the Chicago group, Paul Harris put up several suggestions for a name for the club, including 'Chicago Civic Club', and one of them was 'Rotary'. This was selected and members became known as Rotarians. Later, weekly meetings were held in rotation at hotels and restaurants over lunch, when talks were given designed to educate members in the business of the other members. Other clubs were formed on similar lines outside Chicago.

'In its early years,' wrote C. R. Hewitt in *Towards My Neighbour*, 'Rotary was a loosely knit association of clubs in which, after a good weekly lunch and much conviviality, members stood up and testified to the increased business their membership brought them. They named fellow-Rotarians to whom they had sold this or from whom they had bought that. They filled in forms which showed what business had been transacted as a consequence of membership, and from these forms there were compiled periodical returns showing what "Rotary" had done for its members.'

This was not what Harris had intended. As Hewitt points out, he was dismayed to find that his 'fellowship' club of business men whose main justification, as he saw it, was that it should do something for the community from which it drew its members, had become a self-help organisation with a 'transactions register'. When Harris started to found other clubs on a better basis in New York, San Francisco and elsewhere, the Chicago club's opposition was strenuous. But by 1910 there were sixteen clubs, mainly due to the efforts of Chesley R. Perry who became Secretary of the National Association of Rotary Clubs of America formed in that year.

Thus for the first years there was no idea of 'Rotary' as a philosophy or a body of doctrine which it was the duty of the Rotarian to propagate. This notion developed from the work of a committee appointed just before the convention they held in Portland in 1911 which drafted and submitted what was known as the Rotary Platform. This document concluded with the two 'slogans' – 'Service is the basis of all business' and 'He profits most who serves best'.

From then on 'Rotary' had a philosophy. The Objects of Rotary were six-fold, to encourage and foster

(1) The ideal of SERVICE as the basis of all worthy enterprise.
(2) High ethical standards in business and professions.
(3) The application of the ideal of service by every Rotarian to his personal, business and community life.
(4) The development of acquaintance as an opportunity for service.
(5) The recognition of the worthiness of all useful occupations and the dignifying by each Rotarian of his occupation as an opportunity to serve society.
(6) The advancement of understanding, goodwill and international peace through a world fellowship of business and professional men united in the ideal of service.

The Ideal of Service – the ancient 'golden rule' – was adopted as Rotary's new *raison d'être*, and in the coming years it dominated the whole movement. 'The lowly Nazarene who walked by the Sea of Galilee was the first Rotarian' a speaker was to tell his audience at an American Rotary luncheon some years later. 'The second great Rotarian was that other man who probably did more for mankind than any other man that ever lived, Abraham Lincoln. Could we spread the Rotary spirit to the coal mines, this ideal of service would end all strikes. Could it be spread to the governments of Europe, France would not have entered the Ruhr, Germany would have paid. You remember what President Harding said at a Rotary convention in St Louis: "If I could plant a Rotary club in every city and hamlet in this country, I would then rest assured that our ideals of freedom would be safe and civilisation would progress".'

Many 'civic clubs' were to be formed in America, each competing with the other and constituting a hierarchy in the prestige membership bestowed, but Rotary, the oldest and the most coveted of the civic clubs, represented the aims of all of them. The six characteristics of the newly organised chain of clubs

were the unique basis of membership, the singleness of classification, the compulsory attendance rule, the intensively developed friendships, the activities for the betterment of the
individual member and his business, the requirement that members strive for the betterment of the craft corresponding to their
classification, particularly stressing higher standards of business
practice.

In their book *Middletown, A Study in American Culture*, the distinguished American authors Robert S. Lynd and Helen Merrell
Lynd describe the Rotary chemistry at work.

'These chosen head men, meeting in the best hotel or at the
country club stand about chatting, observing the ritual of calling each other by first names until the president shouts "Let's
go!", whereupon all crowd into the dining room. No blessing
precedes this meal as in the other civic clubs, as the classification
of ministers is unrepresented in Rotary. Eating proceeds vigor-
ously at the long tables for about half an hour. Ten minutes of
lusty song follows – the latest Broadway hits and Rotary songs
chief among them.'

The words of the song written on a roller were hung on the
wall for all to follow. They then heard a talk either from one of
their own members on his own classification, from the head of
local charity, a local teacher or librarian, or an outside speaker
routed to them from headquarters. As part of their civic work
they would invite honour students of high school to a lunch,
give a Christmas party for needy boys, run an annual Easter Egg
Hunt in the local park for local children, give a radio to an
orphans' home, secure summer camps for the YMCA.

Robert Lynd saw the reason for the dominance of Rotary
clubs over the other civic clubs in America at this time as lying,
not in their lunches and speeches or their charity work, but in
the 'instrumental and symbolic character of their organisation'.
'Not only are they a business asset, but by their use of first names,
sending of flowers on birthdays, and similar devices, they tend
to re-create in part an informal social intercourse becoming
increasingly rare in this wary urban civilisation. "It isn't

Edward T. Smith, President of So and So Corporation you're addressing," said a speaker at Rotary, "but a *human being*, the eternal boy in Ed." "It makes you realise *the other fellow hasn't got horns on* and ain't out to get you," said another. These genial, bantering masters of the local group find here some freedom from isolation and competition, even from responsibility, in the sense of solidarity which Rotary bestows.'

'Challenging him and his world at no point,' was Robert Lynd's summing up of his assessment of American Rotary at this time, 'often proving of actual cash value in his business, membership in these clubs may serve a Middletown business man as the symbolic repository of his ideals, assuring him that, by virtue of carrying on his business and being a member of his club, his daily life in the group is its own justification and has dignity and importance. This combination of utilitarianism and idealism, linked with social prestige and informal friendliness, is almost irresistible.'

The Rotary idea was taken up in Canada (Winnipeg), and in 1911 it found expression in Britain. In February of that year an American, previously a member of the Rotary Club of San Francisco, Stuart Morrow, who had settled in Ireland, formed a Rotary Club in Dublin and in July he had formed another in Belfast. In 1912, on the strength of there being Rotary Clubs in the United States, Canada and Great Britain, the organisation in Chicago was re-named the International Association of Rotary Clubs. In Britain more clubs were formed in Manchester, Glasgow, Edinburgh, Birmingham, Liverpool and London, and before the Great War broke out in 1914 these had formed themselves into the autonomous British Association of Rotary Clubs. Some of these were affiliated to the International Association, but in 1916 the clubs in Britain adopted a new constitution requiring that all of them should be affiliated both to Rotary International and British Rotary.

Just after the outbreak of World War 1 an organisation was

formed in America which had aims and objects more similar to Rotary than those of any other civic club, but differed by being in the hands of younger men. This was the Young Men's Progressive Civic Association which Henry Giessenbier formed in St Louis, Missouri, in 1915, later becoming known as Junior Citizens or JCs. The watchword which brought the 'Jaycees', as everyone called them, growing support and remarkably quick expansion was 'service to humanity is the best work of life'. By 1920 the Jaycees had become a national body, and JC had come to stand not for Junior Citizen but Junior Chamber (of Commerce). In that year the Junior Chambers of Commerce of twenty-nine American cities met for a convention in St Louis.

During the war (in June 1917) Mervyn Jones, a young American insurance man, brought under one organisation a number of independent groups of business and professional men as The International Association of Lions Clubs ('The Lions') with headquarters in Chicago. This was a federation of all such clubs in America at that time, and in October 1917 twenty-five of them held a first convention at Dallas, Texas, at which 'Lions International' adopted the motto 'We Serve'. Their name, they said, symbolised strength, activity, courage, integrity. They had no rule limiting the age of those who joined, and membership was by invitation.

In Europe, where all the fighting was taking place, a modest 'Services Club' was founded in 1915 in Poperinge, some six miles west of Ypres, in a house rented from a Belgian, which the army chaplain who was installed as 'host', Rev. P. B. (Tubby) Clayton, named Talbot House as a tribute to Neville Talbot, senior chaplain of 6th Division in the Ypres section, and as a memorial to his younger brother Gilbert who had been killed in July. Talbot House became known as T.H. which army signallers spelt out as 'Toc H', and as such the service club at Poperinge, and the worldwide organisation which developed from it, has ever since been known. When the fighting ended Toc H was re-established in a flat in Red Lion Square, London, and subsequent hostels in London and other towns in England were dubbed Toc H Mark 1, Toc H Mark 2 etc. But from this first post-war attempt to keep alive the spirit which had inspired the Talbot House of Poperinge, grew a very much wider conception of its role. After the granting of a royal charter in 1922, the first Toc H Central Council declared what they regarded to be the essential nature of the movement in a document which became known as the Main Resolution. This stated the ends of Toc H, stemming from a strictly Christian premiss, to be 'to think fairly, to love widely, to witness humbly, to build bravely'. In Britain the growing branches and groups were organised into Districts and Areas, and in the 1920s isolated members began to spread the gospel in Argentina, South Africa, Malaya and other overseas countries. Soon the Lamp of Maintenance, the famous Toc H symbol, had been lit in Australia, a first festival had been held in Calcutta, the first overseas Mark opened in Winnipeg, the first Belgian group formed in Ypres, German groups in Hamburg and Berlin, others in New Zealand and Ceylon. The office of 'Jobmaster' was created to lead each branch, and give force and direction to the voluntary service to which members pledged themselves.

'Some say that Toc H stands for fellowship, others that it stands for service,' writes Geoffrey Martin in *Vista, The First Fifty Years of Toc H.* 'Both definitions are incomplete in themselves, though in any one branch the emphasis may be strongly upon one or the other. Nevertheless it is our belief that a fellowship content to be passive, well-intended but undirected, falls sadly short of that urge to practise the Christian faith in everyday life which from the first has stirred men to action. Hence the Jobmaster, the man who knows something of the human needs around him and tries to meet them by drawing upon the active goodwill of his members. Anyone who delves a little into the present social services will quickly discover that many of them have one feature in common. They were started by small groups of compassionate people who could not contemplate some particular aspect of poverty or injustice without trying to cure it. So it is that here and there, in various parts of the world, Toc H men and women have accepted this tradition as a matter of course, and by drawing on the willingness of friends have themselves started some form of organised voluntary service which has quickly grown beyond their strength to maintain alone.'

The formal aims of the Main Resolution have been expanded in Toc H's own Fact Sheet which states that members try 'to build friendship across the barriers that divide man from man; to give personal service; to find their own convictions while always being willing to listen to the views of others; to work for the building of that better world which has been called the Kingdom of God'. Sixty years later the message was conceived as being that society needed compassion more than competition – and the spirit of humour which knows that if life is serious it is also fun.

The young Prince of Wales, who had seen for himself the horror of the fighting on the Western Front, was an early patron of Toc H, and at their second Birthday Festival in December 1922 he lit the lamps of forty new branches at London's Guildhall.

The material ravages of the war in France gave rise to a group of volunteers of differing nationalities pooling their efforts to restore the war-damaged village of Verdun. They were brought together in 1920 by one Pierre Ceresole who looked for a constructive alternative to war. From his work grew Service Civil International of which a branch was formed in Britain under the name 'International Voluntary Service'. SCI teams worked in disaster areas all over the world. Every year they held – and still hold – international work camps in which teams of SCI volunteers meet, learn to understand each other and together construct a playground, for instance, work with mentally handicapped children, or run a holiday scheme.

It was in 1920 too that Harold A. Rogers, a young man in his twenties returning to his home in Canada after fighting in World War 1, invited a few of his acquaintances to dinner at a cafe in Hamilton, Ontario and fired them with his enthusiasm for forming a club which, like Toc H, would attempt to perpetuate the spirit of comradeship he had experienced in the army. Hal Rogers's father was a Rotarian and gave him every encouragement. Hal called his group The Kinsmen Club, and when one of the original members moved to Montreal he formed another there. Others went to Winnipeg and Vancouver, and Kinsmen Clubs came into being there too. Within four years, by this unaided chain reaction, there were Kinsmen Clubs across the length and breadth of Canada, the first all-Canadian 'service' club, and open to young men between the ages of twenty-one and forty. Its policy was 'to fulfil the community's greatest need'.

Two years after Hal Rogers had established the first Kinsmen Clubs in Canada, a young American from Auburn in California, Paul Claiburne, had a similar idea. Having been the guest of his boss at several Rotary lunches, he enlisted the help of his local Chamber of Commerce and in 1922 rallied several of his like-minded young friends to form in Sacramento, capital of California, a group he called 'The 20-30 Club', specifically for young business men within that age group. He adopted as the club's emblem an hour glass from which only a small amount of sand had run out. Rotary encouraged what they regarded as a welcome adoption of their idea by a section of the community to whom membership of a Rotary Club was virtually excluded due to the rule that the single member filling each classification had to be old enough to be in a senior executive position, and because of his seniority able to influence his colleagues and subordinates and others in his own line of business or profession. It was generally considered that anyone under forty would not qualify. So 20-30 would cater for 'Rotary types' who would be debarred from joining a Rotary club by their age. With help from Rotary headquarters a second 20-30 Club was formed at Stockton, California, in 1924; a third came into being at San Bernardino shortly afterwards, and in 1926 a fourth appeared in San Francisco. By 1926 Claiburne considered the seven clubs then in existence justified the formation of an Association of 20-

30 Clubs. A pledge to undertake service to the community was a condition of membership, and the raising of funds for charitable purposes featured strongly in all early activities.

While the 20-30 Clubs at this time were confined to the western states of California and Nevada, a similar fraternity of young business men was established on the east coast with the first 'Active Club' being formed in February 1922 in Aberdeen, Washington State. With no conscious effort to expand, within three years four other Active Clubs had come into being, and later clubs were formed in other parts of America including 20-30 territory in California and Kinsmen territory in Canada. A headquarters was set up in Spokane, Washington. Active differed from 20-30 and Kinsmen however in that it sought to train its members in salesmanship and public speaking, teaching them the rules of debate and keeping order at meetings.

In Britain the formation of new Rotary clubs under the aegis of the British Association of Rotary Clubs continued apace, and when the war ended in 1918 the responsibility for the new formations was regionalised, with Great Britain and Ireland being divided into six Districts. In Britain this American movement acquired – or rather was given – a peculiarly British flavour. For members of the British Rotary clubs, good-fellowship – or 'fellowship' as the Americans confusingly insisted on calling it – was not enough. By the mid-1920s Rotary clubs in Britain had evolved without conscious direction into 'important centres of social endeavour', to use C. R. Hewitt's phrase. When the significance of this came to be appreciated at British headquarters it was decided that all should be made aware that this was the true Rotary line, and a campaign was launched to educate members in what the powers-to-be wanted them to regard as the official Objects. They began by re-drafting Paul Hariss's original Objects given on page 9 in the following form:

The Objects of Rotary are to encourage and foster the ideal of service as a basis of worthy enterprise and, in particular, to encourage and foster:

1. The development of acquaintance as an opportunity for service.
2. High ethical standards in business and professions; the recognition of the worthiness of all useful occupations; and the dignifying by each Rotarian of his occupation as an opportunity to serve society.
3. The application of the ideal of service by every Rotarian to his personal, business and community life.
4. The advancement of international understanding, goodwill and peace through a world fellowship of business and professional men united in the ideal of service.

In a headquarters pamphlet entitled *Synopsis of Rotary*, these aims were further elaborated.

The public understands and appreciates a movement which stands definitely and solidly for some specific line of action, and it is naturally apt to discount and to ignore one which, by setting itself to unite all men of goodwill and of good endeavour, thereby debars itself in the main from any corporative declaration other than one in favour of certain abstract principles of conduct. And the danger will always necessarily be, of course, one which is inherent in abstractions and generalisations: that they lack the touchstone of reality and of real trial, and are apt to provide a phylactery* for the hypocrite and a cloak for the self-complacent.

This campaign was designed to impose a pattern of behaviour on all British Rotary clubs. 'The primary emphasis at this time was on "vocational service"; the builder, the dentist, the baker could best serve the community by being a good builder, dentist or baker, charging "fair" prices and shunning "unethical" practices.' (C. R. Hewitt)

A leading part in this campaign was taken by the head of the well-known confectionery firm, Sydney Pascall, who showed

* An ostentatious display of piety or rectitude (OED).

17

himself an enthusiastic advocate of ethical codes of the kind that had been compiled by Rotary International based on American experience. He drew up similar codes suited to British business life, but annual conference rejected them as too rigid and replaced them with a more loosely expressed pamphlet giving a Rotarian the guide lines on ethical behaviour expected from him in his business or profession. The pamphlet *Vocational Service* published by Rotary International Britain and Ireland (RIBI) which the British Association had now become, laid down broad principles for a Rotarian's relationship with his employers, his competitors, his suppliers, customers and clients. It went as far as urging profit-sharing schemes, production committees, training in industry, and the setting of exemplary standards in wages and conditions of employment; eschewed bribery, business with firms of ill-repute, and cut-price competition and commended the honouring of contracts and the prompt settlement of accounts. It extolled efficiency, truth in advertising and the aesthetic importance of good premises, manufactures and printing, and condemned any tendency in Rotarians to seek or expect special business favours from each other. Of interest to this story was the section which urged co-operation with, and fair dealing for, employees, and *paid special regard to the bewilderment of the young*.

The 'service of youth' was perhaps British Rotary's main community interest. In 1923 the president of the Weston-super-Mare club proposed the founding of a seaside holiday home for 'under-privileged' (i.e. poor) boys, and in the years that followed established hundreds of Boys' Clubs, took a lively interest in the National Society for the Prevention of Cruelty to Children, and organised talks on 'vocational guidance' to boys leaving school at centres of the Young Men's Christian Association (founded in 1844).

But it is not 'youths' (aged twelve to eighteen) with which this story is concerned, but 'young men' (aged eighteen to forty), and for the latter British Rotary had nothing to offer either at the giving or receiving end, in spite, as Hewitt pointed out, of their awareness of the fact that 'as may be judged from the story of the University settlements [like Toynbee Hall and the Oxford House in Bethnal Green] it is from men much younger than forty that society has usually drawn its most fervent enthusiasts for social service'. British Rotary's shortcoming in this respect was deplored by Archdeacon Lafone, President of Kendal Rotary Club, when he told District 13's first conference at the beginning of 1926 that in view of there now being in British universities so many coloured men 'I feel there ought to be something in the way of a junior Rotary Club which would enable men of prospective qualifications to mix with one another. White men should be able to meet together, before they are actually in business, with these black and yellow men, who will then be able to take back to their own countries the fact that they met on equal terms in their Rotary clubs with the men of this country'.

It was unlikely that the archdeacon had heard of the American organisation which came near to being just that, the 20-30 Club, or the similar associations of Kinsmen Clubs and Active Clubs. Nor will news of these groups have filtered through the pavement grill to the airless confines of the basement Smoke Room (Men Only) of Langford's Restaurant in London Street, Norwich, where the contemporary version of the coffee-house regular – young clerks, office managers, shop assistants and apprentices – congregated every morning for elevenses in the form of a steaming hot cup of coffee provided by the genial, chubby young proprietor with the difficult name, Louis Marchesi.

At twenty-seven Marchesi (pronounced Markaysey) claimed to be the youngest member of Norwich Rotary Club and indeed of any Rotary Club in Britain (which was probably far from the truth, but it became part of the legend). A frequent topic of conversation stimulated by the proprietor at these regular morning sessions of young business men from the nearby shops and offices was this very matter of What was Rotary doing for Young Men? It was true that Marchesi had managed to become a member of the Norwich club under the classification 'catering'. Once admitted, he was presumably on a par with any other member. Officially there was no discrimination between young and older members, but in fact the majority of over-50s dominated the proceedings. As a young man still in his twenties Louis felt unused and unheard.

The Marchesi family belonged to Poschiavo, a village in the Swiss canton of Grigioni near the Italian frontier, where they quarried marble, while owning vineyards at nearby Madonna di Tirano. In the middle of the nineteenth century the head of the family was Luigi Marchesi who ran the village blacksmith shop, flour mill and general store. His brother Frederico was lured to Australia by stories of the gold rush which failed to make him the fortune he dreamed of but won him an Australian wife and enough money to buy a passage to England. The couple settled in Broadstairs where they opened a café-restaurant-hotel on the esplanade overlooking the harbour. King Edward VII had once planted a fig tree in its garden, though what it commemorated nobody could remember.

Luigi's youngest son, Prospero, stayed at home to carry on the family blacksmith shop, but the eldest of his six sons, Erminio, went to England to help his uncle Frederick at Broadstairs. One of Erminio's brothers joined him (Alfonso?), and the business became known as 'Marchesi Brothers' (which still flourishes under that name in Broadstairs to-day). In 1896 the twenty-five-year-old Erminio Marchesi fell in love with one of the waitresses, a twenty-one-year-old Irish girl called Jane Danaher (born in Southsea) whom he married in Fulham in November. The following year the two brothers, having gained the experience they needed, decided to move on. Alfonso went to Scotland, where he disappears from this story, and Erminio, for reasons best known to himself, chose Norwich (which, it should be said for the benefit of non-English readers, is pronounced 'Norritch').

Norwich is one of the finest and oldest cities in England. In the Middle Ages, as the centre for exporting wool to northern Europe, it had been second only to London in size and prestige. In the sixteenth century it gave refuge to large numbers of Walloons and Flemings, and to the Protestants who went by the name of Huguenots who had fled from religious persecution in their native France. By 1587 Norwich counted 5,000 'strangers' among its population, a third of the whole.

The young Erminio Marchesi acquired premises in Prince of Wales Road, Norwich, and opened them as a café-restaurant. Soon afterwards his wife presented him with his first born, a son whose name was given in the canton's Libretto di Famiglia as Erminio Gugliemo Luigi (19 January 1898). But he was always known as Louis. As a small boy he attended St Stephen's Catholic primary school at Norwich.

In 1908 Erminio sent his two eldest sons, the ten-year-old Louis and the eight-year-old Terence, to Switzerland to live for a year with his mother at Poschiavo (his father had died). Here the boys attended the village school, learnt to speak the local dialect, Puschiavin, and helped Uncle Prospero at the forge. In the holidays Louis earned pocket money as a baggage boy at Poschiavo's hotel, Croce Bianca.

After his year in Switzerland, Louis returned to England to attend the City of Norwich School where no one could pronounce his name correctly, and Marcheesey inevitably became 'Cheesey'. One of his schoolfellows was W. G. Quinton who plays a part in this story, and another Walter Clabburn who in 1975 well remembered the exploits of his ever-resourceful boyhood friend.

Erminio Marchesi's family in Norwich grew to three sons and two daughters. By the time Margaret, their last child, was born in 1915, Erminio had opened a second restaurant in Cromer on the north Norfolk coast, and with the aid of his sisters, who had come to join him from Switzerland, a second Norwich café at 5 Davey Place off the market square.

When war broke out in 1914 Louis was sixteen, had finished his schooling and was helping his father. He and Wally Clabburn enrolled in the British Red Cross and were given the job of helping with the reception of the wounded soldiers who arrived direct from the Channel ports at Norwich's Thorpe railway station. This was voluntary work of course, and their services were often required in working hours. Wally had to get his employer's permission; Louis just told dad. In 1976 Wally had happy memories of how, after a spell of Red Cross work, the two of them would repair to the family café and refresh themselves with coffee and cream cakes – 'believe me, there have never been cream pastries like them since those days!'

Many of his school friends were joining the army, and in 1915, not to be out of it, Louis misquoted his age and became a boy soldier in the 25th Battalion, the Middlesex Regiment. Here 'Pudding' Marchesi became a popular character – always ready to do a turn in the regimental concert party or draw funny cartoons in the regimental magazine. But he showed he was far from the softie these activities might indicate by becoming the regimental tennis and boxing champion. He went with the battalion to Mesopotamia. He trained as a wireless telegraphist, and as W/T operators were hard to come by his sergeant refused to allow him to volunteer for front line duties. But after a quick perusal of King's Regulations regarding his rights as a private in the army of King George, he confidently stepped out of the ranks at his CO's inspection one morning to make a personal complaint – which must have needed considerable nerve. He was placed under open arrest, as the procedure which his action had set in motion demanded, and the next day he was marched before his commanding officer who asked him what he had to complain about. Not being allowed to risk his life in the firing line? A commendable offer, but the officer supported his sergeant and permission to go up front was withheld. Any other request? What about my being considered for a commission? The answer was a dusty – or rather a sandy – one.

After a short leave at home away from the wilds of Mesopotamia, he embarked with the regiment for India. But his troopship, the *Tynderius*, was blown up off Cape Agulhas in South Africa and he was picked up by the hospital ship *Oxfordshire* after twelve hours in an open boat and landed at Cape Town. He spent five months recuperating from injuries at Wynberg convalescent camp near Durban. When he was fit enough he went to Hong Kong and thence to India where he contracted malignant malaria and spent most of the time in hospital. He was still there when peace came in 1918. When he eventually returned to Norwich a seasoned campaigner of twenty, as a Swiss national (as well as a British national, for the Marchesi family had retained dual nationality) he had to report to the local police station as an alien. On the first few occasions it appealed to his sense of fun to report in his British army uniform.

The following year his father sent him to Switzerland for a thorough training in the hotel business. As a hotel trainee he played many roles, including that of a porter at the Bahnhof Hotel in Zurich. Returning to Norwich in 1921 he borrowed £2,000 from his father and bought no. 77 Prince of Wales Road, a few houses further up the road from his father's café, and ran this as another Marchesi restaurant. He made such a success of it, he was able to pay his father back within a year. He too became adept at making pastries, and for the people of Norwich a visit to one of the three Marchesi café-restaurants was a rare treat after four years of wartime austerity.

Leisure-time activities in Norwich got into their stride once again in the twenties and the number of local clubs and societies proliferated. The Ancient Order of Druids, the Ancient Order of Foresters, the Independent Order of Oddfellows, the Independent Order of Rechabites, the Royal Ancient Order of Buffaloes had active branches in Norwich; there was an Ex-Servicemen's Club, the British Legion, the Naval and Marine Association, the Fellowship of Freedom and Reform, the Norwich and Norfolk Traders Association, the General

Traders Association, Caley's Recreation Association, the Church of England's Young Men's Society, Toc H; and for those middle-class gents who considered themselves a cut above such groups there were the City Club, the Gladstone Club, the Norfolk Club, the Norfolk and Norwich Club, the Norwich Masonic Club.

No ritual or subscription however was required to become a regular of the Smoke Room at Langford's in London Street which Erminio and Louis Marchesi acquired and the latter managed when Christina Langford, who had had it since the 1870s, died in 1925. It had a well-connected outdoor catering operation by which it organised hunt ball suppers, wedding receptions and the like in other people's houses which Louis took over and expanded. Next door was a rival business offering much the same kind of service, Lambert's London Oriental Café, first opened in 1903 which until 1960 was an all-male preserve, and only closed in 1975.

Each of these latter-day coffee-houses had their set of regulars. At Lambert's as well as Langford's no doubt world-beating notions were hatched, visions dreamed, ideals paraded and vows abjured. But in the cosy *ambiente* created by Louis Marchesi where the world of the street outside and the temporarily abandoned office and shop were easily forgotten – the leather couches, the oak beams, the ingle-nook fireplace, the low-powered artificial lights (vestiges of all of which can still be seen in what is now Moss Brothers' storeroom), to say nothing of the drowsy effects of the coffee, the Chelsea buns and the air heavy with the fumes of Ogden's Mixture – here the dreams of Neville Coe, Billy Quinton et al, inspired by the infectiously enthusiastic Marchesi, *came true*.

One of the notions Louis Marchesi had harboured ever since 1914 when, as a lad of sixteen, he had found himself being given the responsibility of helping with the reception of wounded soldiers at Thorpe station, was how greatly *all* young men would benefit from a similar experience – building up self-confidence and finding that older men were ready to trust them to do a job without supervision – but of course in circumstances other than war. He believed that many young men would share with him the satisfaction to be derived from not being patronised, from being treated as someone capable of making a contribution to a project beyond a robot-like carrying out of orders. This depended on both younger and older possessing an awareness which he believed could be cultivated. It required a mental effort directed at bridging the gulf between the outlook of the older man who had passed further downstream (whose memory of what it had been like in the upper reaches had been overlaid), and that of the younger man who received false impressions of what it was like to be over forty. The bridge building would have to be initiated simultaneously from both sides of the gulf. The older must come to understand it was not precocious to want to be needed; the younger to appreciate the worth of junior status and be content with it.

Louis Marchesi's own experiences between 1914 and 1918 made him an unusually mature young man. They made it easy for him to become the Mr Looking-Both-Ways in the centre of the bridge supporting the spans reaching out from each side of the gulf.

Was it all that difficult a mental exercise for an older man to Do As He Would Have Wanted To Have Been Done By as a younger man? Was a flight of imagination back to the other side of the gulf to re-experience the outlook from the standpoint of the younger man he once was, wounding to his *amour propre*, weak, unmanly, un-English?

If some saw it in this light, the Irish-Swiss Louis Marchesi had no such qualms. He was hardly an intellectual, but he had imagination and considerable *simpatia* for others' stresses and wild ambitions. He was the first to offer encouragement whenever he saw an opportunity. One of his early projects was to form a junior section for the sons of Norwich master bakers, and he started bakery classes at the Old Crooks Place School. He took into his kitchens at Langford's some of the seventeen-year-old 'delinquents' whom no one else would employ to help them readjust themselves. He took boxing classes at Norwich Lads Club. There was no Junior Chamber of Commerce in Norwich on the Henry Giessenbier pattern – the first British Junior Chamber had been formed on the other side of The Wash at Lincoln in 1925 – but if there had been Marchesi would have been a founder member. To reconcile the thinking of the older with the younger, to give young men confidence in their formative stages and help them become aware of their responsibilities beyond their immediate circle and take their part in the community as Junior Citizens, became his life mission.

He had been ruminating on younger–older men relations for so long that when it came to his turn to read a paper, as all members had to do, to the Norwich Rotary Club, it was this theme which was the burden of his talk, linked to what his fellow Rotarians were expecting to hear, a description of the job of his classification, catering.

Whether it was merely the journalistic cliché with which the reporter who covered the Rotarian lunch every week always introduced his piece, however impromptu the delivery or the occasion, the detailed report of Louis Marchesi's address in the *Eastern Daily Press* of Thursday, 23 September 1926, began with the sentence: '"Youth and Business" was the subject of a paper read by Mr Louis Marchesi at the weekly luncheon of the Norwich Rotary Club held on Wednesday at the Royal Hotel, the president Dr Pope in the chair.' Perhaps to the reporter every talk was 'a paper'. But the story arose that this talk was completely unpremeditated, and that the number of the seat at which Marchesi was sitting was drawn out of a hat as the member to give the talk in place of the booked speaker who had failed to turn up. This event in itself might have proved worthy of a news item, along with the fact that Marchesi's talk was given on the spur of the moment – unless the report was submitted each week by the honorary secretary who would have wished to cover up the error of the regular speaker's non-appearance, which was probably his fault. But the report looks too lengthy and too professional for that.

Be that as it may, many years later Marchesi told a reporter in Pretoria: 'I was the youngest member of the Norwich Rotary Club and had at short notice to speak on a subject about which I could claim to have the most experience. They all expected me to speak on catering. Instead I told them they had all forgotten what it was like to be a young business man of twenty-nine.'

He began by telling them that he did not believe a young man made a better job of his business than his father, since age, judgement, and experience would always tell. It was up to young men to emulate their seniors, and then, when they had caught up to them, to try still further to improve upon methods of business. A great responsibility rested upon employers for the ultimate fashioning of useful productive citizens. A youngster valued very highly encouragement and appreciation from his employer, and doted upon being allowed to execute some little duty off his own bat. If he realised that his superiors in business had eyes to see him raise his cap and acknowledge it when off duty, he felt that he was something on the firm, not a mere cog in the wheel, and when he felt that, better service to the firm resulted. A sense of *noblesse oblige* was created in him. That kind of recognition appealed far more than a small rise and the cold shoulder; it cemented a bond higher than a financial advantage, and showed a recognition of the man within the worker and the employer. The desire to do a thing well for the sake of turning out a good piece of work was the spirit that animated a truly successful man, and this could be created only by putting responsibility on the man or youth.

Could not young business men in various trades be induced to meet once a month and express their ideas for an hour or two in a club of their own? If the idea could be developed he would be delighted to place at their disposal a room where they could discuss their individual ideas and problems, eschewing politics, in a spirit of comradeship and helpfulness, with an occasional address by a Rotarian. He would like to see the formation of such a body of youths, irrespective of social status or creed, just out to do their best to make things better by understanding each other's difficulties.

As regards the young man with the spirit of very high adventure and a corresponding low supply of funds and opportunity, why not devote that adventurous spirit to acquiring the funds and making the opportunity? Or was that too old-fashioned an idea for the modern young man? Was not business a great adventure? He found it so even in Norwich. Would not business supply funds for a youth who could not find adventure at home and who really wanted it? Of course it would, especially to a British young man.

Youngsters passed through several stages before finally deciding how they could best exercise their energies and capabilities. He had met young men who were thoroughly fed up with the job selected for them by their seniors, with the best intentions, weary of waiting for promotion, and with the door of opportunity closed to them. In business there was colour and opportunity and every chance for the poor adventurous young man. Given a good straightforward education, common sense, honesty of purpose, and the will to make good, he could carve success and round off and pad the sharp corners himself; moreover he would really enjoy the doing of it and make himself a potential helper in assisting others by providing employment by the furtherance of his enterprises.

The career of a confectioner and caterer held out splendid opportunities to a youth who was prepared to face hard work, and to master the trade. A thoroughly practical training that demanded close personal attention to details was essential and then, after about ten years, a man ought to be able to start business on his own account in a small way. The youngster who intended to follow this trade would have to sacrifice one or two things. His work would be heaviest when others were playing; night work would often be his portion.

He ended his talk by outlining the training to be undergone.

When Marchesi sat down, Dr Pope, the president, said the

speaker had shown them that catering was really a scientific profession requiring very great training. It was a curious thing that in England we seemed to be ashamed of this business; it seemed to be considered *infra dig.*, and wherever we went we found that foreigners monopolised it. There was wanted in Norwich a spirit of enterprise in the catering business.

W. Lincolne Sutton, president of Norwich Rotary Club, fifty-five-year-old Norfolk and Norwich City Analyst, said he hoped the club would not lose sight of the suggestion that it should get in touch with the young business men of Norwich. Hugh Ramage said the spirit of stay-at-home was very strong in Norfolk. So many young people seemed to think they could get into business and earn their living without a struggle, but one could not progress without a struggle. J. Hanly, chairman of the Juvenile Employment Committee, said his committee were being continually faced with the difficulty of finding work for young fellows of eighteen who had got into blind-alley employments. There was no great spirit of adventure among them, and they did not take kindly to the idea of going to a new country. Probably their parents had a good deal to do with this.

Encouraged by the spontaneous reaction of the president of Norwich Rotary to his somewhat ragged suggestions for a club for young business men in the town, Louis Marchesi invited three Rotary friends of around his own age to come for a chat at his other restaurant at 32 Prince of Wales Road on 22 November (1926). In the minutes of this meeting headed 'The Proposed Young Business and Professional Mens Club' W. Smith who was in the chair, H. Ramage, L. Luthorn and Marchesi himself were all referred to as 'Rotarian Marchesi' etc. He had asked Rotarian L. H. Buckingham to come but he sent a letter of apology.

'Rotarian Marchesi authorised the proposition for forming a Club and the rules suggested to govern it.' This was the first minute and it indicated that Marchesi had been mulling over possible rules, but unfortunately they have not survived.

But, details apart, there is no doubt they were from the start couched in Rotary language and forged in the Rotary mould. They were concerned with defining who were eligible for active membership (young men from each trade and profession between the age of eighteen and forty) and honorary membership, the method of election, circumstances demanding 'cessation' of membership, the corporate structure of annually elected 'officers', the subscriptions and entrance fees, how and when ordinary annual and special meetings were to be held, the submission of annual reports and accounts.

The next minute removed all doubt about the proposed club's relationship with the senior organisation: 'In the course of the discussion that ensued emphasis was laid on the desirability of the Rotary Club guiding the proposed Club's progress.'

'A letter from Rotarian Udall was read offering the use of a room at the Y.M.C.A. for six months free of charge. The offer of a Rotarian to cover the cost of hiring Suckling Hall for Club Meetings for six months was also considered.'

The secretary (Marchesi) was instructed to forward to a Dr Claridge (brother of the editor of the *Eastern Daily Press*?) who was secretary of the Service Committee of the Norwich Rotary Club, what is referred to in the minutes as 'the sub committee report' together with a copy of the proposed rules and suggestions. Whether this was a sub-committee of Norwich Rotary's Service Committee (and thus convened by it) and the meeting of November 22 at 32 Prince of Wales Road was a meeting of this sub-committee, is not clear. It may have been a sub-committee of the 'committee' created by Louis Marchesi.

To whomever it was beholden, this 'sub committee' reported as follows:

1. They consider the forming of a club for Young Business and Professional Men a practical proposition and recommend that a strong committee be formed by the co-option of the following Rotarians to your sub-committee: Messrs. C. W. Collinson, E. H. Coe, H. Duncan, Quinton Gurney, R. G. Pilch, G. Poverind, H. Read, and E. G.

Smith to give effect to it with full power to act.

2. A definite connection be maintained between the proposed Club and Norwich Rotary Club.

3. The objects and suggested rules for the proposed Club (copies attached) are recommended to the augmented committee for further consideration.

4. Your sub-committee consider the proposed Club should and could be eventually self-supporting.

5. They further recommend that the club meet on neutral ground. Suckling Hall is recommended.

'Objects' had now been added to 'Rules' – it is significant they were secondary – but regrettably the copies of the suggested objects which accompanied this report became detached, and have not survived. It would be interesting to know to what extent, if any, they varied in their drafting from the Objects which were finally adopted and have remained unchanged, except for an addition, to the present day;* but it is fairly safe to assume that Marchesi's first draft was the one which subsisted. In writing them in his room on the upper floors of Langford's which was the Marchesi home with entrance from no. 6 Opie Street, he will have had a copy of the Objects of British Rotary in front of him. These, it is worth recalling at this stage, were as follows:

1. The development of acquaintance as an opportunity of service.

2. High ethical standards in business and professions; the recognition of the worthiness of all useful occupations; and the dignifying by each Rotarian of his occupation as an opportunity to serve society.

3. The application of the ideal of service by every Rotarian to his personal, business and community life.

4. The advancement of international understanding, goodwill and peace through a world fellowship of business and professional men united in the ideal of service.

* The latest of many attempts to re-draft the Objects was made in 1976.

31

Marchesi's draft for his club will have resembled what it is known they finally became, though (C), as will be seen later, began life in a different form.

OBJECTS

(A) To develop the acquaintance of Young Men through the medium of their various occupations.

(B) To emphasise the fact that one's calling offers an excellent medium of service to the community.

(C) To cultivate the highest ideals in business, professional and civic traditions.

(D) To recognise the worthiness of all legitimate occupations and to dignify each his own by precept and example.

(E) To further the above objects by meetings, lectures, discussions, and other activities.

It was only later that the misleading word 'Aims' was tagged on to 'Objects' – misleading because Round Table had no aim in the sense that the Anti-Slavery Society was formed with the aim of abolishing slavery, only a purpose or *raison d'être*. The phrase 'Aims and Objects' led many to look for an aim where none existed.

Walter Smith chaired a second meeting at 32 Prince of Wales Road on 4 January 1927 at which none of the eight young men who attended were referred to as Rotarians. William Lincolne Sutton who as well as being president of Norwich Rotary had once been president of the Norwich Science Gossip Club which had been founded in 1870 (and closed in 1934), had been invited but was unable to attend. Hugh Ramage was there again, and Louis Marchesi as secretary to the 'augmented committee' (which presumably this was) said the meeting had been called to enable gentlemen who had volunteered in the matter of the proposed club to meet members of the sub-committee who had had the matter in hand so far, to forward suggestions to 'the council' for this body to consider at their earliest convenience. It is not clear of what body these 'sub-committee', 'committee', 'augmented committee' and 'council' were part, but obviously many minds were at work on the form the Proposed Club should take; and at this meeting A. C. Plumstead, a leading engineer in the town, proposed that at least two Rotarians be included in the Committee.

'Various suggestions were given for the name of the proposed club' – but no hint is given of any of them. Seventy-seven-year-old W. G. Chastney, a founder member of Table no. 1 who attended these early meetings, recollected in 1976: 'As regards the name, many suggestions were made; one bright boy said, "Sitting round this table and not being able to find a suitable name seems ridiculous". Brains were working hard and this remark – "Round the Table" – produced the answer.' But at this stage it was only one of many possibilities.

The suggested objects and rules were amended, and the subscription fixed at 12s 6d a year instead of the 15s 'hitherto considered' (but not minuted at the last meeting). Archie Plumstead preferred the 15s, but he was overruled. The meeting considered, and amended, a draft letter to Rotarians 'to enlist their help in obtaining recruits to the Club'. It seems that a General Meeting was held on 29 December 1926, since a 'proposition arrived at' in the course of it was referred to in the minutes of the meeting of 4 January, but no report of this is available. The next meeting was fixed for 11 January at Prince of Wales Road, but this was not minuted.

This concern about the post-war industrial and business scene by a group of young business men in Norwich was reflected in, and presumably to some extent prompted by, the anxieties of Stanley Baldwin's Conservative Government in the same direction. The United States had just completed a fifth year of unbroken prosperity, but Britain's unsheltered industries, exposed to the full blast of foreign competition, had just finished five years of the most intense depression they had ever had – and the coal stoppage and the general strike had completely shattered their hopes of 1926 being a year of recovery. Instead, it had been, in the words of the *Times Trade Review* of 1 February 1927, 'the blackest of black years'. Production of steel had been the lowest for thirty years and of pig iron the smallest for seventy-six years; 123 million tons of coal had been lost, costing the coal companies £20 million. In 1925 Britain imported 6,000 tons of coal costing £11,000; in 1926 twenty million tons costing £43 million. The year 1926 had seen an adverse trade balance of £465,400,000, the largest since 1919. 'Industrial strife on an unprecedented scale set back the clock of economic progress in terms of overseas trade by three years.'

The year 1927 opened in industrial peace but, as the Annual Register observed, it was a peace of exhaustion based on fear of disturbing the existing equilibrium. From every quarter came voices for the need for goodwill between employers and employed as an indispensable condition for restoring Britain's trade to its former pre-eminence. Everywhere there was talk of the need for 'a new spirit in industry' – a *better* spirit.

'Never again' was the cry, as it had been in 1918. Memories of the Great War were still very fresh – Allied military control in Germany only ceased in January 1927 – but the spirit of the trenches, and the sense of the 'we're-all-in-it-together' classless comradeship which it engendered, were evaporating fast. To meet employers' insistence that the government *do something* to see that never again would there occur what the Chancellor of the Exchequer, Winston Churchill, described as 'last year's shocking breakdown in our island's civilisation', the government promised to amend trade union legislation to make a General Strike illegal – the Trade Disputes and Trade Unions Bill which J. R. Clynes, for the Labour Opposition, described as a deliberate act of class hostility. But the government realised something more positive was required to cure Britain's industrial malaise, and invited the industrialist Sir Arthur Balfour to head a Committee on Industry and Commerce to diagnose the trouble and prescribe remedies. This committee issued its first reports at the end of 1926, and in February 1927 came its third report on 'Factors in Industrial and Commercial Efficiency'.

The lengthy summary of its recommendations printed in the *Times* of 16 February 1927 will have been a topic of animated discussion that morning among Arthur Colman, E. G. Cooper, Louis Marchesi and others in the Smoke Room at Langford's. In particular they would have been delighted at the Balfour Report's conclusion.

'It is a matter of supreme necessity in this period of rapid and insistent flux and transformation,' it asserted, 'to maintain unimpaired the qualities of initiative and flexibility of temperament, the power of readjustment and adaptation, and the capacity for free and willing co-operation among all the partners in production and distribution. Any waning of these powers can only mean an increasing rigidity and ossification of economic structure and a progressive enfeeblement of its vitality for which no measures of external support or defensive organisation can compensate. There is no need for pessimism in this matter if the situation is faced with courage and an open mind.'

'In addition to the economic problems which British trade had to face before the war, the vast disturbance and impoverishment caused by that catastrophe dealt a staggering, and for the time a numbing, blow at industry and commerce; and manufacturers are now carrying, and for many years must carry, a very heavy, though it is to be hoped diminishing, load, not only of public charges but of other burdens incidental to, and calculated to retard, the progress of recuperation. Nevertheless, it cannot be doubted that in British industry there lies latent a great power of energetic co-operation and response to changing conditions. But it needs the exercise of the highest qualities of imaginative leadership and of loyal good will to evoke and mobilise this reserve power and direct it to the common benefit.'

It must have been heartening for those who were planning the formation of Round Table in Norwich to hear a government committee echoing their own thoughts in so forthright a way and at so pregnant a moment in their planning. Though sponsored by the Right, the report had an un-typical Conservative flavour. Louis Marchesi and his friends were aware of the potentially divisive nature of 'politics', but in this critical year of 1927 no one calling himself a business or professional man could ignore affairs of a state which claimed to be 'running the economy', and inevitably these provided the richest stimulant to the 'fellowship' which meeting together fomented. Sheering away from the rigid and conventional attitudes of Conservative or Labour, they could have respectably admitted admiration for the views of the mounting numbers who felt a party standing midway between Toryism and Socialism was not merely desirable but absolutely necessary for the welfare of the nation. Liberalism attracted a body of moderate, balanced opinion of the kind with which many who were attracted to the Objects of Round Table would probably have liked to have been associated; and many young businessmen of 1926 and 1927 would have felt more at home in the Liberal Party, now reviving under Sir Herbert Samuel and Lloyd George, than in the parties of government and opposition both of which seemed at this time to be accepting the class war as a permanent feature of British industrial and political life, in a way no 'Tabler' could ever tolerate.

Some of the Smoke Room regulars at London Street may have attended the meeting in Norwich on 19 February 1927 at which Tory MP Sir Herbert Nield had told delegates of Conservative and Unionist Clubs of Norfolk, Suffolk, Cambridgeshire and Huntingdonshire that there was never a time when it was more necessary for Conservatives to instruct their more indolent fellows in the science of politics, and nodded their heads in agreement. Many of them will have been members of these clubs whom Nield declared could do more good than any other agency in combating the virus of Socialism. There were too many soft-soapy and sentimental people about, he said, and it was the duty of their clubs to fight these people and get the country back to sanity.

The Conservative Party and its county clubs doubtless had a

part to play in reinvigorating Britain's industrial life, but the sort of clubs which Louis Marchesi saw spreading all over Britain were not designed to fight anyone but rather to attempt the more difficult and subtle role of building bridgeheads of understanding among all involved in industry and business, and making conflict outmoded and unnecessary.

Two days after Nield's call to battle there opened at the White City in Shepherd's Bush, London, and at Castle Bromwich in Birmingham, 'an excellent corrective to national pessimism in the matter of trade', the British Industries Fair. The idea of a BIF had been mooted in 1915 and this was the thirteenth. It was hailed by the Lord Mayor of Birmingham as 'the harbinger of industrial revival bringing in its train stability, freedom from disputes and a happier condition of things for manufacturers and the public. . . . Any notion that the country is done for will be dissipated by an inspection of the exhibits at Castle Bromwich.'

That evening (21 February 1927) Edward Prince of Wales (motto, 'I Serve') was principal guest at a dinner given by the government in honour of the BIF at the Mansion House in London, with Sir Philip Cunliffe-Lister MP, President of the Board of Trade, in the chair. The Prince made the principal speech of the evening and he had to wait twenty minutes before delivering it to suit the timing of the British Broadcasting Corporation – it had taken over from the British Broadcasting Company on 1 January – who regarded what he had to say of such significance that they were transmitting it to the nation over the wireless. The meal ended early, so to fill in the time His Royal Highness suggested circulating a golden goblet of mulled wine as a loving cup.

Those in Norwich with a crystal set, and maybe a one-valve bright emitter amplifier, who donned their headphones at half past nine that evening and turned the dial of their variometer to where they could hear 2LO, in the expectation of hearing support for their views from the thirty-three-year-old, liberal-minded heir to the throne, were not disappointed. From his attack on the industrial and business Establishment of the day and his call to them to re-think their antiquated methods and face the fact that the pre-war world had gone for ever, they knew he was on their wavelength.

In the previous year (1926), said the Prince, a cloud had hung over them but it had burst and now the outlook was brighter. Manufacturers and traders were looking forward to 1927 with a different spirit and in most cases a cheerful spirit, which after all was half the battle. Enterprise and enthusiasm were the qualities needed at the present time and, he might add, imagination. The present situation called for determined effort to make good the ground lost in 1926.

'Our original industrial development, which dates back a whole century, naturally produced a whole multiplicity of individual plants, and to-day the survival of these necessitates sometimes domestic and even international associations. To deal with these new conditions it would seem that industries must federate more, and by collective action explore and defend their collective interests. This, I think it will be agreed, justifies the best brains being used for the common interest, and here I think lies a great opportunity for younger men in industry to spread a new industrial gospel. Young men should surely have greater opportunity and, if anyone says they lack experience, surely this could be counterbalanced by saying that they lack bias and prejudice.'

He went on to advocate more standardisation 'even though it might involve the sinking of that personal pride sometimes bound up with adherence to traditional methods, possibly a little out of date, or to the sinking of individual caprice'. They must not lose sight of maintaining a high standard of living for the British people; large earnings could only come from large production. 'We must be ready to modify our traditional conservatism and cherished procedure where necessary, whether it be the privileges of the employers or the practice of the workers, when the common good demands it.'

Unorthodox talk of this kind was not the normal fare for those who gathered at the bidding of the Lord Mayor in the

heart of the City of London. But this was no orthodox prince.*
He had already identified himself with many of the pressing
social issues of the day, especially the re-absorption of the men
who had fought in the war into industry, and had co-operated
on unemployment matters with the new National Council for
Social Service which had been created in 1919 to bring together
statutory and voluntary agencies to prevent overlapping.

Such problems, continued the Prince to his listeners at the
banquet and on the wireless, had been examined by Sir Arthur
Balfour's committee whose report had been issued the week
before. It showed that British businessmen were alive to the
problems of the day, but it also showed there was room for improvement. 'I recommend it to all who wish to get out of a
groove (laughter) and develop business on modern lines.'

It was the only laugh that evening.

'We Britishers think we are very efficient and we are at the
head of the world in lots of things, but to keep in the van we
must be conscious of that very valuable thing, the knowledge
that we learn something new every day. To put it in three
words, we must learn to adopt, to adapt and to improve.'

The outlook for the future provided grounds for reasoned
optimism; what was needed was a new spirit of co-operation
and good will between employer and employed in which the
human element was the keynote. The human element played an
enormous part in industrial relations. It was necessary to study
that human element as regards the workers as it was to study
new methods, new ideas and new organisation. The status of
being consulted where appropriate and where possible was the
natural aspiration among the workers. The tendency in that
direction must help forward the improved relations in industry
which had developed since or from the experience of 1926.

The following day, accompanied by his private secretary and
Sir Philip Cunliffe-Lister, he went by train to Atherstone to in-
spect some of his race horses, then took the wheel of his motor

* He reigned briefly as King Edward VIII and on his abdication in 1936 became the
Duke of Windsor. He died in 1973.

car to drive over to Castle Bromwich Hall for lunch with the Dowager Countess of Bradford, thence to the Midlands section of the BIF at Castle Bromwich.

The *Birmingham Post* devoted two columns to an account of the Prince's visit, which however contained no report of any speech – the Castle Bromwich section had been opened the day before. 'The tour was rapidly carried through,' it stated, but 'the Prince found time to express appreciation of the wonderful enterprise and skill of British manufacturers.' He then left to visit Highbury and Uffculme hospitals. John Creasey in his 1953 history of Round Table quotes HRH as saying at the Birmingham BIF of 1927: 'The young business and professional men of this country must get together round the table, adopt methods that have proved so sound in the past, adapt them to the changing needs of the times, and whenever possible, improve them.' Creasey got it from a typed document, prepared for a History of Table no. 1 headed 'Events Leading up to the formation of Norwich Round Table', stating that the Prince used it at the *opening* of the 1927 Birmingham BIF. But in fact the occasion on which the Prince pronounced his new motto for industry* was the Mansion House banquet of Monday, 21 February 1927, and this was the very day on which also the pioneers met in the great hall of Suckling House 'to establish a Club for Young Business and Professional Men of Norwich'.

Suckling House was an old building in the centre of Norwich built between 1345 and 1348, but whose connection with the Suckling family dated from Robert Suckling who was sheriff of Norwich in 1564. This was the meeting for which all the preliminary gatherings of the 'augmented committee' had been preparing. William Lincolne Sutton was there this time, and Walter Smith was again in the chair. There were nine of them altogether including Marchesi as secretary. The Worshipful Sheriff of Norwich, G. Poverind, wrote to regret his inability to attend. Marchesi outlined the history of the idea of the club

---

* This may have been delivered in this expanded form and contracted by the *Times* reporter to the words in his report in spite of being given as a direct quotation.

and thanked those Rotarians present for their support. He told them how he considered 'the changing business and professional customs of the day' made the establishment of such a club desirable, and at once declared the motive which was central to his purpose and was to remain so for the rest of his life.

'He felt the ideals of the Club would assist members in their future dealings with their seniors and with their subordinates.'

Then Rotarian Lincolne Sutton made his point. He 'dwelt on the ideals of service and explained the Rotary ideals and how they would apply to members of the proposed Club. He described how Rotary objects assisted in one's business or profession.'

When P. V. F. Homes asked if it were possible to incorporate the words Norwich and Guild in the title of the club, Walter Smith said no name had yet been definitely fixed; it was up to members to suggest names to a committee which would be appointed for choosing one. At this point 'Mr W. Lincolne Sutton put it as a suggestion that some such name as The Round Table be adopted'. Whether it was really Marchesi's idea, and he had asked Sutton to suggest it on the grounds that the other Rotarians would more readily accept it, is a matter of conjecture.

But quickly passing from consideration of a suitable name which they left unsettled, they proceeded to the heart of the business, endorsed the suggested scheme for the proposed club and resolved that the meeting 'proceeds to form a Club'. When it was proposed that Louis Marchesi be elected secretary, Bernard Durrant, a leading Norwich solicitor but not a Rotarian, suggested that having originated the club Marchesi should be the first chairman; whereupon Louis said he would be pleased to serve in whatever capacity the members placed him. But the meeting elected Marchesi secretary, Bernard Durrant chairman, R. E. Morgan vice-chairman, and C. C. Payne treasurer (all honorary posts of course). In addition William Lincolne Sutton was elected President, plus six Vice-Presidents including Archie Plumstead and Walter Smith, all of them Rotarians.

When non-Rotarian Bernard Durrant took the chair at the 'Committee Meeting' at Langford's Restaurant on 23 February he said he thought it would be in keeping with the spirit of the club to drop formal methods of addressing each other in committee, and they all agreed. Again they discussed a suitable name for the club, and finally resolved to recommend 'the Round Table, An Association of Young Business Men' to the General Meeting they had called for 7 March. This resolution, it is worth noting, was taken the day before the Prince of Wales is alleged to have made his remark about 'getting around a table' at Castle Bromwich. Bernard Durrant, Louis Marchesi and F. V. Donovan were appointed as a sub-committee to formulate rules. When this main committee met again at Langford's on 1 March, Lincolne Sutton said he considered someone younger than himself should be president, but they would have none of it; and in spite of his being fifty-five and all the Rotarian vice-presidents of around the same age, the committee of the Young Business Men's Association insisted that they remained.

The first entry in the old exercise book labelled

The Round Table
no. 1 Norwich
Register

was for the General Meeting of 7 March 1927. The president and seven vice-presidents attended, as well as the four 'officers' and four committee men – F. V. Donovan, H. A. Pank, P. V. Howes, and F. H. Olorenshaw. Thirty 'active members' attended and signed their names, including several who in 1976 still remembered the day, Tom Tillett and Charlie Leveton among them.

Before approving the rules the meeting discussed the suggestion that Edward Prince of Wales should be asked to honour the club by becoming its patron. They agreed to pursue the proposal through the Lord Mayor of Norwich, but nothing ever came of this. Since the rules they discussed have not survived, the amendments alluded to in the minutes have no meaning; though one of the clauses of Rule 2, (Objects) was changed to 'To cultivate the highest ideals in business, professional and civic traditions'. It is intriguing to wonder what it was before.

Louis Marchesi's proposal that, until club membership had reached seventy-two 'committee members' (?), each classification should consist of not more than four members was carried; as was Rule 6 that two votes against a candidate for membership disqualified him. Bernard Durrant again appealed to everyone to drop the formal style of address at meetings – it seems he was up against an inherent love of formality which so many mistook for dignity but others regarded as pomposity. The question of a badge was discussed, and the design of stationery. Archie Plumstead told the meeting he thought the idea of Round Table would grow nationally and then proceeded to present members with a bell for the chairman's use at meetings. The sum of £15 12s was received from members in subscriptions.

The stage was now set for the inaugural meeting. The seed had been sown and it had taken root.

It happened that in 1927 two young men held the two senior civic positions in Norwich: the forty-one-year-old C. R. Bignold of Norwich Union Insurance, Lord Mayor; and the thirty-nine-year-old A. A. Rice, Sheriff. This coincidence seemed to be a living illustration of all that Marchesi was trying to say.

Already thirty-eight young men had become members of the Norwich Round Table Club and there was a waiting list of twelve before the inaugural meeting took place in Suckling House on 14 March 1927. They were welcomed with cups of coffee to stimulate circulation and enable them to make each other's acquaintance which it will be remembered British Rotary had promoted to first place from fourth in their list of objects, and Marchesi made his prime Object too. Coffee was the medium on this first formal occasion as it had been in Jonathan's, Will's and Waghorn's, the coffee-houses which were the prototypes of the good-fellowship circles which Louis

Marchesi envisaged.

In opening the proceedings Bernard Durrant pointed to the youthful Lord Mayor and Sheriff who were beside him on the platform as young men who exemplified all Round Table stood for, young men who had brought enterprise and the spirit of adventure into their work. The young men of Norwich should be inspired by their sense of service; serving the community was the keynote of the new club they were inaugurating that day.

Some hint was given of Sutton's motive in suggesting 'Round Table' as the name of the club when he opened his remarks which followed Durrant's by addressing those present as Knights of the Round Table – not really what Marchesi had in mind. Courtly love and mediaeval chivalry was hardly the image of *his* Round Table.

He had accepted the office of president, said Sutton, to show the goodwill of Norwich Rotarians. Although Norwich Rotary Club had not fathered the new club, officially it was incubated at the Rotary Club. When Louis Marchesi had read his paper on Youth and Business to Rotary in February 1926, his vision had appealed to the imagination of some of his members and they had done all they could to help in the new club's formation.

The new club, he said, had paid Rotary a compliment by adopting almost entirely its ideals and objects, and he considered they had been wise in so doing. The club would especially appeal to post-war young men who escaped the great adventure of the war but now had to face problems far more difficult than any before the war. There were many ex-servicemen's organisations, but Round Table could perhaps be described as an in-service club to include both service and post-war youths.

Walter Smith, who had chaired the first preparatory meeting, said it was most desirable that such a club should exist so that young business and professional men could open out on the great problems before the country. They would bring a fresh outlook to bear upon these problems which older men, if they ever had one, had now lost. The relation between employers and employed was a question of vital importance to the prosperity of the country, and he was convinced that young men could very largely help to bring about a worthy solution of that problem.

The most stirring speech of the day came from thirty-nine-year-old A. A. Rice MC who had served his articles as an architect and surveyor in Norwich, gone to Canada in 1908 to join the engineering staff building the Canadian Pacific Railway and Toronto Harbour. He had fought in the 1914–18 war as a private at Ypres, obtained a commission in the Royal Naval Division and fought on the Somme, was transferred to the Royal Engineers and fought once again at Ypres where he was wounded and gassed and won the Military Cross. After the war he became a director of Rice Brothers, building and engineering contractors, and was actively associated with the Liberal Party in Norwich, became a member of the City Council and worked relentlessly for the British Legion as chairman and president of the Norwich branch. He was a founder of the Norfolk and Norwich Aero Club and qualified as an air pilot. At the time he spoke at the inaugural meeting of the Norwich Round Table club he was serving his term as City Sheriff 1926–27, the last to hold that office who paid all the expenses of office out of his own pocket, as was the case with Mr C. R. Bignold, the Lord Mayor (he was knighted in 1938).

Archie Rice could be said to be the archetype of the kind of young man Louis Marchesi had in mind for membership of his new club.* It was often remarked, Rice told the first forty members of Round Table on 14 March 1927, that the verve, enterprise and energy which characterised the merchant princes of other days was lacking in conspicuous measure from the present generation. They should search among the lumber of evidence for the causes of the temporary loss of business acumen and driving power.

* Rice was elected a member on 28 March 1927, but the attendance rule was waived for him during his year of office as Sheriff. The Lord Mayor who was over forty was elected an Honorary Member.

'The outlook of the young business man of to-day is start-lingly different from that of my father's day. The business man of the eighties had his peculiar difficulties, but the factors arrayed against his modern prototype are stupendous, almost beyond belief. The forces which have driven the men of commerce from a position of stability and independence to one of insecurity and hopeless dependence on the powers-that-be are the incalculable forces of war and politics. To our forebears war was an affair of Governments; having paid their financial tribute, cheered on the sailors to rule the waves, the soldiers to march to speedy victory, they settled down with no worse feelings than that the war might shrink the bank balance a trifle, a matter which would be speedily adjusted by the spoils of victory. War was but an incident in the life of a nation; politics quite a simple affair between different shades of opinion. The business man smiled through it all, developed his industry in peace with the moral certainty of a just reward for his enterprise and energy in due season and the approbation and gratitude of those for whom he found employment.

'But what a change to-day [1927]! What a scene spreads before the astonished gaze of the rising generation! War looms up no longer an incident and annoyance to be settled by professional soldiery, but as a grim and grisly shadow engulfing not only the military but the civilian population, women, children and all.'

In the war that had ended only nine years previously business went to the wall in a night, he said. The doors of those enterprises closed, their founders were reduced to beggary. No wonder young men of 1927 paused and thought. Was it worth while, they asked, for them to pour out their energy, their enthusiasm, their lives, on something which the first shot of war might smash to atoms? Politics was no longer an affair of beer and flag waving, but a grim and stern contest, not so much of political problems but industrial control.

'I do not speak of the merits of individual versus State control. Both have their protagonists in the political field. But leaving

Louis Marchesi as a boy soldier in the Middlesex Regiment, 1915.

Langford's Restaurant in London Street, Norwich, run by Louis Marchesi, where the idea of a Young Men's Business Club which became Round Table was first discussed — to-day a branch of Moss Bros.

The Smoke Room where the founders of Norwich Table met regularly for coffee.

Suckling House, Norwich, where the first meeting of Table no. 1 took place in March 1927.

ADOPT ADAPT
IMPROVE
THIS TABLET COMMEMORATES THE INCEPTION OF
THE ROUND TABLE MOVEMENT
WHICH TOOK PLACE IN THIS HALL ON 14 MARCH 1927
WHEN LOUIS MARCHESI FOUNDED THE
NORWICH ROUND TABLE

The plaque in the Great Hall, Suckling House, commemorating the event; hanging below it a photograph of the founder.

politics aside, the young men of to-day must face the facts that the greatest efforts and dreams for industry are contingent upon what is known as the Voice of the People – a voice that is never constant but ceaselessly changing with the passing fancies of the age. A single election may place a man's life work in the iron and inelastic arms of the State. Another election and it may be flung back at him. No wonder the young aspirant for business honours pauses upon the threshold and asks, Is it worth it? Why bend my will to the construction of an industry which will assuredly become the shuttlecock of striving politicians?' [The Coal Strike leading to the General Strike of 1926 would have been very fresh in his memory and that of his listeners.]

'I take it I am addressing a gathering of men who are determined, come what may, to fling their energies into that glorious sphere which is the keystone of our greatness and the foundation of our prosperity – the sphere of business, a sphere in which energy and resource are prized and shiftlessness and indolence are abhorred. The trials ahead are immense and the rewards uncertain. To thousands you will be but selfish exploiters; to others vulgar men of commerce. Be proud when you are so taunted, for thus it was said of all pioneers by whom you are preceded. It should not offend your democratic sentiments that you are not one of the crowd, for crowds are led by minorities and saved by the few. You must become one of the few in order to become the servant of many. Let that be the consolation of your loneliness. You know the blind hopelessness and insensate cruelty of war; then let your agents be ambassadors of peace and prosperity as well as men of commerce and industry. Thus may you younger men save our industries and England save her soul.'

It was not for Louis Marchesi to play a leading part on this occasion; he wisely confined himself to supporting E. R. Morgan and F. V. Donovan in their vote of thanks to the Sheriff of Norwich, but in doing so managed to insert the point, which for some reason he must have thought required making, that Round Table had not been formed in a spirit of antagonism to Rotary.

He was glad to hear Lord Mayor Bignold express the belief that Round Table would develop into a real force if it went for quality not quantity, for this was the point Marchesi was to lose no opportunity to make when in the coming years he saw those he hoped would follow his lead altering course and wandering off the path so clearly and rousingly delineated at that inaugural meeting.

Setting the Junior Pattern

2

Consolidation
1927-1928

Young Business Men to
Lubricate Wheels of Industry

News of the new club spread quickly round Norwich – though no further afield and certainly not to British Rotary headquarters. Young men who had read the report of the inaugural meeting headed 'Eyes of Youth' in their *Eastern Daily Press* and been inspired by Archie Rice's resounding speech, queued up to become members, and indeed within a few months there were even a few who were being asked to resign because they had not paid their subscriptions. The original founder members brought young men, whom they considered suitable candidates, as guests to the evening meetings which at once took place at regular fortnightly intervals, to listen to papers read by one of their number on subjects like The Need for Economy, Aviation Local Possibilities, The Fishing Industry, The Place of Accountancy in Commerce. But was not the purpose of their coming together – indeed the purpose of their forming the club – to cultivate high standards in business, professional and civic activities, asked one member, and to show how their jobs could be the medium of service to the community? and should not the subjects of their discussions on these occasions be linked with these objects? Homes who questioned the club's purpose in this way was told that 'it was difficult to instruct volunteers as to the content of their paper', though why that should be the case is not clear. He was also told 'members were not all experienced speakers' which again begged the question. However 'it was considered desirable that papers should be given on the aims and objects of the Club sooner or later'. (Committee meeting at Langford's, 5 August 1927.)

Candidates had only to be proposed by a single member, and then, if they saw fit, recommended by the club committee for election by members who attended the next meeting. Young men also wrote in applying for membership without a proposer, and if the committee saw fit to recommend any of them on the strength of their letters, they did so. When elected the new member's name was entered in the Register and he was given a number. The registrar who kept this first register was S. A. Cannell. At the first meeting members sat in chairs according to their membership number, but on 25 March it was decided that they drew fresh chair numbers out of a hat at each meeting to stimulate the forming of new acquaintanceships which was the prime object of the exercise. There was no pre-cast classification list; this formed itself from the jobs of those who presented themselves, on the basis of first come, first served – the first four bakers, the first elected. At the committee meeting which followed the inaugural session of 14 March two candidates were not accepted for recommendation because their classifications were already filled. Amongst the earliest classifications were 'insurance manager', 'architect', 'grocer', 'milling', 'boots and shoes', 'estate agent', 'medicated wines', 'dental surgeon', 'banking', 'optician', 'publisher', 'market gardener', 'printers manager'.

Members of the club committee assumed the right of approving or disapproving a classification, quite apart from the prospective filler of it. When, on 7 October 1927, Louis Marchesi proposed that a 'public service' classification be formed, P. V.

Homes 'strongly opposed this as he felt a greater variety of callings should be represented in the club'. (Presumably there were
already four local government officers filling a classification
with a title slightly differing from 'public service'.) Marchesi
had to withdraw his proposal. At the meeting of 25 March it
was decided 'to form a classification for Clerks for which articled accountants, confidential clerks and managing clerks
would be eligible', for presumably candidates giving all three of
these positions had presented themselves.

By the end of August they had enough members. There must
have been a limit set to the size of the club in the original rules,
and this had been reached in terms both of individuals and
classifications. Now Homes proposed 'that membership be increased to 100 by providing new classifications if necessary, but
the number of members for each classification to remain at
four'.

From the start, the club's objects were given a wide interpretation. In April they sent the Lord Mayor of Norwich a
resolution supporting the Norfolk and Norwich Light Aero-
plane Club and the Norwich Industrial Fair; and in July organised a Crippled Children's Outing, and raised the money for
this by putting a box on the table at meetings into which members were invited to place donations. The following month they
were organising a Shopping Week (?), and when in September
the Rotary Club had to pull out of organising a dance in aid of
the Joint Hospitals and War Memorial Fund in 'Appeal Week',
Norwich Round Table took it over. In September Homes organised a bowls tournament, and in October there was talk of
holding a Club Dinner to mark their first birthday which in the
event took place at the Maids Head Hotel on 15 February 1928
and brought them welcome publicity far beyond Norwich. It
cost the club 6s a head and they sold dinner tickets for 8s 6d. A
'musical event' was provided by members at the end, and community singing was organised *during* the meal.

There was already a draft 'Round Table design' in existence
before 25 March, made by the energetic Homes, because Archie

Plumstead objected to it at the committee meeting at Langford's on that date. He produced one of his own. 'Mr Plumstead had incorporated a Victorian post leg round table in his design, and would like the club to adopt that type for its stationery, etc. The committee unanimously opposed the Victorian round table design, but held over the question to enable Homes to produce other designs. Homes objected to the present design because of the variety of periods represented in its make up.' The committee were not impressed by the drawings Homes submitted on 4 April and decided to invite someone else altogether to have a go, a Mr Lemy.

On 11 June 'a model of a Victorian Pedestal Table was submitted for approval by the Secretary [Marchesi]'. This is thought to have been a miniature furniture-maker's sample, of the kind made by a joinery apprentice for salesmen to take round to customers to illustrate styles better than a two-dimensional drawing. 'During the discussion it was decided that the dice (dies?) to be cut showed one foot of the triangle forming the base in front with the two remaining ones at the rear. Donovan proposed that the dice be cut from the model submitted and adopted as the Club badge for stationery purpose.' This was carried unanimously, and at the next meeting on 28 June, 'a model of a Victorian round table was accepted for the design on all club stationery and the cover of the booklet [containing the constitution of the club, its rules, objects and the names of officers and circulation, not one copy of which seems to have survived].

The design so far discussed has been for printing on the club's letterhead, and booklets. A club badge was on the agenda of the meeting of 2 September, when Percy Homes proposed it should be of silver or whitemetal with an engraving of the club round table in a mahogany brown no larger than a threepence piece. The committee agreed to obtain samples of the badge in whitemetal and brass to submit to all members for their approval. On 7 October they finally chose a 'mahogany brown round table in enamel on gilt metal' for recommendation to the general meeting which eventually adopted it. They cost a shilling – an old shilling – each, and members were charged 1s 6d for the loan of the badge during their membership and had to return it when they resigned.

What precisely Lincolne Sutton had in mind when at the meeting of 21 February 1927 he suggested the Norwich Club should call itself The Round Table is anyone's guess but, knightly overtones apart, he was probably attracted by establishing a link between the senior and junior body through a common 'roundness'. Marchesi's original concept however is well known. He wanted a club which would stimulate young men to meet and talk around a table, not in a spirit of chivalry or knight errantry, but in the more cosy, homely atmosphere which an ordinary domestic table would signify. His brief which inspired the first designs will have been prompted by these considerations which were at the heart of the new idea.

Inscribed on the supports of the bell which Archie Plumstead presented to the Norwich Club for the use of the chairman at meetings were the words 'Adopt, Adapt, Improve'. As seen, this is what Edward Prince of Wales had said British industry needed to do in order to keep it in the van. There is no record of a discussion at any Round Table meeting about making these three words the motto of the movement, but they appeared on Archie Plumstead's bell, and after that on a scroll underneath the gate-legged table badge, on literature and letterheads, to survive to the present day.

As secretary of the club committee Marchesi obviously

attended all its meetings, most of which were chaired by solicitor Bernard Durrant. Other committee members had definite views on most of the matters they were asked to discuss, but the prime mover was the founder who was active in promoting his club in other directions than those formally discussed at the committee table which he minuted. Some time before the end of 1927 Marchesi wrote to a Mr H. J. Nutt, the manager of the Bank of California in Seattle, to whom he had had an introduction, telling him about Round Table and how he saw it developing. 'This year,' he told the American, 'we are starting the formation of branches in England and countries abroad. Already we have prepared the way in Germany, Switzerland and Holland, but we would naturally prefer America took precedence. Norwich is Table Number 1, and it would give us the greatest pleasure to know that Table Number 2 was in America. We should like to be able to announce at the Annual Banquet the receipt of a cablegram intimating that another Round Table was being formed in Seattle, as our present Lord Mayor intends to issue an appeal for funds to build a memorial hall to Abraham Lincoln who came of Norfolk stock. In the event of your deciding to send such a Table cablegram, please address it to Marchesi, Norwich, England. Alternatively, we hope you will mail a letter to reach us in Norwich by 15 February [the date of that first birthday dinner].'

He will have told the old guard who still met of a morning for coffee and cakes in the Smoke Room of Langford's of what he was doing, but the committee's first official intimation of his action was on 20 February 1928 when he read to them the reply he had received from Nutt turning the idea down. 'This city is at all events overladen with clubs, fraternities, associations, civic enterprises and probably anything you might name in this line. . . . It is improbable therefore that such a club as Round Table would achieve success here in Seattle . . . Local orders with local dues would be more acceptable to local men than one with headquarters 6,000 miles away' – like 20-30 which neither of them seemed to have heard of. Nutt was not prepared to start a Round Table club at Seattle, nor were those who received similar letters in Germany, Switzerland and Holland. 'It was decided to drop the correspondence with Holland' minuted Marchesi after the meeting of 20 February.

Though it was not from a letter from Marchesi, a native of one of the three European countries that he had tried to interest in Round Tables in 1927 did seem to receive the message. This was Louis A. Van Leer, a young Dutchman who had come to England as a part-time student of the London School of Economics, and keen to do voluntary service ran a troop of Boy Scouts in the East End of London. He had just started in a factory management job and as a Rotarian had written to fellow-Rotarian E. J. Burrow, the Cheltenham town guide publisher, saying he had accumulated a number of ideals about the duties of employers in industry and was determined to carry them out. He realised his colleagues would do their best to 'knock all that silly nonsense about duties and service out of me' but he meant to persevere.

Burrow was so impressed by the letter that he sent it to the editor of British Rotary's magazine *The Rotary Wheel* who printed it in their December 1927 issue (vol XIII, no. 12) under the headline

ROTARY AND YOUTH
Dutchman's Suggestion for a Junior Organisation

'There is a great revival,' wrote Louis Van Leer, 'of the feeling of responsibility for the public welfare among all classes of people – witness your own Ideas of Youth competition. Now what would be more logical than an organisation in which all these idealists who step into business could find a place, and as from the beginning find a confirmation of their ideals and help in building them up? What we all have to do now is fighting our own battle and losing our ideals one by one until we are so "fortunate" that one of our colleagues who is the trade member of Rotary for our town retires from business or dies, and then we will have a chance to become a member of Rotary, and start either at the bottom again to build up what we lost in all those years.

'It seems therefore to me that Rotary is throwing away an enormous chance of influencing the business leaders of tomorrow. . . . If Rotary thinks it best to remain the exclusive fraternity it is now, the only other course I see open is the formation of a sort of Junior Rotary run by the seniors in which the principle of "one man one trade" could, or could not, be applied. In any case this would be something, though I think that just the regular contact with those at the top will prove to be a jolly good thing for us – perhaps it wouldn't do *them* any harm either.'

What is remarkable about this letter is Van Leer going to the heart of Marchesi's message, which was the benefit to be derived from bridging the gulf in the thinking of the younger men and the older men – and this being to the benefit of those on both sides of the gulf. He had certainly never heard of Round Table when he wrote this letter, neither obviously had Burrow, nor the editor of *The Rotary Wheel*; but the launching of Rotary's Ideas of Youth competition showed their minds were moving in the same direction as Marchesi's.

At the first annual general meeting of the Norwich Round Table Club at Suckling House on 20 February 1928 a credit balance of 8s 3d was declared, Bernard Durrant was re-elected chairman, C. V. Miller vice-chairman and C. C. Payne treasurer. When Louis Marchesi was re-appointed secretary, he was presented with a chiming clock as a tribute to the work he had put into the club as its founder. His old school friend W. G. (Billy) Quinton, now manager of a branch of Barclays Bank in the town, joined the club committee, as did J. L. (Jimmy) Hanly, who was on the management side of one of the several boot and shoe manufacturers in Norwich. When a member proposed that the secretary had an assistant to help him, Marchesi said he thought they should wait a little longer before they did this. He agreed however it would be necessary to nominate an Assistant Secretary later 'in view of the fact that the club would doubtless be extended this year in other parts of the country'.

He had obviously made several attempts to do this already which had justified his confidence in telling Nutt in the autumn of 1927, 'we are starting the formation of branches in England'. The town he was looking to as the father of Round Table no. 2, after all hopes had subsided of Seattle taking that prize, was Whitby.* But nothing was to come of his efforts here either, though no details survive to relate the cause. He will have put out feelers to other towns in England – and it would be intriguing to know which – but all his overtures were rejected. The trouble was Round Table was an unknown quantity and no one was prepared to take the risk of jumping on yet another voluntary service wagon which did not yet seem to be on the move and whose distinction from, say, Toc H or the Junior Chamber of Commerce had not yet made itself clear.

However in the winter of 1928, following the publicity given to its first dinner and annual general meeting, news of Round Table spread outside Norwich. The February 1928 issue of *The Rotary Wheel* (vol XIV, no. 2) carried an article by William Lincolne Sutton headed AN ASSOCIATION OF YOUNG BUSINESS MEN which told Rotarians the twelve month history of Round Table and what it stood for. The club, he said, was broadly framed on the model of a Rotary Club. Some young business men in Norwich had looked on Rotary in operation and found it good 'and yearned for something similar for themselves'.

'On the side of Rotary some of our members took up the idea with enthusiasm, feeling that we ought to help our young business friends to grasp the boon which we ourselves had enjoyed from association in Rotary. We could not hand them Rotary itself, but we could show them how to start and develop an association on similar lines and based on like ideals.

'The Rotary Club did not officially launch "The Round Table", but the enthusiasts in the club called an inaugural meet-

* See *Portsmouth Evening News*, 16 April 1928.

ing, every Norwich Rotarian being asked to recommend a young man to whom an invitation should be sent. The response exceeded the expectations of the most sanguine amongst us. We found that we had gathered together the cream of the young men of the city, and had hit upon the very thing they wanted. A Club was provisionally formed, and eventually launched at a meeting attended by the Lord Mayor and Sheriff, who happened to be themselves young men in their thirties.

'The President and Vice-Presidents are all Rotarians, and are honorary members of "The Round Table". The Chairman is a young non-Rotarian, but one or two of the active members are also Rotarians, whilst the hon. sec. is the young Rotarian L. Marchesi, who was from the first the prime mover in the idea. The Club has gone from strength to strength both in numbers and influence. The limit of membership has now been raised to 100, and there are some 85 members.

'The founders of "Table No. 1" (the Norwich Club's sub-title) are ambitious. They visualise a chain of "Round Tables," throughout the country, or even throughout the world.

'In commending this movement to Rotary as a worthwhile piece of community service, we suggest that "The Round Table" should be developed not as a part of Rotary, but side by side with Rotary as an independent body. The function of Rotary would be to summon the right young fellows together as a sound nucleus of a "Round Table" Club, and show them how to start on the right lines. The experience of Rotarians would be invaluable in choosing the right type of member and helping the young men over the difficult style of inauguration. It is essential that "Round Table" should be an independent organisation and self-supporting financially and otherwise, the actual management and running of the Club to be in the hands of the active members, the young men. The part to be played by Rotarians should be to join the Club, in limited numbers of course, as honorary members and afford evidence of the support, goodwill, and co-operation of Rotary by filling the positions, say, of President and Vice-Presidents. Countless opportunities will arise for exchange of visits and ideas, help and stimulus between the senior and junior organisations.

'Young business is crying to Rotary for bread. Shall we give them a chunk off our loaf? We who founded "The Round Table" suggest that it would be better and healthier for Rotary itself, and for the young men, that we should rather hand them the yeast of Rotary – its spirit and ideals – for them to make their own bread.'

Even wider publicity was given to Round Table by the article which appeared in the *Daily Telegraph* of 16 February 1928 written by Vivian Carter, secretary of British Rotary. It was in fact a weekly column, 'Rotary Week by Week', which devoted its whole space on this occasion to the new Round Table club. It must have been read by hundreds of regular readers, but it was Rotarian C. E. Smith of Portsmouth who not only read it but acted on it.

Charlie Smith who was in his mid-fifties was manager of the Portsmouth branch of the Century Insurance Company and in 1916 had founded the Portsmouth and Southsea Rotary Club of which, in 1928, he was secretary. He read Lincolne Sutton's piece and Vivian Carter's column, and invited some of his Rotary friends to his office to talk about the new project which someone had started in Norwich. What about forming a 'Table' in Portsmouth? They were all enthusiastic, and Charlie Smith had his young managing clerk E. A. Finley Day, who was not a Rotarian, write off to the secretary with the funny name in Norwich to ask him for details of how his club worked and suggestions for starting a similar one in Portsmouth. Louis Marchesi read the letter he had had from Finley Day to Norwich Round Table committee members at that meeting in Langford's on the morning before the first annual general meeting, and told them he had forwarded the writer a copy of their rules and membership book. 'It was hoped that this project would materialise' he minuted. The letter from Portsmouth stimulated the Norwich committee to positive promotion of the Round Table idea – and the exercise acquired the Rotary name

'Extension'. At the next committee meeting on 27 February Lincolne Sutton, Walter Smith, C. V. Miller and Jimmy Hanly were formed into a sub-committee 'to consider the necessary steps for starting branch clubs', with Bernard Durrant and Louis Marchesi as ex-officio members in their capacity of chairman and secretary.

Encouraged by the swift and friendly response from Norwich, Charlie Smith invited people he knew would be interested to a meeting in the Corner House, Portsmouth on 15 March (the day after the anniversary of the Norwich club's inaugural meeting) to explore the possibility of forming a Round Table club from young business men in the town on the lines of that in Norfolk. They included E. W. Ward, a solicitor; A. E. (Bertie) Hooper, a fish salesman; T. Hooper, a draper; L. Palmer, a brush maker; S. Tanner, a dairyman; J. Webb, who ran a petrol filling station; J. M. Whitecross, a paper-bag manufacturer; F. Wilkins, a coach builder; L. Woodham, a credit trader; and of course E. A. Finley Day who had written again to Marchesi who read the letter to the Norwich committee on 13 March.

After Smith had outlined the object of Round Table, the meeting voted to form such a club in Portsmouth, but unlike Norwich to limit membership on the Rotary model to *one* member per classification instead of four, fix the subscription at 15s instead of 5s and hold fortnightly *lunches* in the middle of the day instead of evening sessions. They also decided to limit membership to ten or twelve at first. A provisional committee was appointed and Finley Day became Interim Secretary. Charlie Smith had done his bit as inspirer and creator of the club, and as an over-forty withdrew.

The committee met on 20 March and elected John Webb chairman and Eric Ward vice-chairman. Finley Day read to them the letter he had received from Marchesi congratulating them on having formed a club in Portsmouth and saying he would try to come down for the inaugural lunch on 29 March. 'But it was decided that the secretary should write to

Mr Marchesi postponing his visit till April 12 as our first
lunch would be more in the nature of a business meeting.'

The following month the committee decided to call them-
selves a 'council' and formed four committees to handle the
Rules, Catering and Social matters, Membership, and Speakers.
A report of the club's formation appeared in the *Portsmouth
Evening News* of 16 April which included the information that
Marchesi had told Finley Day that theirs would be the second
club to be formed in England and as such would be known as
'Table no. 2 – Portsmouth and Southsea', though Whitby had
been in the running for this honour.

On that same day fifty members of Round Table no. 1
attended a Special Meeting in Suckling House, Norwich, to
discuss the whole business of 'extension' and try to settle the
way the movement should, in their opinion, develop outside
Norwich. The importance of this meeting justifies quoting the
relevant part of the minute in full:

> The Chairman Durrant presiding, the following business
> was considered in view of the anticipated development of the
> movement.
> 1. The Constitution of a Central Body for the purpose of
> administering the movement nationally for one year.
> This item developed into a consideration of a Committee
> for extension and a separate Central Council of Representa-
> tion of Round Tables as such Tables came into existence. The
> discussion was approved by the Chairman reading the corre-
> spondence between the secretary of Table No. 1 (Norwich
> and District) and Table No. 2 (Portsmouth and District).
> The Portsmouth Table accepted the Resolution forwarded
> by the Extension Committee of Table No. 1 as follows:-
> Every new Table must adopt the Objects and Rules as for-
> mulated by Table No. 1 and no new rules may be made or
> existing rules altered without the written consent of the Cen-
> tral Body. Members' subscriptions may be fixed by each
> Table according to Local conditions. The Portsmouth Club

however did not then perceive the necessity of Affiliation until 10 or 12 Tables were in existence. The reply of the Secretary Table No. 1 (Norwich and District) was to the effect that some steps must be taken to ensure that Tables should not be formed indiscriminately and for that reason it was essential that there should be one centre with which all Tables would be in touch until such time as a Central Body of Representation of all Tables should be elected. The Right to use Table Badge and Motto should also be controlled. It was also obvious that a Central Fund would be necessary to enable the Movement to develop and that each Table should provide for that Fund from the Start.

The Chairman then called upon the secretary to state his impressions and Marchesi said that he felt to develop nationally we should concern ourselves more with the Ideals of the Table movement than with the fact that it originated in Norwich or that Norwich should have any claim to precedence. He stated that the feeling of the Portsmouth Club was very firm and sympathetic.

Mr Lincolne Sutton the President said that one could not expect a finer expression of the ideals of the Movement and the sincerity of the Portsmouth Table than was expressed in their letter. He felt that in the matter of forming a Central Body equal representation should be offered Table No. 2. The consideration of supporting the extension of the movement would no doubt receive considerable attention at the Annual RIBI [British Rotary] Conference at Harrogate in May.

Ellis Jacobs next spoke both as a Round Table member and secretary of the Rotary Club of Norwich. He said that he thought the movement would develop rapidly in view of an enquiry he had received from one of the Rotary Clubs in London. He agreed with the views of the President, that Portsmouth should have representation on the Central Body but suggested 6 Norwich Members to 2 Portsmouth. He thought that the Rules could be altered to meet local conditions by each Table formulating its own bye-laws within the bounds of the general rules.

Marchesi said he felt that Norwich should not have more than a proportion of 3 Norwich Members to 2 Portsmouth Members on the Central Body. Mr W. Smith suggested that 4 Norwich members to two Portsmouth be the proportion. Herbert Smith suggested that the duration of the Council so formed be fixed until a given number of Tables were formed. Ellis Jacobs then proposed that "2 members of Table 1 (Norwich) and 2 members of Table No. 2 (Portsmouth) be nominated to act as a Provisional Council with power to co-opt representation from new Tables as a Council of Round Tables, until such time as 10 Tables were formed when a Conference of Tables should be convened".

This was discussed at length. Many thought that the formation of a Central Council at this stage was premature, particularly if each Table had an Extension Committee. Others considered the Norwich Extension Committee should be the central organisation. Marchesi's view was that some kind of central committee was needed to lord it over proliferating extension organisations at Table level. 'A Central Council is necessary,' he told them, 'for the major role of considering the movement nationally and controlling it'. Bernard Durrant thought Norwich's own extension committee should deal only with extension, and that a Central Council be formed to *control* the movement.

At the end of it all the meeting carried the proposition put by Charles Leveton and seconded by Billy Quinton that 'a Council of Round Tables be formed consisting of 2 representatives from each Table that had received its charter, each delegate to have one vote; this council to function until such time as it considered a change in its constitution should be made'. This was the first mention of a 'charter', which of course Norwich Table no. 1 had never given itself and, alone of the Tables that came to be formed, has spent the entire fifty years without one.

They finally decided to transfer a sum representing 2s 6d a head from the funds of Table no. 1 to a Central Fund but, 'should the necessity arise, a levy of 2s 6d per member be made during the current year and be applied to the funds of the Norwich Table'. They rejected a proposal that their subscription should be increased to the 15s exacted by Portsmouth.

Marchesi sent Portsmouth an account of these events which the 'council' of Round Table no. 2 considered at their meeting of 19 April. They 'decided to take no action in the meantime'. They went ahead with endorsing, with only slight amendments, their own set of rules drawn up by their own Rules Committee.

When another letter from Marchesi was read at their meeting of 10 May 'it was not considered necessary to take any action'. At this meeting 'it was decided to obtain lapel buttons for club functions and the secretary was asked to arrange this at a cost of not more than 1s 6d each'. The design on these lapel buttons was the same Victorian pedestal table as that adopted at Norwich.

Finley Day duly informed Marchesi of Portsmouth's decisions and his letter was read to the Norwich committee on 25 April. It stated that Table no. 2 had adopted the Norwich Rules and Constitution 'with modifications to meet with local conditions'. It would not appear that Portsmouth sent Norwich a copy of these rules, but hoped, rightly, that the latter phrase would mollify any concern which the founder might have that his movement had spawned a rogue elephant which had had no intention of following in father's footsteps and no scruples about giving the Portsmouth club whatever new look it liked.

In Norwich the Round Table club was being regarded as a group which could be relied on to make a serious contribution to the formulation of the community's attitude to problems which affected it. Two of its members had represented the club at a conference on Overseas Settlement, and was now co-operating with Norwich Rotary Club, Norwich Chamber of Commerce and Norwich Traders' Association in organising a public meeting to discuss recent developments of the London and North Eastern Railway Company and the effect of them on the area. Marchesi became responsible for booking the large new Stuart Hall at Suckling House and invited the Lord Mayor to preside. They sent delegates to represent Business Policy in the Mock Town Council Meeting organised by the Norwich Branch of the National Council of Women. This kind of activity was much more in tune with Marchesi's objects. Moreover the committee acquired a sense of 'what did not come under the scope of our activities as an association', namely organising fund raising operations for other organisations. They turned down an application from the Jobmaster of the local Toc H to mount an event in aid of St Dunstan's, and another for help in raising funds for the YMCA. But they seized on the opportunity of having news of Round Table's activities noised round the world by Jimmy Hanly who offered to do so on his coming world tour. An American organisation calling itself the Knights of the Round Table had apparently already heard of the Norwich club and wrote to wish it good luck; Jimmy Hanly might be able to tell them that Norwich's round table had no resemblance to Arthur's, and that their middle-class members had no inclination to emulate the romantic roistering of out-moded cavaliers.

British Rotary was once more turning to the problems which Round Table had formed itself to tackle. In the May 1928 issue of *The Rotary Wheel* E. J. Burrow had an article headed 'Rotary and Youth Again'.

'One of the most interesting features of Rotary in Great Britain during the last twelve months has been the persistent and constantly recurring question, What is Rotary doing to hand on its message to the younger generation? There is an uneasy feeling that Rotary may automatically become an organisation of elderly men with boundless enthusiasm for an ideal which they are too advanced in age (and material success) to use! This uneasiness has prompted the formation of the "Round Table" Club at Norwich and in many quarters there is a "stirring amongst the leaves" which presages action. For the young men of to-day want a message more than the "grave and reverend signors"; their lives and the future of society are inextricably woven and whoever would reform the latter must look to the former.'

It was Burrow who led the discussion at the first of the conference's so-called Group Assemblies of British Rotary's annual conference held at Harrogate from 5 to 10 May 1928. 'Behind all the pleasure-seeking, restless movement of to-day,' he said prophetically, 'there is the consuming desire to rid the world of the hatred, envy and all uncharitableness which led to the last war and which, if we are not alert, might possibly lead to the next.' Calmly and with complete assurance Rotary pledged itself to International Service (subject of the discussion), the greatest and most far-reaching detail of its programme.

The annual general meeting part of the conference had been opened with an address from that year's president, Thomas Stephenson, who told his audience he would make the one object of Rotary the ideal of service as the basis of all human relationships. The original motto of Rotary had been Service not Self, but now it was Service *before* Self. Rotary after all was only an outlook. It was a purely abstract and spiritual movement which directed people's actions into their various relationships.

Rotarian Marchesi missed this opening address. He had not in fact intended attending the conference at all. John Creasey the author of *Round Table, the First 25 Years* must have talked to him about the occasion, which will have enabled him to describe it so graphically.

'He had his business to look after, and could not afford to pay a big staff. He worked all hours as it was, and had not two or three days to waste — but he had them to spare for a cause that seemed desperate. He made last-minute arrangements, hired a taxi at his own expense, started off to Harrogate some 200 miles away at ten o'clock at night, and reached the spa at eight in the morning after dozing for an hour or two just outside the town. He went to a hotel, shaved and had breakfast, and was at the Conference Hall in time to hear Hines's resolution, sitting with a sympathetic Norwich Rotarian, W. E. Keefe. The conference welcomed Hines's speech while Marchesi sat and listened, horrified.'

The subject of the paper by Rotarian the Rev. L. J. Hines of Halifax was 'What can Rotary do for the Younger Generation?', news of which had made Louis send for that taxi. The question, said Hines, was a recognition that Rotary stood outside the domain of youth. By the nature of their constitution Rotary was broadly speaking a movement of middle-aged men.

'Europe is younger to-day than ever she has been. The war claimed the ripe manhood of fourteen years ago, and left us with a generation of children. These now form the ripe young manhood of to-day. It is characterised by a bold and assertive idealism, curiously mingled with an instinctive uncertainty concerning the true aims and ends of life. I suggest that Rotary holds the incentive to youth's idealism as well as the full answer to youth's uncertainty. We, in Rotary, have it in our power to light the lamp of the vision of youth and offer the shield against youth's unpreparedness. Though this be the power of Rotary the existing limits of our organisation decree that our attitude towards youth shall remain, at best, one of detachment. This is of serious consequence to the younger men of our businesses and professions who, by the time they reach the age and status which will qualify them for Rotary, will have already become Rotarian in character and disposition without the aid of and in consequence without the need for our great movement, or they will have reached that static state of life wherein it will prove difficult if not impossible for Rotary to transform them.

'If for no other reason than to avert this tragedy there would seem to me to be but one answer to our question. Rotary must take the young potential business manhood of the world into its confidence; and there is only one way to do this – it must bring it into close and definite contact with its fellowship. Think again of the nature of the task to which Rotary has addressed itself. Can a new world be made in the lifetime of middle-aged man? The task of Rotary demands young life as much if not more than war ever did. Rotary is not something to die for, but something to live for, therefore it must find its way somehow into the hearts of young men. If our great movement could find a way to make some overture to the young business manhood, it would be following the successful policy of all the great ideal-istic movements of history. Where would the Christian Church be to-day if she had ignored this issue? What would have been the fate of the great political parties without their junior organi-sations? These societies have been saved, times without number, by the young life they have been wise enough to foster. Who dare say that Rotary will never stand in need of a like salvation?

'My plea is for the establishment of a junior affiliated society to Rotary throughout Britain. With the official sanction of the Board of Rotary, junior clubs could be brought into being through the activities of our local Rotary organisations. This af-filiated movement would call into its fellowship young business and professional men between the ages, say, of twenty-one and thirty-five. These young men could officer and control their own movement along certain prescribed Rotary lines. The parent clubs of Rotary could assist these junior clubs by the ap-pointment of a small number of honorary members to help and guide, though never to direct or control. I should favour the holding of weekly luncheons for these junior sections because I believe that this form of fellowship has meant much to Rotary.

'There is the problem of what would become of these young men when they reached the age which would disqualify them for further membership of a junior affiliated society. This diffi-culty would be no greater than it is for Rotary itself when cir-cumstances prevent perfectly good Rotarians from continuing their club membership. We know that in reality a Rotarian is never really lost to Rotary. We have heard the honoured claim: "Once a Mason always a Mason". In a very real sense we may make the same claim for all Rotary men. These young men would go out with several years experience of Rotary ideals and Rotary influence behind them; an experience they would never forget.

'Another and probably more serious difficulty would be that of classification in an affiliated junior movement. It has been pointed out that such a suggestion as the one I advocate would mean the widening of the term "Rotary". In my judgment this difficulty is purely technical. Let us suppose that Rotary gave its official blessing to this undertaking; that the clubs in Rotary were encouraged to promote the foundation of junior affiliated societies in their own towns and cities; and that these societies were recruited from young potential principals in their own callings and were classified in the customary Rotary way. In what sense would Rotary itself lose its original identity? An affiliated junior society composed of "potential" business executives would be a society of "potential" Rotarians only. The distinctive entity of the parent organisation would remain unimpaired.

'I am not asking that our movement should embrace men who, constitutionally, have no right to admission, or for the duplication of existing clubs in Rotary. All I seek is a widening policy in Rotary activity for the propagation of our principles and ideals through the medium of a separate yet affiliated society of young business men. While we are thinking of what Rotary can do for the younger generation let us not forget to ask ourselves "What can this younger generation do for us?" Youth has as much to contribute to our needs as we have to theirs. Probably our greatest need is just that passion and vim which can come to us through the contact of men at an age when the flood tide of enthusiasm runs high.'

Leonard Hines was born in the north of England in 1889, brought up a Methodist but became a Congregationalist. He held a commission in the Royal Naval Reserve in the Great War after which he was made a minister of the Unitarian Church at Huddersfield where he remained during 1919–20 and then moved to Sheffield. In 1923 he became minister of the Northgate End Unitarian Church in Halifax where he stayed till 1937. He joined Halifax Rotary Club in 1926, becoming president in 1934. He resigned in 1937. A writer of fiction and drama – several of his plays were presented on television and he was an adjudicator of the British Drama League – he held ministries in Bath from 1942 to 1946 when he retired to Sidmouth where he died on 16 November 1975 aged eighty-six – his obituary described him as 'joint founder' of Round Table.

In 1928 the Reverend L. J. Hines was thirty-nine and 'a young man' who qualified for membership of the new club just formed in Norwich which made his remarks forceful and pertinent, but to Louis Marchesi, listening with growing uneasiness, somewhat alarming. He was horrified not so much because what he heard indicated that though Round Table had been operating a year or more, and it had been written about in the Rotarian journal, Hines had obviously never heard of it, but because it left him literally speechless.

Creasey again: 'He had prepared a speech, very carefully. He had never made one to a conference session before and meant to get every word right. Everything he had written down was being said by Hines. Marchesi was left without a note he could use. "I wasn't exactly nervous," he said afterwards, "I knew I had to say something before I started disagreeing with the Junior Rotary idea. I just tore my notes up and started talking. And I've never used notes for a speech since".'

In the official report of the conference Marchesi's remarks were contained in three lines:

> MR LOUIS MARCHESI, of the Norwich Round Table, said that Club had 96 members and Portsmouth 80. They in the movement asked only one thing of Rotary – its interest in the furtherance of the spirit of service.

As soon as he had sat down, British Rotary's Immediate Past President rose and said that Rotary was well aware of Round Table even if Mr Hines was not (though not in so many words); it had come before Rotary's Aims and Objects Committee who wished it every success. At best all Rotary could do for youth was to give it an opportunity of finding its own salvation. But they could accept the overture made by Mr Marchesi and the young men of Norwich and Portsmouth, and as a token of this he moved a resolution that was seconded by Wilfrid Andrews and carried:

> That this Conference recommends the Rotarians of Great Britain and Ireland to foster the promotion, wherever possible, of clubs of young business and professional men on lines similar to those actuating the Norwich Round Table, and that where such clubs are formed advantage be taken of the experience gained by the Norwich Round Table.

The use of the word 'youth' instead of 'young men' by Hines and others led Rotarian Hargreaves into the pardonable mistake of suggesting that the new movement should cater for people between the age of sixteen and twenty-one, but doubtless he was soon enlightened on this point by those sitting next to him.

The Immediate Past President who had moved the encouraging resolution was Sydney Pascall, managing director since 1918 of James Pascall Limited, the sweet manufacturers, president of the Manufacturing Confectioners Alliance, then aged fifty-one, to whom reference has already been made. He had long been interested in the problems of young people in industry and was devoting a great deal of his spare time and energy to a wide variety of voluntary activities. He was first chairman of the Association of Whitley Councils, sat on the Government Committee which dealt with the medical examination of young people in factories, pioneered the National Movement towards a Christian Order in Industry and Commerce. He was a regular speaker at gatherings of the Christian Conference on Politics, Economics and Citizenship (COPEC). Since 1923 he had been chairman of Rotary's Business Methods Committee.

As already noted, Sydney Pascall, whom C. R. Hewitt describes as 'one of Rotary's strongest and most respected leaders', had led the campaign to formulate a Rotarian code of behaviour, and been one of the first European presidents of Rotary

International. At the League of Nations World Economic Conference at Geneva in 1927 he was a British delegate, and successfully enlisted the League's interest in a campaign against bribery in commerce and industry. At a conference in London in 1926 British Rotarians had passed a resolution asking the League to initiate machinery to study and compare standards of business practice in industry and commerce in different parts of the world – and particularly to note the levels of bribery, unfair trading, cornering of markets, misleading prospectuses, disregard for sanctity of contracts, piracy in trade marks and patents. Pascall told the Geneva conference that an immediate object of Rotary was to secure the abolition of bribery as an unethical practice of business in all countries of the world. At the Harrogate Conference he offered the hand of friendship to the incipient Round Table movement which he was to continue to guide and influence for many years to come.

At the Group Assembly on 'Community Service' at the end of the Harrogate conference L. J. Hines confessed that when he prepared his paper for the main session he was not conscious that Rotary's obligation to youth had had the consideration it had received at headquarters. William Lincolne Sutton took the opportunity of telling the Rotarians present what the Round Table clubs at Norwich and Portsmouth stood for. Norwich Rotary Club had helped establish the Norwich Round Table club and now the Harrogate Conference had set its seal on Round Table as a worthwhile piece of community service. Its membership was 'vocational' (a word with clerical overtones but which in the American Rotarian parlance, which had infiltrated British Rotary and unfortunately coloured Round Table jargon too to the confusion of a later generation, was applied to all kinds of non-manual employment – or was it?). The age limits, Lincolne Sutton explained, were between eighteen and forty.

Hines suggested if British Rotary intended advocating the institution of Round Table as existing at Norwich, that they reconsider the name in view of *Round Table** being the name of a

* A quarterly journal of Commonwealth affairs founded in 1910 by Viscount

journal which had a strong political flavour. Wilfred Andrews who was chairing the group said the Aims and Objects Committee did not wish to 'go out on this work' without having first thought about it.

Another clergyman, Rev. W. Thompson Elliott of Leeds, said he hoped Round Table would be allowed to develop as freely as possible from the beginning without being tied down to follow a particular form. Rotarians must be careful they did not get so far into the movement as to fail to give young men an opportunity to shoulder their own responsibilities. W. Cockburn of Rugby pointed to another movement already in existence outside Rotary with similar ideals and work, Toc H. H. Bowles of Worthing suggested joint committees of Rotary, Toc H and the British Legion.

The last word on the matter was had by Vivian Carter, British Rotary secretary, who said seven years ago what impressed him least about Rotary was its usefulness as an adjunct to charity. It impressed him most by its action through the individual in his vocation. In 1928 however one had to be a collectivist as well as an individualist. 'We must look upon Rotary as an energiser of social activities.' In regard to the young men's movement, perhaps Rotary had been rather hasty in committing itself to one particular organisation. But it was interested in Round Table because many Rotarians were conscious of the fact that Rotary could not thrive on middle age and therefore every Rotary Club should have some interest in developing Rotary ideals among young men.

His morale considerably boosted, Louis Marchesi returned to Norwich determined more than ever to go ahead with forming the Central Council they had debated at such length on 16 April, in spite of there being only two Tables to federate. He

---

Milner (1854–1925) who was British High Commissioner in South Africa from 1897 to 1905, a Conservative member of Lloyd George's war cabinet 1916–18 and colonial secretary 1919–21. In 1977 *The Round Table* is still an influential and authoritative voice in Commonwealth affairs.

and Billy Quinton were appointed 'national delegates' to represent Table no 1 on whatever central organisation was envisaged. British Rotary were as good as their word and agreed to lend their headquarters at 34 Norfolk Street, Strand, for a meeting between the two Round Table clubs on 25 May to hammer out the details of whatever kind of controlling body they thought would suit them best. John Webb and Finley Day were appointed the delegates of Table no. 2, and when on the day before the meeting the Portsmouth secretary suggested they draw up an agenda for the guidance of Webb and Day at the meeting, it was decided 'to leave the matter in the hands of the delegates'. The Norwich couple were briefed on 22 May and told to insist that the rule regarding party politics and sectarian religion be inserted in the Portsmouth rules which must have omitted this ban.

They called the body which they met on 25 May 1928 to form 'The Central Council of Round Tables of Great Britain and Ireland'. John Webb was appointed 'president' of this body until 31 March 1930, and Louis Marchesi Honorary* Secretary and Treasurer. They agreed to send a letter to British Rotary broadly defining the position of the one organisation in relation to the other.

'This council has been formed to take over control of the Round Table Movement as a national organisation,' stated this letter. 'We the undersigned members of the Council desire to convey to you our thanks and keen appreciation of the Harrogate Conference resolution concerning the movement, from which we feel sure much good will result.'

The letter went on to inform British Rotary that the Council has passed a resolution 'that the "Round Table" will be complementary to Rotary in its activities, having similar aims and objects, with the intention of doing for the business leaders of tomorrow what Rotary is doing for the leaders of to-day.'

* The positions held by members of Round Table clubs as annually elected 'officers' were all honorary, and it is not intended in this story to append the adjective 'honorary' to secretary, treasurer etc, every time they are mentioned.

After lunch the four of them considered how to reconcile the rules which Norwich and Portsmouth had drawn up independently and establish a Standard Set of Rules for the guidance of other Tables. They agreed any new Table must 'accept the title and badge' – presumably this meant call itself 'Round Table' and not Knights of the Round Table for instance, and use the badge created by Norwich. A new Table must adopt the Objects 'as they stand'. They must also adopt 'any ruling of the Central Council on questions arising out of local Table bye-laws'.

The new Standard Rule they agreed on regarding the eligibility of active members differed from the existing Norwich rule: 'Any young man not less than 18 years or more than 40 years of age actually engaged in a business or a profession. Such candidate to be accepted by the local membership committee in the first place, then by the Table General Committee or Council, and finally by the Table at an ordinary meeting.'

There were no guide lines on how members of a membership committee should set about recruiting club members in order to gather in Lincolne Sutton's words 'the cream of the young men of the city', or that that should be their motive. Indeed choice of the word 'accept' indicated a passive role for the membership committee – no going out and positively *selecting* young men and then *inviting* them to join, but sitting back and waiting for young men, at the instance of a Rotarian maybe, to present themselves and then to accept the first to do so if suitable. But perhaps this is unfair reading of a rule which was only designed to define eligibility. But what a young man was being asked to do by accepting an invitation to join a Round Table club was not really very difficult to understand, nor was it particularly glamorous. He was being asked to attend meetings and discussions which it was hoped would attune his mind to considering problems of the day in the sphere of industry and business, spur him to discover in what area his training and background would best suit him to assist; and then, *as an individual,* and as a member of a Round Table club, to act.

'The question of inserting in Standard Rules a rule expressly forbidding matters associated with the Party Politics and Sectarian Religion was then raised and strongly advised by Marchesi. It was decided to insert in the Portsmouth Rules and alter the Norwich Rule regarding the above as follows:

Party Politics and Sectarian Religion shall be excluded from all Round Table discussions. No business which, in the opinion of the majority of active members in attendance, is of a contentious nature shall be transacted at an ordinary meeting unless a quorum of twenty active members be present and concur.'

This let-out clause prevented the new movement from totally cutting itself off from the mainstream of public affairs to which many like Archie Rice and Walter Smith looked to it to make so useful a contribution. But in fact few of the Tables which came to be formed availed themselves of this thoughtful escape hatch from 'safe' deliberations into the risky arena of Life with a capital 'L'.

A paragraph attached to the third minute of this first Council meeting read: 'It was considered advisable to instruct prospective Tables that in view of the similarity of ideals not more than 3 per cent of members be Rotarians, and that preference to be given to non-Rotarians'.

They agreed that the Norwich and Portsmouth rules as now amended would constitute the rules of Round Table nationally, that each Table should send the secretary of Central Council a balance sheet and annual report, and submit local bye-laws to Central Council for approval. The financial year for everyone concerned should end on 31 March. Each Table was to levy what they decided to call a capitation fee of 2s 6d a head payable to a Central Fund, of which Webb and Marchesi would be trustees. No decision was made about common nomenclature, and presumably Portsmouth went on calling its committee a

King Arthur's Round Table at Winchester Castle which in 1928 Granville Howard of Southampton suggested should become the Movement's symbol in place of the Victorian pedestal table originally adopted by Norwich.

'Adopt, Adapt, Improve' first appeared as the Round Table motto on the supports of this bell – presented to Norwich Table by Archie Plumstead in 1927.

Three of Louis Marchesi's contemporaries in Norwich who helped him form Round Table in 1927: Bernard Durrant (left), James Hanly (below right) and Archie Rice.

Tablers of Area 5 pose for a group photograph outside the Imperial Hotel, Blackpool, for their Area Conference 1933/4.

Dolly Buddrell – the manageress of Langford's Restaurant, Norwich, who became Mrs Louis Marchesi

The Rev. Leonard Hines of Halifax whose speeches at the 1928 Rotary Conference at Harrogate and elsewhere were a major contribution to Round Table philosophy.

council, in spite of the new central body being given that name.

Marchesi was asked by British Rotary to attend a meeting on 6 June called to review relations between the two bodies. Reporting on this to his Norwich committee a couple of days later he said Rotary had been most considerate in their attitude to Round Table aspirations, and that the Rotarians of Halifax had promised to further the movement. Rotary had formed an advisory body of three to consult with Round Table Central Council if the occasion arose.

At this meeting of 8 June 1928 members of Round Table no 1 heard that Tables were in the process of being formed with the aid of Portsmouth at Southampton and Bournemouth. Letters of enquiry were read from Liverpool, Hampstead, Rugby, Bradford and Guildford – the first four of these Tables eventually became registered as nos. 8, 403, 113, 31. Guildford was the third Table, and on 6 July Norwich heard of the formation not only of this but of Southampton (no. 4) and Bournemouth (no. 5).

New cells bred from the original nucleus of two. An original member of Norwich or Portsmouth moved to a new job, resigned from Table no. 1 or 2, and set up a substitute Table on the same lines in their new abode, taking full advantage of the right to alter the rules to meet local conditions. This was certainly the pattern in Bournemouth. Shortly after the formation of Portsmouth Table young Bryan Buswell, who had been an early member with his brother Keith, left Portsmouth to go as a trainee to Plummer Roddis, the Bournemouth department store. He had enjoyed the Table at home and determined to set up something similar in his temporary place of residence. He consulted local Rotarians about likely candidates to set the Table going. Sir Dan Godfrey, founder of the Bournemouth Municipal Orchestra who was president of Bournemouth Rotary that year, and Cyril Whitemore, who had been agent to Lord Egmont at Ringwood and was now in insurance, both took to the idea enthusiastically. Buswell called a meeting at the

Wilkins Café which opted for forming what became Round Table no. 5. This inaugural meeting of 16 July 1928 attended by twelve founder members, which in 1975 Bryan Buswell remembered well, was followed by an inaugural supper at the New Cadena Café on Monday 13 August with fillet of sole, roast chicken and gooseberry tart. John Webb, as president of what had become the National Association of Round Tables, proposed the toast of the new Table, and the distinguished guests included the secretary of Bournemouth Rotary, the president of the Chamber of Commerce, and the mayor. Thus it was launched with high civic acclaim – another group who had the well-being of the town's business life and government at heart.

Within a year there were fifty-eight members of Bournemouth Table. Their record in these first twelve months must have been typical of the way all of these pioneer Tables developed in that first year. They held twenty-two supper meetings at nine of which a member gave a talk and at seven an address was given by a visiting speaker. They held two series of 'mystery speeches' and one musical evening. All other meetings were devoted to business matters 'for the welfare of the Table'. They sent six guineas to the relief of miners' children in South Wales and presented a challenge shield for the local Musical Competitions Festival. 'We have been approached by several bodies with a view to their obtaining our services,' wrote the secretary in his report at the end of the first year. He expected that the first actual 'service' would be given by the organisation of a Motor Ballot in aid of the local hospital Saturday and Sunday Fund (this in fact raised £1,892).

There is little evidence here of any appreciation of the distinctive objects of Round Table but much of the assumption of an 'adjunct to charity' role which was not really what Marchesi had in mind. But no one saw fit to arrest them taking the path of least resistance by plunging impetuously into the money raising activities they wrongly assumed everyone was expecting them to do. Even Norwich Table members showed themselves deviationists as early as 6 July 1928 when they accepted the invitation of the Lord Mayor to send representatives to a conference on unemployment and at the same meeting reported that the collection in aid of the Crippled Children's Outing organised by the Norfolk Motor Club amounted to £2 17s 7d.

The Norwich founders were aware of the temptation to run up side-tracks of their own laying, and in order plainly to delineate the main line they gave Jimmy Hanly the job of writing a booklet on *Round Table, What It Is and What It Does.*

A year after the inaugural meeting of Table no. 1 at Norwich, he said, the ideals of the club were appealing so much to the enthusiasm of young business men, and were meriting the approval of all the older generation to such an extent, that a national development of the movement was bound to follow.

'Owing to the necessarily restricted travelling facilities available to young men whose professions are as yet whole time jobs, the work of organizing this development contained many difficulties. A sub-committee, drawn from the general committee of the Norwich Round Table, was appointed to go thoroughly into the question of Table formation throughout the country, with the view to solving these difficulties of personal communication, and modifying the disadvantage of operating from a city which is geographically badly situated as an organising centre. . . . We are told that "Unity is Strength," and this, when applied to the Club, means not only unity amongst ourselves, but unity of ideals and objects. To achieve this first desirable unity is a comparatively easy task, because the act of becoming a member of the Club is a personal guarantee to forward its interest, but the idea contained in the Committee's decision was the desire for a similitude of management in Tables throughout the country.

'It would be impossible, and highly undesirable, to attempt a rigid standardisation of all rules, as local conditions must vary according to circumstances in different centres, and it is, therefore, left to the various Tables themselves to adjust such matters as the annual subscription and times of meeting according to their specific requirements. It will be seen, however, that there are many matters in which all Tables can act alike, and it cannot be too strongly emphasised that where the individual activities of Tables can be governed by a collective adherence to agreed methods of management, it is highly desirable that this foundation for solidarity and progress be adopted. It is the hope of the Norwich Table that this booklet will make possible a similitude of Table management, and also act as a link between the founder Table at Norwich and all other Tables which may come into existence.'

He outlined the events leading to the formation of Table no. 1 and the work it had accomplished so far 'with the idea of giving new Tables some indication as to how integral a part in the civic affairs of the city an organisation of young men may become'.

'An appeal by the Lord Mayor for the Hospitals and for a War Memorial was receiving the attention of all citizens during one week, but, unfortunately, owing to a misunderstanding, one day was left unprovided for, and it gave the Round Table a chance to show its worth. In spite of the short notice, its committee got together, and, working until midnight, took the responsibility on its own shoulders, with the result that the otherwise blank day had a bowls drive in the afternoon and a brilliant dance in the evening, while the Lord Mayor's Fund benefited to the extent of £108.

'Although this accomplishment will always stand as one of the most gratifying successes of the Table, every member is perhaps still prouder of a letter which was received at a later date from the Norwich Employment Exchange, asking that two representatives from the Round Table should be appointed to sit on a Committee formed to investigate the questions in connection with Empire Settlement. *This invitation was a recognition that the Round Table was a force whose opinion and advice were to be appreciated*, and it is the hope of the pioneers of the movement that, in every city where such a table is formed, the members may be able, in divers ways, to perform, individually and collectively, the highest service of all – the service of Citizenship.

'It is the wish also of those responsible for the drafting of these rules and guides, that readers will observe the spirit rather than the letter, and will, by endeavouring, with the aid of this book, put their minds in harmony with the ideals behind the rules, and forge, by their own enthusiasm and stability, *another link in the great chain of industrial common-sense*.

'One can truthfully say that the Rules and Objects of the Round Table, as set out in the official handbook, are as expressive of the true aims as brevity will permit, but the underlying principles are so morally and industrially vital, and offer such opportunities by their observance *for a better commercial world* that they are here expanded at length, so that even the sceptics of modern business methods may find perhaps some solution for their grievances. None of us are perfect, and pray Heaven none of us will ever be, or the world will have upon it some very unpleasant and monotonous beings, but *the striving to attain business integrity* must tend to bring about honest prosperity, not only individually, but to our cities and to our country. Let us be keen business men by all means, let us profit by our own work, but, when the total is reckoned, let it not record profit at the cost of misery to others.

'Turning our attention to the Rules, we shall find that, *underlying the formal words, are the precious secrets of increased knowledge, commonsense, reasoning, and peace in industry*.

'The Round Table is one of the few Clubs which are based upon a vocational basis, and, whilst not desiring to speak unfavourably about the principles of membership of those clubs not based upon such conditions, it is apparent that these few clubs mentioned do gain very material advantage from this vocational membership. Our pleasure, or otherwise, of meeting a person depends to a very large extent upon the medium through which we meet him. We may greet him heartily as a kindred follower of some sport, but, on the other hand, shudder at his political views, and it would be a very difficult matter indeed to run a club which depended for its success upon uniformity of ideas on so many different lines. As far as business or professional obligations are concerned we all have a common object in view, service to the community by our own efforts, and this forms the mutual ground which has made such a club as the Round Table possible.

'By causing business to be the foundation of the club, it has been possible to make the highly controversial subjects, which concern the few rather than the majority, such as Party Politics and Sectarian Religion, not only unnecessary in club discussions, but also, to render them by Rule 11 inadmissable. It would be a breach of this rule to discuss them here, and it is not proposed to do so, not because of this rule, but because of the idea behind its incorporation – business is a collective effort, and its progress must not be obstructed by individual bias.

'It will be seen, therefore, that one of the open secrets of the success of the Club is that its members meet upon a common footing, and, whatever the varied results architecturally of the great industrial world we may build, the foundations will always remain solid by reason of the unity in their construction.

'The Round Table has one of its finest ideals in teaching that we have no need to envy those with ten talents; we have in our own number, whatever it may be, chances to give service equally as valuable as those better equipped for industrial life. The day, fortunately, is long past when one country can feel itself independent of all other countries, but the interdependence of individuals, is even now, sometimes misunderstood. There is no legitimate occupation which does not thrive by its own merits. All will admit that, but not so many are ready to admit the worthiness of certain occupations. It amounts to class distinction of a very unpleasant nature, unpleasant not only in the fact that it is unjust, but because, by its existence, it is retarding industrial understanding and marring a co-operation of effort, which none of us can afford to neglect.

'Let anybody so inclined stand by the side of some great machine, and they will learn from this production of man the importance of apparent insignificant factors. Each wheel and cog has been designed by the engineer to carry out some specific task. Is it carried out by that little cog itself for its own achievement? No. The work of each cog is dependent upon the work of something else, and their various contributions of energy help to provide the grand total of the efficiency of the machine. Each of the occupations of men depends upon, and contributes to, day in and day out, the work of their fellow creatures, and the total is not an individual total, but the measure of efficiency of the great industrial machine which we have built up, and upon which we are dependent for our existence.

'The Round Table is undertaking a service of world value in attempting to promote a more generous feeling among followers of all occupations, and if they can, by good fellowship, lubricate, as it were, the bearings, the wheels of industry will run more freely, and make for more efficiency in production. The recognition of every legitimate trade as of equal service to the whole is the first step to happier conditions for all engaged in trade.

'There is no need to point out the many discrepancies in business morals. For one reason, this is not a sermon, and for another, most of us are fully aware of the opportunities for the establishment of higher ideals. To be a keen business man should be the legitimate aim of every person engaged in trade, but it is a hard pillow for reflection in our declining years to know that our prosperity has been gained by doubtful methods, and by deliberate indifference to the well-being of others . . . Loyalty to our city is not a sentimental expression based on love of its past history. It is a far cry from the days of gallant knights, spectacular pageants and heraldry of the history books to these days of clattering machinery, social upheaval, and the thousand and one things which seem to fill our lives to the exclusion of the very phrase "civic tradition". Tradition is often quoted as inspiration for young men to work for their city, but not less an incentive should it be to glance forward. The future men of our city must have something to inspire them in their work. Our object is by our own endeavour to uphold the honour of our work in every direction, to maintain a loyal standard in our civic effort, and to pass on to our sons a heritage equally worthy as that which our forefathers have given us.

'However great the ideals of such a club as that of which we are members, these ideals must find expression in a tangible, efficient and useful form. At no time in the history of the industrial world has the importance of cool reasoning been so needed as in the present day. Workers and employers are finding the value of level-headed discussion previous to drastic action, but preference for the former can only be accomplished either by economic necessity or an inbred desire for order. "Kill or cure" is a motto which the country cannot afford to adopt to-day. Our aim must be the prevention of the one and the elimination of the necessity for the other; thus shall we seek to establish in the minds of future business men the importance of clear reasoning before they are brought face to face with the indispensability of it by some contingency. A meeting of the Round Table, which is based upon a vocational basis, gives to each individual the knowledge of the whole. He receives first-hand information given by those expert in their calling, and has presented to him the objects under discussion from various points of view, and thus involuntarily enlarges the reception of his brain. The result is that he sees the thing from the other fellow's point of view, and after all, this is surely a sound foundation for a better understanding generally.

'The invaluable results of these meetings are not by any means confined to the numbers attending. Each will have occasion, sooner or later, to use the extra knowledge, and in so doing, will spread to the community not a biased view, such as is probably already held, but a well-balanced, broad-minded outlook, which contains the main essentials common to the various points at issue.'

Jimmy Hanly, who in 1976 was still enjoying energetic retirement in Norwich, concluded his booklet by emphasising the importance of uniformity in rules and management though each Table should decide its own subscriptions, times of meeting and constitution.

'The young business man who has joined a Round Table

Club has become something more than an ordinary club associate. *He represents the link between the last generation and the next.* It must be his aim to pass on to his son the world of business into which he is now entering, and to pass it on richer by his efforts.

'Rotary has, in the words of Mr Lincolne Sutton, given the Round Table the yeast of opportunity, and it is the job of the Round Table to bake the loaf. It is no easy task, this knitting of the old with the new, and the value of discernment will be a very important feature. We have got to realise that the foundations upon which business has been built must be pretty sound to have withstood the test of time as they have. It is not in our sphere of activities to destroy and rebuild. For one thing, we have not the time, and if we had, it would be a waste of time; for by the end of our lives we should be no further than at the beginning. The great edifice of industrialism has concreted its foundations by countless years of existence. Our task lies in perfecting its architecture and preserving the rock-like foundations.

'The Round Table is not a movement of imperious youth urged on to destroy and rebuild, efface, and start again, but a *whole-hearted*, sensible attempt to adopt the fundamentals of industrialism, to adapt *them to changing conditions, and, wherever possible, to improve them.*'

3

Heart-Searching

1928–1935

Association for a Purpose
or Mere Gregariousness?

By the time of the second meeting of what had become the National Council of Round Tables on the neutral ground of the Hotel York in Berners Street, London, on 4 October 1928 there were seven Tables: Norwich no. 1, Portsmouth no. 2, Guildford no. 3, Southampton no. 4, Bournemouth no. 5, Reading no. 6, and Doncaster no. 7.

The latter is distinguished for being the first Table to be formed outside the south of England. A traveller who regularly called on Langford's Restaurant in Norwich in 1928 was thirty-three-year-old Edgar Taylor of Doncaster who journeyed all over England as a representative of A. Bellamy & Co., a Birmingham distributor of raw materials for the food trade, calling on bakers and confectioners. Taylor had a number of Rotarian friends and he struck up a particularly firm friendship with Louis Marchesi who told him of his Round Table plans. He discussed these with his Doncaster friends, including solicitor Frank Capes and Wilf Wicks of Peglers, on Saturday mornings over a jar of ale at Maw Barker's in the High Street, and in

October 1928 they decided to form a Round Table of their own and hold an inaugural meeting. John Webb came up to present them with their charter on 29 October 1929 at a café in St Sepulchre Gate, with Marchesi at his side and in the presence of the usual Rotary and civic dignitaries.

Edgar Taylor was the first chairman of Table no. 7, but he was unable to attend the second meeting of Council in London on 9 October owing to illness. All the other six Tables sent representatives, two each except Reading who sent one. All eleven of them could vote individually as they wished; there was no block voting. After ratifying the National Constitution and electing Sydney Pascall and William Lincolne Sutton honorary vice-presidents, they came to item six on the agenda which was 'Consideration of New Badge'.

Granville Howard, a bank manager, who was chairman of Southampton Table and their representative at this meeting, had recently been attending assizes in the hall of Winchester Castle and found himself staring all afternoon at the big 'King Arthur's Table' which hung on the wall above the judge's head. Winchester had once been the capital of England and may have been the legendary Camelot. The wooden table was of uncertain antiquity, but had been repainted by King Henry VIII in 1522 in the Welsh national colours of green and white, with a double rose in the centre in the white and red of the Houses of York and Lancaster. Granville Howard, who remembers the occasion well, thought to himself how very much more inspiring an emblem this would make than the homely Victorian table which some took for a 'T' and standing for Toc H or others (as Arthur Colman recalled) thought indicated membership of a furniture makers guild.

On 4 October Granville Howard proposed the substitution of a design based on the Winchester Castle round table divided into twelve black and twelve white segments for the current badge. He was supported in this by fellow member C. F. Carr, editor of the *Southern Evening Echo*.

Portsmouth had told Norwich of their plans to supplant the

badge with one of their own design, and at their meeting of 20 August Marchesi, Durrant and their friends felt 'that the proposed design was not an improvement on the present one and savoured rather of an attempt to copy the Rotary badge'. The view of all Table no. 1 members was sought at a Special Meeting on 17 September, when 'T. F. Newman opposed the adoption of the new badge on the grounds that the present one was the original one and that a change would create a precedent which the other Tables joining might adopt when they felt they were in a majority. It would be the wrong policy to allow the badge to be changed if it could be avoided.' Another member wanted Quinton and Marchesi to oppose the adoption of the new design at the Council meeting or at least obtain a postponement of a decision to another Council meeting when more Tables would be represented.

On 4 October the two Norwich delegates did as they were instructed. Marchesi pleaded with the young men, who seemed to have a better idea about how his association should be run than he did, not to change so fundamental a part of the new movement 'in view of the fact that the new badge associated Round Table with the Arthurian legend and not with the modern idea of discussion and co-operation "around a table" which after all was the original idea'. But when it was put to the meeting they all voted for Howard's new design except Marchesi and Quinton – nine against two.

Obviously the new movement needed an official journal to act as its mouthpiece, but Marchesi urged that at the moment they could not afford it. Members of Norwich Table had subscribed £75 to pay for the booklets and lapel badges which had been supplied free to new Tables. If Portsmouth thought there was plenty of money available, a priority in his view was assisting Central Fund by paying for the old badges issued, now that they had become obsolete and unwearable. The old badges had cost 1s 6d each; the new ones were going to be sold at 3s 6d each.

They broke for lunch with guests Arthur Chadwick, president of British Rotary, Fred Broad, a Rotary director, F. C.

Hickson, executive secretary of British Rotary, W. W. Blair-Fish, editor of *The Rotary Wheel,* and Rotarians Sydney Pascall and William Lincolne Sutton. Rev. L. J. Hines had been invited but he sent a letter of apology in which he advised closer affiliation with and more control by Rotary. Marchesi's letter to delegates of 29 September stated that the subject for discussion at this important luncheon was 'consideration of the appointment of a joint committee of Rotary and Round Table to act as an advisory and consultative body'. Round Table council members had agreed among themselves to ask the Rotarians who were their guests to use their influence with their headquarters to ensure that Rotarians again be asked to assist the Round Table movement in the manner and spirit of the resolution passed at the Harrogate conference.

When the Round Table Council resumed its deliberations (without of course their Rotarian luncheon guests), Marchesi suffered another reverse when, on the proposal of C. F. Carr, the journalist who was a Southampton delegate, and H. H. Norris of Guildford, the Council resolved that in spite of the last paragraph of minute no. 3 of the meeting of 25 May, the sense of the present meeting was that it would be *inadvisable* to instruct prospective Tables to elect as members no more than three per cent of those who were Rotarians, and that preference should be given to non-Rotarians. After that lunch they could hardly have done otherwise.

Carr proposed Granville Howard as treasurer, but in deference to the obvious convenience of having secretary and treasurer in the same town, Billy Quinton was appointed to this 'national' office.

Carr had promised to write a piece about Round Table in *The Rotary Wheel* and assured the meeting he would make no allusion to the Arthurian legend in it, in spite of the new badge. Since Rotary had given so little room to youth in its ranks, he wrote, 'that much discussed individual the Young Business Man had been seeking alternative accommodation'. There was no new spirit of youth abroad, but there was a new spirit of service.

To give this full expression was the joint responsibility of youth and age. 'At present in business circles in this country 50 per cent of that spirit is running to waste. Somebody ought to see about it. Round Table is willing to accept the responsibility'.

Round Table realised, he said, that Rotary could not be expected to rhapsodise over or sponsor any new organisation as soon as the first little shoot showed through the top of the flower bed. It realised that first of all the plant must come to some show of maturity so that it could be determined without any shadow of doubt whether it was something of which the gardeners could be proud or whether it was a mere weed. That fact must be to most Tablers complete justification for the some-what non-committal attitude of Rotary towards Round Table. What one did want to show was that its present stage of devel-opment warranted for Round Table a place in the sun – if not exactly opposite to the Rotary rosebush, at least somewhere in the kitchen plot amongst the more humble but equally useful vegetables. One wanted to go even further; to ask that Rotary might take an active part in the nurture of this young but prom-ising organisation. 'One main reason is that Round Table, being so very similar to Rotary in its principles and in its personnel and, I trust, identical in its ideals, will draw upon a great reserve of service power that so far remains untapped (December, 1928).'

Before the Hotel York luncheon on 4 October W. W. Blair-Fish had written an editorial in *The Rotary Wheel* for October 1928 headed 'Rotary and Youth'. At the Harrogate conference, he said, this topic had arrested attention. Too often platform successes in a month after achievement, let alone five months, counted for nothing. There was little sense in hoping for too much from movements of any kind. 'So we see without disquiet-ude that in many Rotary centres Round Tables are to be more or less passing fashion. For "Rotary and Youth" was not solely a conference high spot. Had not Norwich previously *done* some-thing, and is not the present heightened activity due to enthu-siasm spreading out from the Norwich and Portsmouth examples? Which all brings us to a word of warning. On every hand one hears the supposedly supporting arguments that these junior clubs are to be reservoirs of strength for Rotary ranks, that our clubs are to be thus recruited. But we must not think of ourselves. The only concern for us is to what extent can we help these youths. Of all the service clubs in the field they are the most securely founded.'

Rotary influence was particularly pronounced in the case of Table no. 8 at Liverpool. At the first and foundation meeting at 15 Lord Street on Friday 9 November 1928, J. Rutherford Lindsay, a thirty-two-year-old barrister, opened proceedings by giving the twelve young men who attended an account of the progress of Rotary, and made a statement of its objects and, in the words of the minute, 'explained the relationship between Rotary and the Round Table, and the similarity of their aims'.

'It was decided to adopt the procedure of the Rotary Club of Liverpool in having a weekly (or fortnightly) luncheon to be followed by a speech or address on some subject of interest to the Club. No party politics or subjects of a sectarian nature to be discussed.' They decided to assemble at 12.55, have lunch at 1, the secretary's notices at 1.30, the main speech at 1.35 and dismiss at 2. Their first lunch (2s 6d a head) was held in the board room of the Liverpool Trade Protection Society which must have had similar objects. They fixed their entrance fee (for founder members as well) at half a guinea (10s 6d) and the annual subscription at one guinea.

At the inaugural meeting on 27 November 1928 at the Bear's Paw Restaurant Rutherford Lindsay who was the club's chairman said that Rotary, composed as it was of the leaders of industry and commerce and unable to admit more than one representative of each trade, inevitably failed to make any allowance for the younger generation. The Round Table had been set up as a junior club on the same lines as Rotary but for younger men. Two young men between the age of 18 and 40 would be admitted from each trade. The objects of the Liverpool Club had been 'cribbed wholesale' from Rotary.

Throughout they had had the full backing of Rotary. He hoped that Rotary in its turn would regard the Round Table as a feeding ground from which to draw members when there was a vacancy in any particular trade representation.

At the meeting W. Gibbons, president of the new club and also president of the Liverpool Rotary Club, welcomed Liverpool Table no. 8 as 'the nursery department of Rotary'. 'The age of chivalry is not yet dead and there is still great scope for the work of men who are, in the best sense, gentlemen.' Rev. Hunter Rodwell, former chairman of Liverpool Rotary, said if they kept the ideals of the Round Table club before them and elected as new members only men who had the Round Table ideal, they would make a success and grow automatically.

Table no. 8's Application for Membership Form asked the candidate to sign a statement undertaking, if elected, to comply with the requirements of the club's constitution and by-laws 'which have been explained to me'. A final paragraph over his signature read: 'I acknowledge the ideal of service and fellowship as the basis of all worthy enterprise and accept the obligation to attend regularly the weekly meetings of the club or to explain unavoidable absence therefrom.' The proposer and seconder had to sign a declaration that 'the undermentioned gentleman' was personally known to them and 'is eligible according to our rules with which he is acquainted'. But there was no assurance that the candidate was acquainted with and prepared to work for the *objects*.

The precise nature of these was still being hammered out by the founding fathers in Norwich. Was it within their terms of reference to stage either a mock town council or a mock trial, they asked themselves at their meeting of 10 December 1928. Billy Quinton thought it was not. He felt the Table should concentrate on minding its own business and improve the standing of discussion at its own meetings. What advantage would accrue to the Table or the town, asked another, if the Table took upon itself to do work which others had discarded? Marchesi made the revealing observation that it did not matter what the Table took up so long as discussion of it resulted in an *ac-tivity*. Whereupon a member declared he had entered what he believed to be the Ideal Organisation, insofar as he could fulfil the club's objects by indulging in masterly inactivity with congenial companions.

Just how hollow was the laughter which followed that remark was not recorded in the minutes.

Quinton thought they could probably mount a mock town council without being accused of party bias; as individuals they all had their views, though as a club they were not allowed to discuss them at a meeting. Others thought the club should turn their thoughts to 'community service'. Toc H were doing all they could in this field, but there was still much left to be done. They should appoint a sub-committee to explore possible lines of action.

Norwich Table, it seems, was on the defensive. There had been criticism of it from some quarters on the grounds of it not being seen to be *doing* anything. One member thought that to think of appointing a sub-committee to take counter-action was the result of panic. 'After all, criticisms were inevitable and any movement carrying out its own interpretation of its objects would be subject to it, but that was no reason for being influenced by it. He felt that in meeting as they did, regularly, and expressing their views on service and business ideals they were fulfilling the objects of Round Table.'

The panic that hit that meeting of Table no. 1 in Norwich on 10 December 1928 seized every Table in the course of time, and very few of them managed to stand firmly on the base of their foundation and refuse to be shaken off it. In the pursuit of objects which made them different from other movements they were ill at ease and lonely, and preferred to herd in with the rest and enjoy the comforts of orthodoxy. Eschewing subtlety, which might need close explaining and produce instant boredom, certainly had the effect of making the multiplication of clubs that amount easier.

New cells bred easily, and by the time the National Council

met for the third time on 21 February 1929 delegates came from twelve Tables. The newcomers were Liverpool, Bristol, Brighton and Hove, Stourbridge, Poole. Only three of the twelve Tables had paid their capitation fee so the net balance at the bank amounted to only £2 14s. Bernard Durrant tried and failed to persuade them to change to a block vote, but by nine to seven they retained individual voting. The Bristol Table delegate on his first appearance wanted to alter two of the Objects – the first of many attempts to do the same thing – but they all thought this was asking too much of a movement which had only been going two years. They decided to leave them as they were.

That spring the National Association of Round Tables held its first annual conference – Louis Marchesi insisted that it be at Norwich and he won his way. It lasted two days – 3 and 4 April 1929. Lincolne Sutton received the Tablers at a tea party in Stuart Hall and later there was a civic reception by the Deputy Lord Mayor, C. R. Bignold. In the evening there was a banquet for 160 presided over by chairman Bernard Durrant wearing the badge of office presented to him by fellow members of Table no. 1. The speeches were distinguished by the harsh observations made about Round Table's dependence on Rotary. In proposing the health of the National Association Judge Herbert-Smith said he supposed Rotary stood in the relationship of step-mother to Round Table, one not redolent as a rule with particular affection. The pedigree of Rotary was American, and of all places in America it came from Chicago, the most lawless place in the world. Round Table came from Norwich the most law-abiding city in England.

Jimmy Hanly proposing the visitors bravely tried to put the record right by pointing out it was profoundly untrue to say that Round Table was an offshoot of Rotary. The answer to the question What was the relationship between the two?, was that Rotary stood where Round Table started. If members of Round Table were going to make themselves worth while they must get out of their heads the doctrine of material wealth and pursue the higher path which would lead them to a higher position – a position of leaders of government and of democracy.

But in spite of Hanly's apologetics, Arthur Chadwick, president of British Rotary who was a principal guest, was plainly shaken. Rotary made no prior claim to superior position in the matter of ethical conduct, he said. It simply sought to give a lead and co-operate. He did not know to what extent Rotary was responsible for the birth of Round Table (!), but he thought those responsible had taken some of their pages from Rotary literature and got some of the spirit which Rotary stood for.

Chadwick was able to expand on this at the conference session the next morning. The remarks made at the dinner, he said, were not intended to be unkind, although the criticism of Rotary had been rather harsh and a little trying, if not irritating. They were due perhaps to a lack of understanding – the reference, for instance, to Chicago and to Rotary being a product of America. They had much to thank America for in conceiving the idea of Rotary. 'The Rotary movement to-day better understands the aspirations and plans of Round Table. At first I was a little distressed about it, because I thought there was a tendency towards disparagement which I think would be fatal. To my young friends I would say, avoid disparagement of other organisations. There is room for all of us, and there is certainly room for Round Table. I admit I have difficulty in understanding the point of view of the young men of to-day, but I must allow that since the war progress among young men and women had been greater than that of middle-aged men.' He finished by paying tribute to Louis Marchesi who must have warmed to hear the president of British Rotary refer to his difficulty as an older man to understand younger people's point of view. He had touched on the mainspring of Round Table's distinctiveness.

At the dinner Marchesi took up Bignold's expression of hope that Round Table would be extended to 'the colonies' by announcing that he had already been in correspondence with a Rotarian in Australia and believed that something would develop not only there but in Canada. John Webb too looked forward to rapid expansion; next year instead of twelve or fourteen Tables he expected to see 120 – an optimistic forecast at a time when total income for the first year of operations amounted to £108 14s 6d. Expansion to date had been almost entirely due to Louis Marchesi travelling at his own expense all over the country (leaving Langford's in the competent hands of manageress Dolly Buddrell) to inspire young men belonging to the section of the community to which he himself belonged with his simple, uncomplicated purpose.

His aim was to encourage the formation of clubs on the lines of the one he had founded in Norwich. But his disposition was not of the kind that rammed ideas down other people's throats in a spirit of take it or leave it. He planted the seed and left growth to take whatever form reflected the thinking of those who had been interested enough in what he had told them to 'have a go' themselves.

Table progress reports read out at the first Norwich conference showed the variety of ways they were developing. 'We hope,' stated Table no. 4 of Southampton which had sixty-seven members, 'to be recognised as a power for good, for efficiency and straightforward dealing and for service; this latter is thè chief justification for our existence.' Doncaster Table (no. 7) had formed a committee to work with the local labour exchange to attend at the railway station to wish godspeed to friendless emigrants who would otherwise leave the town without a cheerio. The entrance fee for Bristol Table (no. 9) was 3s 6d and the annual subscription 12s 6d.

The conference ended with a dance in the Arlington Rooms and the pattern had been set for the next fifty years. On the following day, the editor of the *Eastern Daily Press* contemplated Round Table's future. 'Wisely directed,' he wrote, 'the Round Table movement may well become a vital force in national social progress. The conference which has just been held shows that the movement is energetic enough in the pursuit of its ideals to make a stir, and that it is also wise enough to profit by

the experience of other organisations and avoid antagonising
public opinion by too flamboyant advertising its ideals before it
can see its way to translate them into useful service.'

As the founder of a single club at Norwich Louis Marchesi
could ensure that it began and developed on the lines he
planned; though once a committee had been formed to run it his
was only one vote among several. On the National Council his
voice once again was only one among many, and as more and
more Tables were formed and the size of Council grew there
was less and less chance that his views would prevail. In any
event Tables, in spite of being affiliated to the National Association, never had an opportunity of learning of Council's deliberations or the policy decisions which resulted from them. In the
spring of 1929 Marchesi must have felt he could only let things
ride, that the movement had to take its own course wherever
that led it. Direction of the movement he had created had been
taken out of his hands in the interests of 'democratic control' –
in this it had not copied Rotary. But he took back some of his
lost influence when he persuaded Council to allow him to be responsible for publication of a bulletin for circulation among all
clubs which he called *Round Table News & Views,* the whole cost
of which once again he paid for out of his own pocket. This established a line of communication not only from the would-be
leader to club members in the field, but also between one Table
and another. If it had occurred to anyone to attempt to arrive at
a consensus of opinion on any particular subject, a Round Table
corporate view, the journal would have provided the medium,
but the mood was against not only seeming to dictate a policy
from above but to frame one for public consumption from
within. Round Table would only thrive through exchange of
ideas of the entire membership, stated Marchesi – 'hence our
bulletin'.

It was the kind of ideal of which idealists often dreamt. But
members rarely have ideas about the movements they join, let

alone the urge or ability to express them. Marchesi was on firmer ground when he saw his bulletin as a means of making sure that members had joined for the right reason, of reinforcing the purpose he hoped had inspired their joining in the first place. 'Our future as a movement depends entirely upon the proper assimilation and subsequent expression of our Aims and Objects by all who undertake to uphold them.' Membership, he said, was not merely belonging to a Table; it was personal acknowledgement to the community of one's responsibilities throughout one's life. 'Being of the community, living in it by the exercise of our different vocations [occupations] it behoves all Round Tablers to do our bit for it – not a mere spasmodic effort, but a continual sustained one in our daily round and common task.'

It recalled Thomas Stephenson's assertion that Rotary was an attitude of mind, an outlook – attributes of the individual, not the group.

He returned to his original concept of cultivating understanding of other people's jobs and a realisation how many of the problems were shared by each; and to the cultivating of understanding between old and young. 'Let us in these columns lend an attentive ear to the voice of age and experience; let us be, in truth, the link between each passing generation and each new one. Let it be our aim to pass on this world of [business] affairs in which we are entering the richer for our efforts. Such is progress.'

Though some would have considered the wording and the sentiment high-falutin', that great in-word of the period, the message was not after all so very difficult to comprehend, let alone execute. But the message never got through. Bernard Durrant, first chairman of the first Table and close associate of Louis Marchesi, looking back over the whole span of Round Table's life in October 1975, said, 'His idea was the exchange of ideas between younger men to see how these could be fitted into those of the older people, so we work as one unity instead of two separate ones. This was never realised.'

Perhaps to most this is of little consequence beside the fact that the chain of clubs have survived and are continually growing in number.

Round Table being an essentially provincial institution did not prevent the formation, a year after its establishment in the country, of a club in the metropolis – Table no. 13, London East End, West End and Metropolitan Area. 'In September 1929,' recalled Keith Pascall, son of Sydney, 'I heard from my father of a group of young businessmen who used to meet together and I managed to attend one of their meetings at Suckling House, Norwich, with Bernard Durrant in the chair. The proceedings were not of great interest, but at a smaller gathering afterwards in Louis Marchesi's room over Langford's restaurant I soon came under the spell of the bubbling, spluttering and excited founder.' On return to London he gathered together a dozen sons of Rotarians and at a meeting in the hall of the Worshipful Company of Bakers, attended by Marchesi and representatives of eleven of the twelve Tables then in existence, the decision was taken to form the thirteenth, meeting in the Olde Cocke Tavern, Fleet Street.

Durrant's forecast of eventually having to divide the British Isles into sections had to be realised somewhat earlier than he anticipated. By the end of June 1929 Council, with two representatives from each Table, had already become too unwieldy and, though John Webb was against it, on 27 June it elected an inner Executive Committee of four members from three 'districts': one from the North (Liverpool, Halifax and Doncaster); one from the West and Midlands (Stourbridge, Newport and Bristol) and two from the South (Reading, Guildford, Brighton, Ryde, Southampton, Bournemouth and Poole). The absence of Portsmouth and Norwich is accounted for by the decision to exclude from the Executive Committee any representative of a Table with an officer in it who was automatically an ex-officio member.

At this meeting Council agreed that only Norwich should call itself 'Founder Table' – and its president's medallion so inscribed – and not the first four other Tables as well. When it was reported that Table secretaries were being sent charity lottery tickets for sale among members, Marchesi took the opportunity of declaring that it was bad policy to allow Round Table to become a channel through which members would become overwhelmed with local charity appeals. Any young man could of course take any part he wished as an individual in fund raising schemes organised by other bodies, but Council agreed it was out of order and undesirable for members to raise money for local charities by appealing to the movement nationally.

The dangers were underlined by Leonard Hines of Halifax who attended the meeting as a guest and was invited to express his views. Rotary was inundated with all sorts of appeals, he told them. If they gave way they would be simply flooded. How and where to draw the line was difficult, but they would be advised to try and hold the balance very rigidly right from the start. 'Refuse to encourage excessive zeal in regard to what is known as Community Service.'* Round Table had got to be true to itself, and to Rotary. 'It is not what we are doing but what we are, and it is very easy for Round Table to make a mistake.'

Thanking Hines for his contribution, Marchesi said Round Table was an association of young business and professional men trying to develop that feeling of fellowship and service in their jobs whereby the path of business could be made smoother and broader. They were getting members to give what he called 'Round Table Service' by interesting themselves in the welfare of all concerned in their jobs and in matters of interest to the communities in which they lived. The object of each member of a Round Table club was to *be* something in his own sphere.

* It was questionable whether many on first reading the phrase 'Community Service' did not take it to have the same sense as 'Community Singing', i.e. service by a community (as singing by a community), instead of service *for* a community; and that much confusion arose as a result of this and the pursuit of group community work in the belief that this was an Object of Round Table.

Hines amplified this theme in the speech he gave at the inaugural dinner of the Halifax Table (no. 14) on 18 April 1929, when he said if Round Table was to have value and purpose its influence would be largely felt in the future enrichment of the town's civic sense and citizenship. Rotary was seeking to give expression to an ideal (of service before self) that was universal. But Round Table was not just an extension of Rotary to young men but of its ideal. It was not consistent with the purpose of Round Table to ask of members what they were going to do, but rather what they were going to be. Round Table like Rotary was a function of being. If Round Table regarded itself in that way it would never come into conflict with young men's service organisations already in existence, and would never become involved in its own expensive and burdensome service machinery or 'committed to futile ventures of philanthropy which can be more efficiently carried out by other societies existing for the purpose'.

Hines advocated Round Table giving equal place to the young man who toiled faithfully with his hands as for those who followed a business or professional career. He saw Round Table fashioning a young manhood healthier in body because healthier in mind, having a love of life and of the toil of life for its own sake, seeing a dignity in all service and opportunity in all human contact and fellowship, and possessing a world sense which felt in its heart the larger patriotism of race, not unfamiliar with the best things and the inward things. 'Until Round Table has had time to try its hand at this mighty business we will be content to say "Thank you" for the God speed you have given us and for the hopes and expectations you have expressed.'

How these young business men assembled in the Hotel York reacted to these words can never be known, but from subsequent events it appears the message that a Table would not necessarily be a 'better' Table by virtue of what it did, and what it was shown to be doing, never penetrated. Moreover if any vestige of inspiration on this level had ever managed to seep into the body of any of the first dozen Tables, by 1929 it was beginning to seep out again. Young men who joined on the crest of the first wave of enthusiasm failed to keep to their vows of regular attendance, a reluctance reinforced by pecuniary considerations as Britain entered the greatest economic crisis of its history. In 1929 even Norwich reported: 'Attendance at meetings leaves much to be desired . . . . A score of real live members are of greater value than fifty lukewarm . . . . There is no provision for nominal members in the Rules.'

The Depression had hit Australia as hard as Britain, and in 1930 three young men of Geelong, the great wool and mining centre, Ewen Campbell Laird, Langham Proud and John Buchan, appalled at the effect it had on a young man just starting out on his career, decided to form a club to 'rescue him from his loneliness' and break the prison of his soul. 'With so many difficulties to be faced,' wrote R. S. Love and V. M. Branson,* 'with so much evil to be matched, a man fighting single-handed could wreck himself financially and physically without making any lasting impression on the forces opposed to him. His high purpose and great courage could go for naught. No man alone could hope to succeed against the deadweight of the Depression. It is necessary to enlist and organise the forces of decency and to raise the morale through friendly intercourse.' Here again the motivation was inward looking; to benefit the member, to enrich the member's life.

Geelong had plenty of clubs already, including a Rotary Club, and Laird, Proud and Buchan met in a room of the latter where they decided to form a Geelong Young Business Men's Club to hold monthly luncheon meetings in a café for men between the ages of eighteen and thirty-five, limiting membership to 100. The first lunch meeting was on 3 December 1930 and

* In *Apex, The First Twenty-Five Years* (Rigby Ltd, Adelaide, for the Association of Apex Clubs of Australia, 1955).

soon sixty members had joined. It also acquired objects similar to Rotary – to create an interest in other men's work, to foster high ethical standards in business and the professions and encourage members to take an interest in the civic, social and moral welfare of his community, and exchange ideas. Fellowship with service was the key.

On 10 March 1931 they changed the name to The Apex Club of Geelong and adopted a symbol of the sun's rays rising within an equilateral triangle, the base of which was Citizenship and the sides Fellowship and Service.

Other Apex Clubs were formed and when they met in conference at Geelong in 1932 Paul Harris, founder of Rotary, sent them a message: 'Where there's a will there's a way. Assuming of course that the will is strong enough. Nothing is impossible to one possessed of a will which is indomitable. Accomplishments whether they rank as great or relatively insignificant are generally the result of the application of someone's will power.'

Back in Britain a battle of wills was taking place around the way Round Table was to develop. In February 1930 T. A. Spittle of Bournemouth said he thought all the talk about what they *were,* and not what they were doing, was overdone. Round Table should be a body of healthy, enthusiastic young human beings with an organisation at hand for being of practical service. What better way was there of doing and being than to help a less fortunate body over the stile? The spirit of Round Table should embody fellowship, and surely the hand of fellowship should be held out primarily to those most in need of it – charitable organisations? Bournemouth were about to raise £2,000 for local hospitals.

Marchesi's idea was being too subtle; and for many too simple. A wish to extend *charitas* as opposed to practising *agape* was undoubtedly noble, but Marchesi's Round Table was not designed to foster it.

Perhaps Round Table's energies were being diverted into these channels because it had cut itself off at the start from the main stream of life by outlawing Politics (which it should have called Political Science or Social Management) and Sectarian Religion (which it should have called the Spiritual Life or Mystical Experience). Hines poured scorn on this when he saw his own Halifax Table silting up. 'This taboo is a wicked confession of spinelessness,' he told his members. 'To protect ourselves from each other's opinions is the sort of thing we despise in our elders and betters. . . . We shall be driven to revoke this decision sooner or later, or resort to sewing meetings.

'When we talk about service in Round Table we are talking rubbish unless we have in our minds the equipment of ourselves for any service we may want to perform. There are hundreds of things afoot in this town which we know of only by hearsay. Suppose we get a move on and investigate them for ourselves, instead of sitting like stuffed rabbits.'

Table no. 1 saw informing themselves of what was going on in Norwich as a key part of what they chose to call Social Service, and for this purpose they had members sitting on the city's Hospital Week Committee, Deaf and Dumb Committee, Blind Institution, Unemployment Welfare Committee, Chamber of Commerce, Publicity Association, and the local branch of the British Empire Leprosy Relief Association.

But was 'community service', as most called it, a central or subsidiary part of Round Table's programme and, if so, was it service for the community by the individual member or by the Table as a group? A lead was wanted to direct the movement into the 'right' paths, and the Elders discussed their duties in this respect at the Council meeting of 30 June 1930. Marchesi had no difficulty in spelling out the 'official' line – the founder's line, that is. 'If every fellow in the movement put the spirit of the objects into his vocation (occupation), he would almost unconsciously be carrying out some form of community service.' At the other extreme some delegates wanted the rules altered so that it became an obligation for a *Table* to do a certain amount of community service every year. Another thought Council should make a pronouncement whether community service was a moral obligation of the individual or of the Table as a body. There was nothing in the rules about it now. The movement was waiting, not for the last time in its life, for the lead which never came.

If the matter was ignored by the Rules and Objects it was something which, if a particular Table wished, could be rectified through the form of declaration each required a member to sign on joining. Wolverhampton Table no. 17, formed in 1929, had a 'charge' read to each member: 'You have been chosen to membership of the Round Table of Wolverhampton because we believe you to be the representative of your profession (trade) and because we believe you possess those qualities of mind and spirit which fit you to interpret and impart the message of Round Table to your fellow men. Round Table requires you to do your utmost to carry its true spirit into your own profession (trade), and in your private capacity and as a citizen to strive to live up to the ideals for which the organisation of Round Table stands. Your membership involves definite obligations, including regular attendance at meetings and general support of the Table's activities, and it is our earnest hope that you will endeavour to carry out those obligations to the best of your ability.'

Here was evidence of positive selection of members of the kind calculated to fill Round Table with young men best suited to give the movement the life which Marchesi had envisaged. Selection of speakers and their subject matter was also central to giving Round Table a character which would distinguish it from other clubs (apart from its age limit), and prevent it from embracing the tempting cosiness and lethargy which had always kept 'movements' from moving – the Land Surveyors Club founded with such high ideals in 1834 is a notorious example. When Marchesi warned Tables against the danger of becoming mere lecture or social clubs for the entertainment of members in winter evenings, he was sniping at the tendency to close in the summer altogether. But the attack made by Tom Green of Halifax Table in October 1930 had deeper implications. 'A movement like ours cannot live unto itself alone,' he asserted. 'It is very easy to meet in a very comfortable room and discuss with our friends various problems in an academic way; but we do that only at the peril of our souls. We have to watch carefully any tendency to degenerate into a mere literary or debating society. The test of health of any Table is its ability to apply to the practical concerns of life lessons taught through contact with the ideals and members of Round Table.'

Pricked no doubt by Leonard Hines's jibes about sewing meetings, Green was proclaiming that richer and truer good-fellowship could result from discussions directed at a declared end than whatever the speaker chose for himself. A coffee-house might generate good-fellowship which had to be regenerated every evening; but in a club like Round Table good-fellowship could build up over the months if all concentrated on a common end which bound them together with more potency than coffee, brandy, or heartiness. And for those who saw good-fellowship as the by-product of the adventure of pursuing an end in concert with others, the fun lay in *that* pursuit and not the pursuit of fellowship as an end in itself.

To lend authority to his recommendation Tom Green might have quoted the much quoted remark of Benjamin Disraeli,* 'I prefer association to gregariousness. It is a community of purpose that constitutes society [in the sense of companionship].'

Halifax Table formulated a policy of subjects and speakers emphasising the social and ethical side of life rather than addresses which were purely constructive. 'And it is hoped that an increasing earnestness of purpose and a quickening of the social consciousness of members will soon be made manifest.'

It was a brave report, laying itself open to taunts of over-intensity. For the cynics 'earnestness' had a forbidding tone about it which they mistook for solemnity. But at last it seemed that someone had taken Marchesi's message. But Halifax were an exception.

* His Young England movement had no affinity with Marchesi's Round Table.

The run-of-the-mill young business man to whom membership had been flung open without much attention to his readi-
ness or ability to absorb the club's Objects, was not going to
knuckle down to *that* kind of activity after a hard day's work at
the office, even if his intellect had been up to it. When Tom
Benson talked to Littlehampton Table on the Ethics of the
Round Table, the secretary reported it was an exceedingly fine
paper 'but unfortunately rather over the heads of most of our
members'.

Firmness of purpose however signalised the movement which
was open to young men of the same age group (eighteen to
forty) and walk of life as Round Table – the branch of Jaycees
International which had formed in Britain in 1929 as 'British
Junior Chambers of Commerce' with G. M. Bone of Lincoln as
their first president. 'Service to humanity is the best work of
life' was the British Jaycee creed as in America; making themselves useful to the community while equipping themselves to
develop their own skills as managers and executives, was their
driving force. There was no shilly-shallying on what *these*
young men had clubbed together for. Earnest maybe, but determined. 'To develop powers of leadership and a sense of responsibility to society' was the first objective of the Junior Chamber
of Commerce for London, a leading unit in the movement, as
would be expected, though the main strongholds were in the
North-East and Midlands. 'Personal development and community involvement' was what BJCC stood for.

Another potential competitor for the subscriptions of the
same young men as were attracted to Round Table was The
National Business Men's Association, though this had no age
limit. In 1931 it published a report on Unemployment, the main
social issue of the day, which recorded that between half a million and a million people outside the two million officially unemployed were suffering acute poverty which neither the State
nor any social insurance scheme did anything to mitigate. Most
of these were of the middle middle-class who formed Round
Table membership whose worry from being out of a job would

have overlaid many a good intention to participate in any form
of community service.

In 1931 the economic crisis and the general bankruptcy of
political ideas to pull Britain out of it prompted the foundation
of Political and Economic Planning (PEP), an organisation
with Kenneth Lindsay as its first secretary, formed to study
questions of the day and issue reports and broadsheets. The first
broadsheet, on Iron and Steel, was issued in April 1933. It also
formed a PEP Club with regular fortnightly speaker lunches.
Of course there was only one of these and in London – but it
was in the Round Table tradition. PEP reports were read in
the corridors of power and, as Kenneth Lindsay has said, 'in
some cases they influenced policy. Such bodies as the Social Science Research Council, the Nature Conservancy and in some
measure the Arts Council, owe much (and in some cases their
existence) to PEP enquiries.'

This would have been heady stuff for the average Round
Table member who preferred his subject matter more on the
lines of Gypsy Lore, Impressions of Shanghai, Fur Felt Hat
Making, Modern Wireless, the Lightning and Lighthouses,
Soap, Electricity, Priests Holes and Hiding Places, Fingerprints,
and every now and again The Indian Question, Proportional
Representation, Prohibition, and The League of Nations. Two-
minute speeches on subjects drawn out of a hat were popular:
Should Savages Be Exterminated?, Red Noses, Racing at
Brooklands, Corporal Punishment. And every so often a Ladies
Night, a fancy dress ball, a Christmas Market.

The ladies were always on the fringe of Round Table, though
of course never invited to sit down and take part with their
menfolk in the routine activity. But when eight wives of members, led by Mrs Lee, formed a committee in June 1930 to collect
funds to provide visiting ladies with a gift for the 1932 annual
conference at Bournemouth, they continued to meet and called
themselves 'Ladies Circle'. The same motive led the wives of
members of Manchester Table no. 29 to meet in April 1933 in
anticipation of the 1934 Liverpool Conference on ss. *Doric* – and

to continue meeting. They too formed a permanent group and Mrs Edina Headon and her colleagues, without having had any contact with Bournemouth, also hit on the name 'Ladies Circle'. Mrs Win Hussey, wife of Fred Hussey, vice-chairman of Hastings Table no. 21, accompanied her husband to the Liverpool Conference, attended the Open Information Meeting for Ladies in the ship's sun lounge, and took the message back to Hastings where the 1935 conference was to be held. And so the Ladies Circles snowballed, until, with eight in existence by 1936 – Bournemouth, Manchester, Hastings, Liverpool, Middlesbrough, Wolverhampton, Doncaster, Southampton – a National Association of Ladies Circles was formed with Win Hussey* as national president and Mrs Theresa MacKinnon as secretary. The object was 'Friendship and Social Service for Knowledge and Progress'. A full and highly entertaining account of Ladies Circle International and the growth of Sybil White's Tangent Clubs for 'retired' LC members (an association was formed in 1970) is to be found in Jean Robinson's *Circle, The Story of NALC*, published by the association in 1974.

Round Table was not for women, and the common sense of keeping it for men, emphasised by the formation of the separate Ladies Circle, was plain for all to see. But not all saw the inconsistency of trying to change a constitution which specified *young* men. That Round Table was for under-forties was as much a distinguishing mark as that the Young Conservatives was for young Conservatives. But many members wanted to have their cake and eat it by staying within the fold on reaching forty and becoming an 'honorary' member – a club for under-forties but sort of not, don't you know. They would have had no vote but hung around and 'helped' those who for so long had been waiting to take control without help. It was knowing that such help was not forthcoming that gave the final year or so as an officer its value.

The double-think which enabled the Bournemouth member to feel that 'Round Table could ill afford to lose the driving

---

* She died at Hawkhurst, Kent, in 1975.

power and influence of active members just passing the age of 40' cannot have been shared by many, but that anyone should have missed the point of what Round Table was all about to that extent must have given cause for considerable hilarity in Langford's Smoke Room.

A more level-headed, Northern view came from Bradford: 'The founder cherished the idea of a movement governed and financed by young men and young men only. We should not forget that the young men entering the movement to-day [1931] feel as the founders did four or five years ago. It is our duty to accept the age limit with good grace.'

That was putting it mildly. If you were not prepared to accept it, you did not join. But it was a heartening indication of respect for what the founder had founded, as against the easy mental sliding that justified pulling the structure apart on the grounds that it was honouring the principle embodied in the motto's word 'adapt'. Its place there, as those who have read so far will have appreciated, was to exhort members to be adaptable in their outlook to the needs of the changing times, not change the movement's *raison d'être* whenever the whim dictated.

Such little control as Marchesi still exercised over Round Table from his command post of honorary secretary of the National Association was now coming to an end. In February 1931 he told Council he and Billy Quinton wanted to know whether their appointments, made when the movement was launched by the only two Tables then existing, was endorsed for another year by the current thirty-two Tables. He said both of them would accept Council's ruling, knowing it would strengthen their position 'and enable them to continue with increased vigour'. But Council would give Marchesi and Quinton no such endorsement, and merely observed that nominations for national officers would be received three months before each annual conference.

A new club was not officially recognised until it was formally affiliated and it had been presented with its 'charter'– the wording of which had been drafted by lawyer Rutherford Lindsay. The ceremony of the presentation of this document, usually at a dinner attended by civic dignitaries, was an occasion for the attendance also of the founder. Marchesi had almost certainly been the instigator of the club in the first place, and he was then able to come down and put his seal on it.

But by May 1931, when there were thirty-three Tables, serious consideration was given to devising some form of Area Administration; and Marchesi, in his last term as secretary, submitted a report in which he warned Council that if such a development was approved it was essential that they, Council, should remain the supreme authority in deciding national policy. It would be a hopeless task to consider international expansion before they could be assured of harmony, loyalty and goodwill towards the rulings of Council. No individual Table or group of Tables who might form an Area could be accepted as the mentor of national policy, though he agreed that circumstances differed in certain districts and national rules had to be kept as broad as possible. John Webb supported Marchesi in not wanting to set up a multiplicity of new 'officers' involving work for more secretaries. It would increase the expense too. The general feeling was that they should wait till there were fifty Tables.

Bournemouth Table watched Marchesi's influence 'behind the scenes' with undisguised concern. At the Council meeting in London in September 1931 they accused him of making alterations to the Draft Rules not authorised by a rule passed at a national conference and thus committing a breach of Article IX, paragraph 3. Marchesi admitted this, but defended his alterations on the grounds that they were 'correct interpretations of customs adopted, notwithstanding the absence of an express rule to justify them'. He had made what might be considered 'unorthodox improvements' to the Draft Rules, but this was a result of 'keeness in the movement and a desire to save unnecessary expense by having to print another set'. It must have been

National Association of Round Tables of Great Britain and Ireland

ADOPT · ADAPT

IMPROVE

This is to Certify that No._____

ROUND TABLE_____

being duly organised and agreeing through its officers and members to be bound by the constitution and by-laws of the National Association of Round Tables of Great Britain and Ireland, such agreement being evidenced by the acceptance of this certificate, is now a duly elected member of

THE NATIONAL ASSOCIATION OF ROUND TABLES OF GREAT BRITAIN AND IRELAND

and is entitled by such membership to all the rights and privileges of such Association.

In Witness whereof the seal of the National Association of Round Tables of Great Britain and Ireland is hereto affixed and the signature of its officers duly authorised, are subscribed hereto the_____day of _____anno Domini 19_____

Signed_____

President R.T.B.I.

Signed_____

Secretary R.T.B.I

The Charter

an uncomfortable meeting. They finally agreed to appoint a Rules Committee of six excluding Marchesi 'to investigate the minute books of national Council meetings and conference meetings with a view to framing Rules according to such minutes for approval and acceptance at the 1932 national conference'.

In April 1932 Louis Marchesi and Billy Quinton submitted their resignations as secretary and treasurer, posts they had both held for five years. Before quitting as secretary Marchesi was able to utter one more (official) word of warning about trying to develop too quickly. Expanding the movement internationally in the present state of their finances, as had been advocated by Middlesbrough, would be a waste of time. They must cut their suit according to their cloth. It was not Round Table but its ideas which should be noised abroad. There were societies in other countries fulfilling Round Table's objects and he did not think they ought to encroach upon their preserves. Contact and a friendly exchange of opinions was the only practical way of developing Round Table's ideals, as they had already done with the Loyal Knights of the Round Table of America and the Kinsmen Clubs in Canada.

Liverpool's call for more active leadership from headquarters, for regularly issued guidance and instruction in the best methods of promotion, development and the realisation of the objects of Round Table, was a symptom of the calm that had settled upon Round Table after the early ferment. It was not to be the first of such calls or the first time no heed was paid to them. However much Marchesi would have liked to have answered Liverpool's appeal, the Secretariat or Headquarters was about to leave Norwich together with the Editorial Office of the movement's journal.

It was decided to split the office of secretary and editor. T. A. Spittle of Bournemouth, one of Marchesi's severest critics, was appointed secretary; W. T. Barnard of Poole treasurer; and a professional journalist, Brian Whiteaker, news editor of the *Express and Star* of Wolverhampton, editor of *News and Views*.

But Marchesi could not resist shooting from the sidelines when he attended the Council meeting in March 1933 as Norwich Table delegate by disapproving the action of the Executive Committee in involving the movement in an association with the Local Knights of the Round Table of Tintagel which he said would affect the autonomy of Round Table. But when it was pointed out to him that his resolution might be considered a vote of censure on the Executive Committee he withdrew it.

The new leadership began by instituting a number of annual Round Table debates on a matter of national importance, like Disarmament; but at the very next meeting (May 1933) the Rules Committee recommended deletion of the sentence by which business of a contentious nature could be transacted if a majority of twenty members agreed. The rule became 'Party politics and sectarian religion shall be excluded from all Table discussions' without any escape clause. It was a step which a young Merton builder who joined Round Table in 1933 was to go on deploring for the next forty years – Cyril Marsh. His preaching of the Marchesi version of Round Table had yet to get into its stride, but he already had an ally in lawyer Rutherford Lindsay who told members, 'Too often a member who becomes engrossed in the more social phases of Round Table loses sight of the principal reason for his election to membership, namely that he can represent his particular classi-fication in a way no other member can fulfil'. Round Table was as yet inexperienced in 'community service'. Members must curb their enthusiasm to be up and doing a form of vol-untary service in which there was much duplication, waste of time, effort and money. In every town there were organisa-tions with programmes for 'doing good'. They must profit from the experience of these organisations whose failures were due to misdirected effort, lack of funds or sponsoring an unneeded service.

When he asked members to ask themselves whether they had given due recognition to employees, he might well have had in mind the exemplary step taken by Geoffrey Mander

MP, chairman of Mander Brothers, the Wolverhampton paint manufacturers, who in 1933 gave his work people forty-seven hour wage rates for a forty-hour week. 'It was possible for us to offer our workers either increased pay or increased leisure,' he said. 'They have, we think, wisely and considerately chosen the latter, thereby not only securing for themselves a more interesting and healthy life by securing a free Saturday and Sunday, but also keeping at work a number of people who would otherwise have gone inevitably to swell the number of unemployed. We think that if other firms faced with a similar situation would look at the matter in this light they would be able to make arrangements of the same kind.'

It was an enlightened attitude, well ahead of its time, of the kind that Marchesi's Association of Young Business Men could well have been seen publicly applauding. Geoffrey Mander had been an active member of the Wolverhampton Rotary Club for many years, and was here putting Rotary/Round Table ideals into action – a fine expression of that confusing phrase 'vocational service'. Another member of the family, Sir Charles Mander, who was an honorary member of Wolverhampton Round Table no. 17, and mayor of Wolverhampton and a Past President of British Rotary, lent further authority to the same view. There were still firms who employed labour as water from a muddy well, he wrote in *News & Views* of October 1933. The future of the country depended, he said, on the imagination and courage employed in dealing with the problem of human association. Dealing with the other key object of Round Table, business ethics, which rank and file seemed so anxious to keep at arms' length, he asserted that some thought it did not pay to be honest. 'The dubious half-light between what is admittedly dishonest and obviously fair extends until many things, which in better times would be shunned, become sharpish practices and condoned with a laugh, hardly shamefaced. . . . If one is careless of the foundations then dishonesty may pay as a make-shift, and the hard-boiled perpetrator can still read the lessons on Sunday and if necessary salve his conscience by donations to charities. It is human nature however to avoid this anodyne by keeping one's mind departmentalised.'

This was dangerous ground, an embarrassing topic to most business men of the 1930s anxious not to be considered prigs and made vulnerable to the accusation of taking a holier-than-thou stand which their friends would resent. It was more 'contentious' than arguing whether Round Table was a Christian society (which all agreed it was not), or hearing the merits of the new regime in Germany of Adolf Hitler whose leaders were all under forty, which Dr Ernst Deissmann of the Anglo-German Bureau extolled to a joint meeting of London Tables, or the benefits which Sir Oswald Mosley proclaimed the small trader of Britain would derive from Fascism.

Many Tables which sheered away from the 'difficult' object of Round Table concerning high standards in business life, took little notice on the other hand of Council's ban on the discussion of what was officially held to be 'contentious'. Bromley sought to commend to members the Cause of Peace which it considered Round Table could adopt without joining forces with the League of Nations. Attracted by the title 'Poverty Amidst Plenty – a Solution', members would find themselves listening to a talk on the Douglas Social Credit System, the greenshirts. Many debated the rights and wrongs of Disarmament. Keith Pascall proposed that it was necessary for the peace and goodwill of the world at a London Table debate; on Empire Day 1933 Harold Bing, a university professor, plunged into an attack on the sinister role played by private armament firms in a debate staged by Hull Table. Worthing Table debated the very relevant subject 'Should Corporation Trading Be Abolished?'. Violet Markham MP addressed Chesterfield Table on 'Wanted – A New Technique for Democracy'.

Subjects such as these should have been the leaven of the talks given by members themselves on the problems of their own occupations which would have fulfilled the prime object of Round Table, but they did not feature in the programmes of other than the defiant few. It was 'Rites of Ancient Egypt', 'The

History of Photography' and 'The Life Boat Service' which made it easy for the average member to fulfil his quota of 50 per cent attendance, buoyed up by the groundswell of the less taxing whist drives, motor rallies, tennis tournaments, boxing matches, dances, charity bazaars, collecting and making clothes for the unemployed, visits to the local sewage works, beauty contests, pageants, treasure hunts, golf competitions, hospital fêtes, carnivals, transporting the sick, organising children's outings – though for many this was the main current. If it could be said that not losing members had become a principal aim of Round Table, it was these social activities which made sure it was achieved.

The Bradford member who proclaimed 'We stand for applied common decency' was probably representative of most. 'Where is the Association heading?' he asked. 'I don't know and I don't care. It can take care of itself.'

With no permanent head or director as Toc H or the Motor Union had, the National Association of Round Tables was endeavouring to take care of itself as well as it could. In his five continuous years as secretary Louis Marchesi had managed to lay down what he hoped would be a permanent way on which Round Table could voyage through time, but after he resigned the secretary was changed every two years. In October 1933 T. A. Spittle handed over to another. At the same time Marchesi, who had refused to be made a vice-president when he resigned the secretaryship, agreed to become an ex-officio member of Council until he reached the age of forty in five years time, which meant of course he could advise but not vote.

The main committee of a Table and its sub-committees on one of which, at Manchester for instance, every club member had to serve, had a greater sense of continuity. The number of sub-committees varied. Manchester had eight: Propaganda, Speakers, House, Social, Community Service, Inter-club, Finance, Rules. They also ran their own bulletin. Nottingham had only four: Service, Classification, Programme, Publicity and Club Service. Some deplored this lack of standardisation in the movement's organisation, but 'headquarters' consistently refused to lay down the law or even to suggest guide lines.

The main medium of communication was the magazine *News & Views*. The editor, who was a member of Council, wrote what he liked but had to account to them *after* each issue. He thus had considerable power over the way the movement, as opposed to individual Tables, sustained itself. The editor had the platform of his regular editorial in which to make observations about any aspect of Round Table he saw fit, and to mould what could be termed the movement's philosophy as no one else could. The professionals like Brian Whiteaker and his successors Charles Ramsden of Halifax and Milner Riley also of Wolverhampton, took full advantage of their opportunities, as had Louis Marchesi in his five years as editor. The *potential* was great, but in the event it seems that few of their messages were received, let alone understood; only a minority of readers read any part of the magazine other than the report of their own Table's activities.

A second main opportunity for the dissemination of the Round Table message was the annual conference, but again it was only a minority who had the time or the money to attend, and it was probably the same nucleus who turned up each year; though a full report was given in the magazine. But in 1934 at any rate, when it was held on board the White Star liner *Doric* moored in Liverpool Docks, an attempt was made to pull the occasion into focus and give members and the outside world something to concentrate on, by giving it a theme, 'Planning for Tomorrow'.

A third way of issuing pronouncements was to issue an official policy booklet, and this is what the members who happened to be the officers of the Association did in April 1934. As 'the view of the National Executive Committee on Round Table policy', it was intended to be the movement's new 'Bible' and to satisfy all those who had been looking to headquarters for a lead. A considerable amount of 'interpretation' of the rules and constitution was exercised, and acquired the status of law.

The Executive Committee for instance saw two conditions of membership: being under forty and occupying at least an executive position or being an articled pupil. These ensured selection of young men of recognised standing and influence, and well qualified to represent their occupations. The first object of any club was to enable members to make each other's acquaintance, and the second to impress on them the importance of high standards in business and professional conduct. 'If the Association did no more than maintain those standards of professional and business ethics in this way its existence would be amply justified.' Serving the community came third – by doing his job efficiently the member earned not only a living but the gratitude of the community, and if he found time for voluntary service in unpaid local government work or voluntary social action outside his office hours, so much the better. Round Table, reiterated the Executive Committee, was not primarily a charitable organisation. The objects made no specific mention of charity or social service. But young men joining a Table would have before them the prospect of many genuine friendships and a widening of their outlook, and an opportunity of doing their share in serving the community. They would be obliged to attend regularly and to give their Table general support. 'Before they reach the stage when the operation of the wisely conceived age limit puts an end to their active membership, they may see the Association wielding an influence for good of dimensions undreamed of even in the visions of its founder and his band of pioneers.'

Area Councils were set up in April 1933 for an experimental year and the 500 delegates who paid £2 15s a head for the 1934 conference on the ss. *Doric* and heard guest speakers F. J. Marquis (later Lord Woolton) and Godfrey Winn, the *Daily Mirror* columnist, agreed to adopt Areas as permanent parts of the movement's national organisation. There were fifteen of them, and from February 1936 Council was composed of Area and not

Table delegates. Each Area had its own committee or council, with numerous sub-committees, its own chairman or president and its own officers elected annually, its own bell and 'jewels'. It held its own annual meeting and banquet, everyone dressed in dinner jackets and black ties. A main function was to take charge of the formation of new Tables in the area, and make sure that none were started without its approval and indeed official sponsorship. It also provided a reference point for one club to get in touch with another for joint activities. Tables now sent delegates to Area committee meetings instead of to Council.

There was already an embryo Area 15 in the Yorkshire Ridings with Tables at Middlesbrough, Hull, Bridlington, and York when in 1934 another Table was started at Scarborough, typical of the now many Northern England clubs which for the most part differed in character from those in the south. York Table was the midwife of Scarborough, and when eight under-forties met in the Esplanade Café in December 1934 at the bidding of J. M. Gray of York they heard that potential Round Table members had to be under forty, 'of responsible executive status, of varied occupational classification, and of such character as would cause them to give of themselves for the good of their fellows'. Seven were enthused enough to form Scarborough Table no. 88 – two solicitors, a chartered secretary, an architect, a dentist, a ladies outfitter, and a department store manager. They decided to meet every other Friday for lunch in the Grand Hotel between 1.10 and 2.25 – cost 2s 9d including a threepenny tip. They formed a Fraternity Committee 'to promote a fraternal spirit within the Table and foster its social life by arranging various activities such as dinners and dances'. A Membership Committee recruited new blood.

'The attempt was made,' recollected S. D. McCloy, the solicitor first president, 'to assess fully before election whether a particular candidate could contribute something to the Table. The principle was adopted that we should go slowly at the start to build a Table of members who were congenial and representative, rather on Rotary lines, of a fair cross-section of the community. We were always in the early days careful not to allow the Table to grow so fast that the new members could not be readily absorbed, thus enabling the fairly close ties of friendship to be built up.' They agreed to elect not more than four members in a month.

A Speakers Committee prepared a Table programme. 'Current topics were discussed and debated,' wrote Maurice Horspool in his excellent history of Scarborough 88 from 1934 to 1968. 'Speakers were found who spoke authoritatively on Scarborough itself, on local government, on unemployment and other social problems of the day, and on matters of wide general interest. Quite early for example the Table debated two topics that to-day (1969), after more than thirty years, are still remarkably up to date: That the extensive practice of selling goods on hire purchase is to be deplored; and Is the present tendency of exaggerated advertising effective?

'The Table's own membership threw up speakers on the various aspects of their own jobs. Such vocational talks not only had a continuing interest to the listener, but in some cases gave a novice his first audience, a sympathetic and friendly (but not necessarily uncritical) audience within the fellowship of the Table. This was not peculiar to Scarborough. In Tables all over the country there was a membership varying in age between the early twenties and the late thirties, a hand-picked membership selected not for what it could get from, but for what it could give to, the Table and the community. But in giving it gained. This duty of having to get up and say something, whether to make an announcement, to give a talk, to propose a vote of thanks, to give a toast or even to say Grace, is but one of many things that have helped a shy and diffident youngster to gain poise, to overcome butterflies and often to emerge with a quiet confidence into wider spheres.'

Creation of the Areas brought into being a duplicate set of occasions for getting up and saying something, for the expression of fellowship – Area meetings, rallies, anniversaries, debates, sports events, dinners, dances. They also acted as strategically placed lynch pins round which the movement could be securely tied and consolidated.

Another expression of this sense of Round Table being a national movement was the establishment of a club in London for use of any member of any of the eighty-one Tables now in Britain. This was at no. 2 Hamilton Place, Park Lane, then occupied by the Territorial Officers Club whose membership was too small to justify their having the whole building. The plan was for the club to be available to existing members of the Territorial Officers Club, Round Table members and Rotarians. It was to be renamed The Rota Club. The annual subscription was to be three guineas for town members, two for Home Counties members and one for country members.

It was a place in which Round Table members might well entertain the young men of similar organisations with whom they were now beginning to make contact overseas. In 1934 Ealing, Wolverhampton and other Tables had been in touch by correspondence with Apex Clubs in Australia – Brian Whiteaker, chairman of Wolverhampton Table no. 17, had been made an Honorary Member of the American 20-30 Club no. 17. At its annual convention in California in September 1934 the Association of 20-30 Clubs extended a hand of friendship to Round Table, Apex and Active International.

The promotion of international fellowship had now been adopted as a fifth Object of Round Table, and how to set about this was discussed by a group presided over by Keith Pascall at the 1935 Hastings conference. A request for particulars had already come from Copenhagen, he told them. Rotary was represented in thirty-eight countries. Should Round Table start with the Empire, and then Europe? The group recommended setting up a central committee to co-operate with Apex, 20-30 and Kinsmen.

Visiting speakers always paid Round Table the compliment of taking it seriously, and Lord Eustace Percy was no exception at Hastings when he invited members to look with a full sense of their responsibilities at the whole method by which in each of their Areas young men and women were recruited for industry, the relation between permanent employed and the volume of recruitment of the very young. 'You should try to plan the business of your area so as to ensure as far as possible that we get rid of this evil of boys falling out of the bottom of life between 21 and 24 just as life is beginning to open up its vast possibilities to them.'

Here was a definite project of national importance which Round Table clubs could embark on in the knowledge that their efforts had a social significance of the highest order. It was a challenge calculated, one would have thought, to appeal to the imagination of even the most hidebound businessman. Captain Euan Wallace MP, the other speaker, rammed the message home by insisting that some form of external assistance was essential to deal with unemployment – industrial transference, keeping boys longer at school, earlier pensions. He was perfectly certain it was an ill which the young men of the country of the kind he was addressing could treat by showing the unemployed man he was not forgotten, by creating improved public opinion. The derelict areas remained derelict in spite of growing prosperity elsewhere.

Lord Eustace Percy was not content to leave the matter to his speech at the conference. He sent a message to the Round Table movement for *News & Views*: 'Social power in this country rests, notwithstanding any national organisation . . . with the hundreds of centres of local life. That is why what we call democracy in this country has succeeded while it has failed elsewhere.' The time was coming when a great national effort would be made to focus all the private enthusiasm and voluntary initiative which existed in all parts of Britain where unemployment was acute on the cure of that great social evil. It was within the power of Round Tables, and *it was their great responsibility*, to take such an active interest in the problems of employment, and especially of juvenile employment in their areas as would enable them to offer effective service in any national mobilisation of voluntary effort.

Edgar Taylor, the Round Table president, promised Captain Wallace he would ask Tables to discuss his address, send a summary of their conclusions and plans for action to Barnard, the Round Table secretary, who would forward them to Wallace. Helping to reduce unemployment, announced the president to the movement in its journal, could not be a better form of group community service, but first of all the problem must be understood. Members should make an effort to find out how it affected their towns and the specific problems in their community. They must come to grips with the problem at grass roots, in terms of *people*.

Table no. 87 in Londonderry, Northern Ireland, responded to this call by forming the Londonderry Round Table Welfare Scheme and starting a self-supporting club for unemployed in a disused factory which they rented. An appeal for £500 was quickly subscribed to. York Table considered whether they should admit 'artisan workers' as members (as Hines had advocated in 1928), but they felt the time was not yet ripe. Leeds made an effort to study the problem, as requested, by holding a series of lectures on Unemployment. Nottingham members attended the employment exchange every Monday to make contact with the unemployed, hear their problems, offer advice and help. Two of their members who were lawyers attended every Tuesday.

Were these demonstrations of serious endeavour, of the kind demanded by the Prince of Wales whose Mansion House speech had given Round Table its motto, straws in the wind that was to blow through all parts of the movement and put it back on the path on which it had been set by its founder and from which all others from now on would be regarded as deviations?

It looked for a moment as if they were.

4

Momentum
1935-1958

Wartime Containment; Post-war Expansion Home and Abroad

For Louis Marchesi who succeeded Edgar Taylor of Doncaster as president at the end of 1935 it must have seemed that perhaps after all Round Table was going to get up off its knees and rise to the occasion which Euan Wallace and Lord Eustace Percy had provided, and take a place in the national life (though of course it was not this *group* action which he saw at the centre of his idea at this time). He had an added reason for elation – his marriage to Dorothy (Dolly) Buddrell, his manageress, at Sheringham on 11 October 1934.

He and three others were entrusted with the job of giving a final polish to a revised set of rules and submitting them to the Executive Committee to bring into operation. He had a message printed on the first page of the journal stating it was necessary that they should all know where they were. As founder he wanted to see the revision of the rules definitely settled during his term of office so they could get down to other matters. He was concerned that the greatest care should be taken in the forming of new Tables. None should receive a charter until authorised by the relevant Area Council.

It was felicitous that it was during Marchesi's term as president that the number of Tables topped the hundred mark. At the end of his year he tried to visit as many of them as he could. He found a disquietening degree of parochialism, a disregard for the national aspect of Round Table. He told those he met that without a national organisation the movement would have fizzled out, 'and it will still fizzle out if the necessary support morally and materially is not forthcoming'. He looked to the Area Councils to reverse the inward-looking tendency. A new sign of the times, and a healthy one, was the considerable number of ex-members who had passed the age of forty but wanted to maintain their Round Table links. Early in 1936 Liverpool Table hived off its top-heavy wing of honorary members into a 'Forty One Club' with its own rules 'to continue and further develop the friendships formed under the auspices of the Round Table movement'. They had a lunch meeting on the first Tuesday of each month and three evenings in the winter. It was open to any ex-members of Round Table, not just those who left Table no. 8. Their motto was 'May the hinges of friendship never grow rusty'. It was the first of many such clubs.*

Much of the fun content of membership of Round Table was the ceremony and the dressing up. On charter nights in particular everyone wore their regalia – the chairman his medallion (£4 7s 6d or £5 5s with town crest), the past chairman his jewel (£2 8s) and everyone their lapel badges (3s 6d). A few might have sung the song by two members of Kingston Table, no. 19:

> In Round Table you will find,
> Men of every sort and kind,
> Brains and brawn go side by side
> Meet for fellowship and cheer,
> With ideals and hearts sincere,
> In this movement far and wide.

* The London Old Tablers Society was formed in 1939; a third at Lytham St Annes in 1941; a fourth at Wakefield in 1943.

Chorus RTBI

> In this movement we're proud to play our parts
> RTBI
> It's a cause that appeals to manly hearts.
> We are tied to no convention,
> But devote sincere attention
> To the cause we hold so dear.
> RTBI for friendship, peace and cheer.

There is no evidence of the song ever being adopted officially.

Because Round Table 'meetings' were in fact either luncheons or suppers at which members sat round a dinner table and, after the secretary had read out any 'business' notices, listened to a talk, every club occasion (as opposed to the wholly business meetings of the club committee and its sub-committees) had a social air about it. Consumption of food and drink added to the conviviality, and the object of good-fellowship was achieved in full abundance. But it was at the purely social activities organised at annual conferences that good-fellowship reigned supreme – driving in coaches to local beauty spots, sampling the mayor's hospitality at the civic reception, gossiping with old acquaintances and making new friendships, savouring the elaborate dishes and heady wines of the Metropole and Grand in white tie and tails at the long banquet tables, laughing at the cabaret and dancing the night through beneath the chandeliers in paper hats to a throbbing big band, beating out the foxtrots and the one-steps, treading the streamers underfoot and enjoying every minute of it. For many this escapist week-end justified the whole exercise. In such an atmosphere old issues raised in banquet speeches were listened to with new attention. When the 524 guests at the 1936 London conference banquet in the Connaught Rooms heard A. W. Graham Brown, chairman of Area no. 3, begin to say he did not think it was the wish or the intention of the National Association to deny members the right to discuss events of a political nature, there must have been many who groaned at the resurrection of this hardy annual. But Graham Brown had a fresh angle on a matter that no self-respecting Round Table member would ever want to see permanently buried. 'The object of politics as I understand it', he said, 'is to enable men and women to solve the problem of insecurity, and enable each individual to develop physically and mentally; and I think we are called upon individually and collectively to try and find a solution. It is within our organisation that we can learn to like people and admire them for their personalities as human beings while directly opposed to their political views.'

At the banquet before bowing out as president, Louis Marchesi proudly claimed that out of the 118 Tables then in existence there had only been two 'failures'. It was also a great source of pleasure to him to be able to announce that a first Round Table had been formed outside Britain at Copenhagen, the capital of Denmark, though it was not yet affiliated to the National Association. Modesty prevented him from referring to the high standard being set in the fund raising field by his own Table with the eminently successful *Snapdragon* magazine produced annually throughout the 1930s in aid of local hospitals – the prototype of several other Round Table sponsored magazines using the same lucrative technique. In 1936/7 Norwich's *Snapdragon* raised the large sum of £2,357 for the city's hospitals; 15,000 copies were to be sold in 1938.

The 313 members who registered for the London Conference of 1936 (the other 200 at the dinner had been guests) had found it very worth while, but, as Cyril Marsh pointed out, they only represented a quarter of the Tables and a very small proportion of the 4,000 members. The movement's Objects were being twisted, he claimed, to suit each enthusiast's hobby. The need to consolidate nationally was urgent. 'Are we reaching a state of mind in Round Table when we believe that if we can clap the other members on the back and buy them a drink or raise some money for charity, we are heralding the millenium?' New members might think so when they heard trumpets being sounded over a money-raising effort, and found out that after eight years they still spent a great deal of time at national level discussing small points of procedure. 'Let us boldly discuss the problems of our day and endeavour to make a contribution to their solving.'

A move in the direction of national consolidation came in 1937 with the acquisition of a headquarters office near St Pauls on Ludgate Hill, and the engagement of a retired army officer, C. R. Chambers, as full-time, paid Organising Secretary. He was able to relieve the annually elected honorary secretary who kept the correspondence going from his home by handling much of the routine business arising from rapid 'Extension' now rampant in parts of Britain which were late in taking to the Round Table game, the South-West, the North-West and East. The Area Councils bore much of the burden, but there was still a hypnotic amount of concentration on the Rules – over-concentration in the view of the 1937 president, Harold Norris of Guildford, who took over at a time of tension which brought national issues into sharper focus than ever before and put procedure adjusting into proper perspective.

'We shall be happier when we are less conscious of the machinery of the movement which exists solely to enable each member . . . to express in his life and work the objects of the Association. We have in this country during the course of centuries evolved a certain mode of life peculiar to and suitable for our temperament. We are faced to-day by two antagonistic philosophies in the struggles between which we may, unless we can demonstrate that there is an alternative which is workable, become involved and bring down what we most value.

'Are our standards of value in business life and in public life becoming lower or higher? While our business standards may be improving, can the same be said of those of public and community life? Is material efficiency in all things the only object in view, or is there something greater to which absolute efficiency may be sacrificed? . . . These and similar questions must arise in the minds of any member of Round Table as he considers the objects of his movement and how to put them into practice. On the answer which we, as young men, who have the future of our country in our hands make to them, depends the grave issue which lies before civilisation – whether it takes a step forward or falls back into the ignorances and prejudice of the dark ages.'

For P. E. Rowlinson of Camberley Table at any rate it was no good looking to Round Table for help. For him it gave a sort of fellowship, but one without any solid foundation. As yet it had no traditions and did not seem to be forming any. In the three years in which he had been a member he could recall only one lecture that pointed a way to a higher ideal. 'Never have I heard a talk which explained how one could fall short of the highest ideals, nor indicated what the essentials were of a "square deal" in that particular calling. . . . Of course no one wants to listen to a pious "honesty is the best policy" sort of talk, but something a little more serious than usual would not be out of place now and then. I now seem to have arrived at the conclusion that Round Table, although well conceived, is in practice a failure and indeed redundant. I often think it is; but I know that many will disagree with me for the most cogent reasons.'

He appealed to everyone to prune the tree of Round Table of unnecessary verbiage, so it could put out new and stronger shoots towards the goal which it was the founder's ambition to reach.

But as the war clouds loomed larger thoughts did seem to concentrate on altogether more serious subjects. Less 'Mesmerism', 'Over the Rockies', 'Whaling'. Harold Nicolson spoke to Leicester Table on Recent Developments in Foreign Policy; there were talks on the Economic Depression in South Wales, 'Fuel and National Defence', 'The Problem of

Enforced Leisure', 'The Special Case for the Special Areas', 'Some Aspects of Trade Unionism', even 'The Future of Round Table', which at that moment looked fairly bleak, though not financially. There was enough spare cash to warrant investing £500 in War Loan, and it was decided to incorporate the Association so it could hold investments in its own name, have its own seal and coat of arms and a licence from the Board of Trade as a corporation limited by guarantee.

Louis Marchesi reached his fortieth birthday at the end of 1937 and had to resign from Norwich Table. But at their November meeting Council passed this resolution: 'Wishing to recognise the unique services rendered to the National Association by its founder, it is resolved that Louis Marchesi be elected a Founder Honorary Life Member of the Association'. It was a form of membership to be conferred on him alone.

As already noted, moving from age thirty-nine to age forty had always presented difficulties to some who had tried to erase the finality of that passing with devices like honorary membership and ex-Tabler Clubs. Others saw injustice and 'a loss to the movement' too when a member changed his job and moved to another town where there was no Table. E. M. Tatlow who had been president in 1936 thought headquarters should keep a register of such cases so they could be asked to help with Extension work; but Marchesi opposed developing a free-lance class of membership of this kind. A member leaving a town should be allowed to continue being a member for the remainder of the Table year.

There should never have been concern at the number going down unless it meant loss of quality. The real work of Round Table, fulminated Charles Ramsden in *News & Views*, could not be done unless the membership was 'sound'. 'Within broad limits it scarcely matters what types of men collect for charity, run dances for the local hospital or help at the carnival. But it does matter enormously when it comes to any attempt to exert influence in wider civic and national affairs. The sort of reputation Round Table wants to create is that which would lead a

man to say, "Mr Tomlinson? Well, I don't know him personally but he belongs to Round Table so he must be pretty sound
in every way." Membership should in fact be an honour and
privilege recognised as such by the public. I am convinced that
only through the sterling character and vocational enthusiasm
of its individual members can Round Table ever hope to be anything more than a good-fellowship debating society – and how
very much more it *could* be!'

A concept such as this had yet to penetrate the rank and file,
except those whose work caused them to think other than par-
ochially like solicitors Fred Rea and Eric Ward of Portsmouth
Table no. 2. Their professional activities brought them closer to
the affairs of the nation than most, which made them more acu-
tely aware than others of the serious nature of the international
crisis which everyone was reading about in the newspapers.
They felt that Round Table as a movement should, and could,
exert an influence; or at least make a gesture to try and stem the
turn of events which seemed to be about to engulf the national
life.

Fred Rea had had dealings with Sir Thomas Inskip when he
was attorney general, and now that prime minister Stanley
Baldwin had appointed him the nation's first Minister of
Defence, he used the contact to see him at the House of Commons and find out in what area, if any, a movement like Round
Table could help. He took Eric Ward with him, and the two of
them sat on a bench in a corridor in the House to await the
Minister of Defence's pleasure. When Inskip came up to them
he had the Foreign Secretary, the Rt. Hon. Anthony Eden, PC,
MC, MP, with him, and the two representatives of Round
Table and the two most powerful ministers of state in the British
government had a pow-wow. In 1975 Eric Ward vividly
remembered this historic meeting 'at the summit', and how he
and Rea came away determined to rouse Round Table Council
to action. Marchesi had never had the personality to lead Round
Table in anything resembling a crusade; he had never been able
to inspire that kind of fervour for, say, an attack on business

malpractices, as well he might have done. But now Eric Ward pleaded with Council at their meeting of 29 November 1938 to enthuse over what he called the 'Portsmouth Table Scheme'. 'What can Round Table do at this time of international uncertainty to let the people of this country know how serious the situation really is, and give other nations the knowledge that we, as a nation, are truly united in our efforts?' He told them how Portsmouth Table on their own initiative had sent a deputation to the House of Commons which, in spite of his having two important meetings that day, had been seen for forty minutes by Sir Thomas Inskip, Minister of Defence, who had shown great interest.

'The deputation,' continued the account of Ward's report in Council minutes, 'also had talk with Anthony Eden who had assured them of the gravity of the situation. The question was "How interest in national defence can be created amongst the population of this country as a whole". Portsmouth proposed setting up a Committee of Six at once to investigate and see how Round Table can help. The need was urgent. Anything they could do must be done quickly. Otherwise the apathy which has already set in may not be checked and reversed.'

Council thereupon empowered the Executive Committee to call a National Meeting of Delegates in London, to which a committee on the lines suggested by Eric Ward should submit a plan of action (via the Executive Committee, the smaller body which Council had set up to execute policy). It was all a bit tortuous – and all too late. Events overtook Round Table. Within weeks the Government had introduced its civil defence plans as Air Raid Precautions.

Council returned to considering such weighty matters as the Extension Sub-Committee Report, the Finance Report, the Administration Report, the drafting of model Table Bye-Laws and 'the promotion of a true Area spirit'.

For the anonymous 'Cardi' of Area 4 it was exasperating. He was the latest in a long line of those who asked the question, Where *are* we going? They had high sounding ideals but no guidance on how they should be carried out. The Executive Committee had still to make a declaration of the movement's collective aim. In ten years' time Round Table would be able to look back on an aimless wandering in the wilderness with no collective work of any value to the country as a whole.

If by now the meaning of the movement's Objects was still unclear – and to many, perhaps the majority, they were – to haggle over their obscurities at this late stage would seem a misplaced use of energy when more pressing matters called for attention. In any event, it was not as if the originator of them had passed beyond consultation; Louis Marchesi was still alive and well at 6 Opie Street, Norwich, and could have been called upon to state, to those unable to understand them, if he was capable, *precisely* what he had meant when he wrote the Objects. The tradition had grown that there was an intrinsic merit in keeping the meaning indeterminate and that allowing 'freedom of interpretation' was a gain to the movement.

Could the Objects have been re-written as follows?

(1) To enable young business and professional men between 18 and 40 who are invited to join the movement to make and develop the acquaintance of other young men in similar positions and similarly attracted by the movement's objectives.

(2) To call the attention of such young men to the extent to which their business and professional appointments can provide a means of voluntary service to the community in addition to serving their clients, customers and patients for remuneration.

(3) To remind them how the continuing and unobtrusive example of the dignity and honesty with which they have chosen to conduct their own successful enterprises is likely to stimulate others in their community to follow it, with the more general effect of cultivating high ideals in business, professional and civic conduct nationally.

(4) To enable them to reach an appreciation of the equal worthiness of the occupations of others, a comprehension of their problems and an awareness of their complexity.
(5) To provide them with a base for the furtherance of world peace and goodwill through international relationships.
(6) To encourage them to inform themselves through meetings, lectures, discussions and other activities of the nature of the various fields of voluntary action in which they are invited to participate, so that they can plan lines of action which will be both efficacious and satisfying.

If so, why were they not? The answer is that perhaps for its perpetuation Round Table had no need of Objects.

'One of the most vacuous national institutions of to-day' was how thirty-year-old sports dealer David Simpson, who founded Darlington Table, summed up the Round Table of 1938. Perhaps it was never intended that it should be anything other than it was, so why worry? said some; but for him such a view was unwarranted. He saw discussions of a high tone making up for missing a university education. Round Table should first acquire a name for forceful thinking, then *a voice*.

Area 9 (Leeds, Wakefield, Bingley, etc.) agreed with him. The report they wrote in the spring of 1938 urged that talks given at Table meetings should be chosen to develop intelligent discussion of current civic needs and trade customs, and 'when necessary the fearless condemnation of abuses and encouragement of enterprise and improvement, aided by publicity and a friendly Press, and thus building up a local reputation for serious thought and unbiased views'. Members who gave talks about their occupations should air the difficulties, not just give an ABC of their bread-and-butter routines.

The new president, George Gallimore, thirty-seven-year-old accountant from Leicester, backed their attitude to the hilt. 'If we allow ourselves to drift into being a number of luncheon and dining clubs or a species of debating societies, our movement will slowly but surely fade out. And similarly I am convinced we shall suffer the same fate if we allow ourselves to become merely a further addition to the already long list of purely charitable organisations.'

Area 14 (Leicester, Nottingham, Derby, Northampton, etc.) also urged Round Table to enter the national arena by openly discouraging party politics in local government, commending adult education, studying town planning and the drift from the country.

If all this had led to a rift between those who agreed with the point of view expressed by the Area reports and those who disagreed, and resignations had resulted, it would have done Round Table little harm. On the contrary, if it had not got the mix right, it was not too late for a purge.

One way of shoring up Round Table explored at the suggestion of Cyril Marsh at the beginning of 1939 was closer relations with the older and more firmly established British Rotary. President George Gallimore had talks with their secretary, Mr Banner. That old friend of Round Table's Sydney Pascall was one of the members of the five-men committee which British Rotary set up to discuss the matter with Round Table; his son Keith was a member of Round Table's committee. Round Table administration suffered with the resignation of Captain Chambers, the organising secretary who had to return to his previous appointment at the War Office, but the running of headquarters became easier with the move to more commodious offices at 38 Buckingham Palace Road in May 1939 at which twenty-seven-year-old Clifford Attwell took over as new full-time Secretary.

As armed warfare drew nearer it became obvious too that Round Table's impact in working for world understanding had had little effect. As Milner Riley, the new editor of the journal wrote in November 1938: 'It was certainly rather ironic at a time when more encouraging reports were forthcoming from the International Relationships sub-committee, to find ourselves preparing for war against the very type of young man whose acquaintance we are trying to develop. Fortunately the crisis

[Munich] was averted and, as it happened, produced I know in many quarters a much fuller appreciation of the meaning of that much abused word "fellowship".'

No action of Round Table could have prevented the young men of Nazi Germany becoming our enemies; but what could be done was to tighten the bonds with Britain's probable allies in the coming conflict. In May 1939 came an invitation to affiliate with the 20-30 Clubs of America who suggested in fact that Apex of Australia, Kinsmen of Canada, Round Table and 20-30 should all unite to found an international body of which each should be a member, retaining its own name, legislation and age limit. Twenty-Thirty submitted 'that the new organisation endeavour to create a lasting understanding and friendship between all English speaking young men'. They hoped each would send a delegate to the California conference planned for 1941.

It was heartening at a time of extreme gloom. Evidence of interest in overseas Round Tables also began to show itself in June 1939; a second Table was being formed in Denmark at Aarhus; two had been started in New Zealand at Invercargill and the country's capital, Wellington, by James Ramsay, once a member of Poole Table no. 12. Contact had been made with English colonies in Bruges, Ghent, Antwerp and Brussels.

But the greatest boost to Round Table's morale was undoubtedly the fact that Anthony Eden, who had resigned as Foreign Secretary in February 1938 and been succeeded by Lord Halifax (whom he was to replace once again in December 1940), saw fit to come down to Southampton for the 1939 annual conference and, taking Round Table to be Britain's bright young businessmen in microcosm, appealed to them in no uncertain terms to shoulder their responsibilities. At forty-two he was himself only just over the Round Table age.

The young world statesman said he was proud to be among them because he felt Round Table had great possibilities. He believed the movement could do much valuable work for the country by creating goodwill and understanding between all sections of the community. Without this, democracy could not carry on.

'These are the kind of questions Round Table members should be asking themselves,' he said; 'Are we satisfied that our education system is perfect? Does it give an opportunity for all? Does it place at the disposal of the State the best that is possible for business life and public service? There are many good friends of this country who do not think our educational system is perfect, that it is too narrow and does not afford opportunities. We have to prove that results achieved by the democratic system is better, more satisfactory and more inspiring, than those achieved by other systems elsewhere. We have to prove that our methods of living handed down to us through the years meet the vast challenge of modern conditions.'

Harold Nicolson MP showed the same confidence in the potential of Round Table in his address to the conference at the Palace Theatre. 'I always regard your association as one of the most potent influences for good that we have in this country. Your members are one and the same time widespread and intimate, pervasive and permeating. You provide and stand for, those qualities of courtesy, co-operation, and kindness which I fear are about the only lubricants we can hope for in our sadly mechanised world.'

Did those who had come out of the sunshine and had sacrificed a tour of the ocean liners to listen to these words recognise themselves? Did the few who read them in *News & Views*? If so the selection committee had done what was expected of them.

But within five months 'service' meant 'national service' which meant one of 'the services' to which conscription would call them according to their age groups in the immediate or near future. Those who prepared for this moment by joining the Territorial Army or Reserves as Round Table membership had encouraged them were of course at once recalled to their units. Many Tables decided to close down soon after war was declared on 3 September 1939; others to hold informal mid-day meetings from time to time in each other's homes; yet others to make no change whatever and carry on as usual. The cameraderie of the 1914 trench warfare, which Round Table had in part been formed to perpetuate, was re-created in the air raid shelters throughout the country and in London, in particular in the deep-level tunnel stations of the Underground tube railways. Good-fellowship had no need of artificial stimulation in these days of common peril, but the re-assurance of regularly meeting old friends at lunch, however meagre, was a soothing and steadying influence at a time when 'the old world' seemed to be disappearing for ever – as it indeed did.

For those not whirled into the strange routines of army life or the rigours of naval or airforce training, the long evenings provided an opportunity for mulling over the twelve-year-old question of what Round Table was all about – if anything. The archaic flavour of 'vocational service' had been there from the start but, not wishing to show disrespect or ignorance, few had ventured to say so. But now they could puzzle over it openly and wonder what the hell it meant. Was the average member just too embarrassed by it all and by those confusing 'Aims and Objects'? To such a member the down-to-earth no-nonsense pronouncements of Merton house builder Cyril Marsh must have come as a beacon in the Black Out. He pointed out that the difficulty with the actual, as opposed to the assumed, aim of Round Table membership was that the former was so simple. 'Its very simplicity is disarming and for that reason there is real danger of it escaping the majority of members' attentions, of it being thought unworthy of their attention because it was not "grand" enough, not spectacular enough. But the fact remains for those humble and clever enough to assimilate it, that what distinguished Round Table from the run-of-the-mill federations of clubs was the emphasis it put on the individual. The message was that a young man was judged not so much by what he did as what he was. Many might say there was no need for an organisation to concentrate young men's minds on as simple a proposition as that. Marchesi thought otherwise.'

When Clifford Attwell left to join the Auxiliary Fire Service,

Cyril Marsh, who despite wholetime involvement in his building business, volunteered to take over the work in an honorary
capacity, and Council gratefully accepted his offer to remove all
the office equipment and files from 38 Buckingham Palace
Road to his home at 105 Dorset Road, S.W.19 where he still
lives in 1976. Council standing orders were suspended *sine die*;
the Executive Committee was given authority to act on behalf
of Council until twelve months after the cessation of hostilities.
All future conference arrangements (which embraced annual
general meetings) were cancelled – at the 1938 conference it had
been agreed to hold the 1940 gathering at Londonderry in
Northern Ireland, but when the invitations went out not a
single Area accepted, much to Jock Macauley's indignation, and
Portrush was substituted. There was no question of the National
Association suspending activities 'for the duration' – any fear
that that might be necessary was dispelled by Cyril Marsh's gallant and immediate stepping into the breach. The Buckingham
Palace Road office was closed but the Association kept the lease.

For the first time the Tudor Rose on the Round Table emblem had some meaning, for in the unique circumstances of
World War 2, when communications became difficult, normal
life was suspended in the face of the Black Out, the Rationing
and the Blitz, ARP duties and the rest, Cyril Marsh became the
benevolent despot of Round Table. By doing so, it is no exag-
geration to say that he saved the movement from disintegration
and that it would have been very difficult ever to have put it together again. In such circumstances there were times when perhaps he acted 'illegally', but always for the movement's good.
The Executive Committee met fairly regularly in London in
spite of the bombing and the depletion of its ranks to feed the
forces. With the aid of the Area Councils, it kept the main structure of the national organisation in being at minimal cost.

At a special meeting of the Association in London on 19
February 1940, attended by 103 delegates representing sixty-
three of the 140 Tables, with Rodney Lillicrap, president, in the
chair, members voted to suspend the age limit of forty until after

the war for all active members on the register before 1 September 1939, though it would apply to all those elected after that date.

Commendably members now turned their attentions to the way they, in their capacity as young business and professional men, could help Britain in the reconstruction that would come when war ended. Standards of honesty in public life acquired fresh significance – and other groups, like the Oxford Movement which had renamed itself Moral Rearmament, were enlisting leading British figures like the Earl of Athlone to speak on the wireless emphasising the new spirit which must animate human relationships after the war if it was not to happen all over again. Round Table was not prepared to figure as a national movement to this extent, and the BBC would not have regarded it in this light. The war kindled no urge to lead a crusade. Cyril Marsh received many a plea for 'HQ to give a lead'; but as the one-man headquarters he shrank from playing the role of policy-maker. He wrote to *News & Views*, which continued publication throughout the war, saying it was not for HQ to give a lead; it was for Tables to formulate broad policy and give HQ instructions to attend to the details.

A more positive note was struck by Marsh at the end of his letter when he declaimed: 'Round Table's opportunity will come in the years immediately following the war. Let us be ready as a national organisation to take full advantage of the opportunity so that the National Association and its Tables may operate with greater service to the individual and the community than the policy now.'

A Committee of Action was formed at the top to provide inspiration. At the end of 1941 Round Table was recognised by the Council of Voluntary War Work, but there was no rush by the Cabinet Committee for Post-War Reconstruction to accept an offer of help – available evidence of the movement's pre-war record in this field would have been difficult to come by. It was the moment to make up for lost time. As Milner Riley said in an editorial in November 1941: 'It gives one a feeling of pride to know that one belongs to a movement which is now well on the way to overcoming its apparent former reluctance to expound its theories publicly and which is beginning to lose its youthful shyness of speaking aloud its inner thoughts'.

In a 1942 piece he believed 'the mood in Tables now points to a strong desire to see Round Table released from its dangerously lethargic state and taking a much greater part in the affairs of the country; a determination to recapture and restore the movement's progressive spirit'. In 1943 Sir William Jowitt KC, MP, Paymaster General, who had spoken to the annual conference in Cardiff in 1938, sent a message saying, 'I want the help of members of the Round Table movement because they are among those determined to carry out the post-war policies in the framing of which I am deeply concerned. It is with particular interest that I have noticed the articles on various problems of reconstruction that have been appearing in *Table News & Views*. A wide range of subjects has been treated with a refreshing independence, boldness and freedom from prejudice.'

A 'National Investigating Committee' was charged with investigating the post-war evolution of Round Table – and not the British Nation as many members thought who received one of the 500 questionnaires. To avoid further confusion it changed its name to Internal Reorganisation and Development Committee. The decision to appoint this committee was prompted by a report on Round Table Reconstruction by Liverpool Table – 'young men returning from the war will have changed minds'. The questionnaire revived the whole question of What is Round Table all about, and who is it for? Discontinuance of the 'executive' qualification was a popular wish. Council considered the Committee's report on 19 September 1944 and threw out the recommendation that the maximum age of *entry* be thirty-five though the limit was to remain at forty. They declined to give the report official approval, leaving that to a general meeting of members when everyone had returned from their wartime service.

Even more comprehensive was the Reconstruction Report

submitted by York Table in March 1945 'to deal with the long-standing failure here [at York] and perhaps at other Tables, fully to determine what Round Table really stands for and can achieve', seen in terms of the single club. It touched on every aspect of Table life; the better selection of members, the objectionable executive rule, the unnecessary restriction of two members to each classification, more support from Area Councils, abolition of social functions at annual conferences, etc., etc.

It was a pity that so much energy was expended on the means and so little on the end product, but of course the nature of the latter had not yet been determined. A chance came for the nation to hear the views of the Young Business Men of Britain on the revolutionary document known as the Beveridge Report, but predictably it was thought this would be 'political'. Round Table relied largely on events to suggest suitable ends, and the event of total war brought to Britain's shores large numbers of foreign and Commonwealth young men of a greater variety than ever came, or would ever come, as tourists. Suddenly Object no. 5, haltingly pursued in peacetime by the indirect method of correspondence, was lifted on to a new and vivid plane – face-to-face confrontation. Members of British Tables seized on the opportunity to invite these men of the Allied Forces to Table meetings, and to their homes, to make their acquaintance, to ply them with questions and seek to understand their way of life and work problems – and to give as much similar information about themselves as they learnt from their guests.

From 1945 onwards perhaps it could be said that this Object or Purpose (as York sensibly called it at last) was the main justification for the Round Table's claim to be other than a loosely federated chain of social clubs. It was in this area that it was able to record its most significant successes. Because of the upheaval of war which forced so many out of Britain to see how the other (foreign) half lived, and brought so many foreigners to Britain, the pursuit of establishing international goodwill and understanding became an exercise which was not only comprehensible but real.

Just before the European War ended Round Table was invited to a meeting in Chicago on 8 April 1945 to form a 'World Council of Young Men's Service Clubs' consisting of Kinsmen, 20-30, Active International, Apex and Round Table. Neither of the latter could send representatives but they both ratified the Chicago resolution creating the World Council and all five associations became founder members.

The objects of the World Council were declared to be: (1) to develop young men and create in them a desire to participate actively in service and civic work; (2) provide a common platform for regular interchange of information and opinions; (3) to facilitate extension of such clubs in all countries; (4) to procure through this unity a recognised voice of young men in international affairs.

Even more heartening was the way war-torn Europe rose to the Round Table idea. The first club outside Britain, as has been seen, was formed, before war broke out, in Copenhagen and owing to the efforts of Bulow Jacobsen a second Danish Table had taken root in Aarhus. Astonishingly five new Tables were formed in Denmark while the country was under German Occupation. John Creasey gives interesting details of the circumstances:

'Bulow Jacobsen was in charge of a motor assembly plant, and he was secretly assembling sten guns from parts dropped by British aircraft; and several Danish Round Tablers were also active members of the Underground. It was felt that if any one of these were caught the Gestapo would get a lead to Round Table and might well arrest all the members and put them into a concentration camp. This wasn't considered to be worth the candle, and the meetings were "suspended", although members continued to meet clandestinely.'

Karl Christensen, who became president of the Danish Association of Round Tables formed after the war, when there were seven Tables, wrote, 'Apart from the insecurity which everyone felt, there was always a certain risk in arranging meetings. You never knew with complete certainty who was reliable, and for long periods we had to meet privately. In spite of these circumstances we opened five new Tables, and one of our members [Erik Dupont] succeeded in starting the first Round Table in Sweden at Helsingborg in 1943.'

Henk Bruna who had served his apprenticeship in Reading before the war formed the first Dutch Table at Utrecht in 1946, with sixteen members, and soon there were four others, enough to justify the establishment on 7 June 1946 of the De Nederlandsche Tafelrond, the National Association of Round Tables of Holland, of which Bruna became president.

In January 1947 these European Round Table associations expressed a wish that there should be some form of machinery for closer liaison with all national associations calling themselves 'Round Table', and Reg Bates of Liverpool, the then president of what must now be referred to as British Round Table (RTBI),* was strongly in favour of a body being created for this purpose. In June, when there were 133 Tables in Britain, eighteen in Denmark, seven in Holland and five in Sweden, Council discussed the possibility of founding 'Round Table International' (RTI) with headquarters at the RTBI offices in London.

Cyril Marsh, now forty-six, who had resigned as honorary secretary the previous summer and been made an Honorary Member of the Association in recognition of his service to the movement by virtually keeping it in being single-handed throughout the war, warned of the danger of forming a Euro-

---

* When Rotary crossed the Atlantic, Rotary International Britain and Ireland was the title of the new district and is always referred to as RIBI. In 1911 the whole of Ireland was politically part of the United Kingdom of Great Britain and Ireland. When the independent Irish Free State was set up in 1922, RIBI ignored this distinction and continued to call itself RIBI. Round Table followed Rotary's example in this. It called its national association 'Round Table Britain and Ireland' which in documents is referred to as 'RTBI' and of course covers the two islands, and the Irish Republic and Northern Ireland in the smaller one. In this story 'British Round Table' is used to denote the National Association of Round Tables of Great Britain and Ireland: and 'Council' for the National Council of RTBI.

pean bloc within the World Council of YMSCs. World Council were consequently kept fully informed of the new development, and a report on RTI sent to its Montreal convention that summer to which British Round Table sent a delegate.

The international quartet of Erik Emborg representing Denmark and Sweden, Henk Bruna the Netherlands, and Leslie Crew of Hastings who had been a member for nineteen years (he was elected at Harrogate in 1928), and Reg Bates, put their heads together to draft the thirteen articles of a RTI constitution. They decided to charge one shilling a head capitation fee from each member association, which meant British Round Table paying £250. A Round Table International Council was established, and Crew and Bates were nominated as Britain's members, Reg becoming the first International President.

But interest had also been shown farther afield than Scandinavia. In 1946 Penang Table, with Charlie Chislett, once of Rotherham Table, as chairman, and ten nationalities represented in its thirty-six members, became the nucleus of an 'International Round Tables of Asia' with the motto Understanding, Friendship, Service.

At Hastings in 1948 were held on following days in May the first conference of Round Table International, the conference of the World Council of Young Men's Service Clubs, and the conference of the National Association of Round Tables of Britain and Ireland. It was an event that made glad the heart of Louis Marchesi, who considered it the most important in the history of Round Table. He saw in this great tripartite gathering the culmination of all that he had done in 1927. The machine he had designed to generate international understanding and goodwill, though as yet low-powered, was *working*.

He had satisfaction too in seeing British Round Table soon climb back to its pre-war strength of 4,000 members. Active membership had sunk to about 1,000 in the war, with seventy to ninety Tables out of 140 still meeting. It had been decreed that after 1 April 1940 members in the armed forces could retain their membership if they wished without their Tables having to pay a capitation fee to headquarters, and that they could not lose membership because of their non-payment of subscriptions to their Table or no longer residing in the town. About another 1,000 members in the services in this category remained 'on the books' at Cyril Marsh's Merton HQ throughout the war. Council were told in February 1945 that there were 1,334 members and 958 in the forces. By January 1947 there were 100 chartered Tables in operation; thirteen had been re-opened but not yet chartered; and seven new ones had been formed. But there were still forty-one of the pre-1939 Tables which had not yet seen fit to start up again, about half in the south of England.

The serious intent of the last years of the war was largely dissipated in the euphoria of peace and the excitement of being reunited with those whom one had been prepared never to see again, in the exchange of stories of the Blitz, of narrow shaves in the Desert, of horror on the Normandy beaches. It was great to be alive, and celebration of that took priority. Thoughts of reconstruction necessarily took second place. In any event most of those who had thought of 'after the war' were those who found themselves no longer members on 31 March 1948 when the age limit suspension came to an end. They were swept out with the rest of the over-forties into the ex-Tabler clubs whose numbers now warranted an Association of their own. But well before Retirement Day the small proportion of the total membership who assembled for the three Special General Meetings in London considered and, for the most part, rejected the York Report drafted in the dark days of the winter of 1944/5. They refused to let the Executive Committee choose a national act of corporate service and invite Tables to join it.

There was a swing back to 'fellowship' as the main purpose of Round Table in Britain – though perhaps it had never departed from it to any appreciable extent. Be that as it may, this was the image of Round Table now encouraged by Cyril Whitaker, the no-nonsense Bradford wool merchant and member of the town cricket and rugger club, who took over from Cyril Marsh as honorary secretary for the next two years and set up headquarters once again at Buckingham Palace Road. The two of them had nothing in common except their Christian names, and any sense of mission which Marsh might have injected into Round Table during his wartime stewardship quickly fell away. The calls to national responsibility of Anthony Eden and Lord Eustace Percy no longer fitted the mood of the times, even if any had nursed their memory over the years in the hope of an inspiring renascence of a Round Table determined to take an exciting part in the nation's affairs after its near-oblivion. It was not to be that kind of re-birth. It was to be on a lower, safer level. The movement, probably with relief, embraced once more the cosy role which suited it best, with little in common with what Marsh had in mind for it, the development of the individual in taking his place in the community. And perhaps Louis Marchesi's satisfaction at Round Table's post-war survival was tempered by regret that it was being achieved at the cost of abandoning the central ideas which he had tried to make its *raison d'être*.

Every now and again Horace Cotton used his position as editor of *News & Views* to try and steer the boat round, but as soon as professional editors were dropped, the magazine ceased to be the voice of the movement which Marchesi had meant it to be, apart from giving Tables information. Presentation and design became wholly unworthy of the image which Round Table should have insisted on maintaining. In 1948 Cotton invited six members to take part in a Discussion in Print on Where Do We Go From Here? George Greaves of Stoke re-discovered Object 3. 'I would suggest that it should be our first aim, if not indeed a major campaign on behalf of the movement as a whole, to seek in the most emphatic way to bring about a re-birth of moral consciousness in business life. If we are to retain our position as a worthwhile influence in our national life . . . there can be no greater task in front of us.'

It was not however a question of retaining it, but of creating it – for the first time. But no one was interested.

Areas picked up the reins again and President Roland Covell spent much of 1947/8 attending Area rallies, Table revival meetings and re-chartering dinners. Headquarters had no record of the second Table being founded at Portsmouth and in the absence of any documentary evidence to substantiate their claim – all their papers were destroyed in the bombing of Portsmouth Docks – they were about to be given a new number among the 300s when Bertie Hooper remembered they still had a deposit account in the bank. It was only the 1928 date of this entry which saved Portsmouth from the ignominy of losing its cherished rank of Table no. 2.

Table no. 1 in the meantime was celebrating (on 12 March 1948) its Coming of Age with a lunch at Suckling House, Norwich, where it all began, attended by representatives of thirty British Tables and messages of congratulation from Penang, Denmark, Sweden, Holland, Belgium, Finland, Australia, Canada. Louis Marchesi, who was now fifty, took the opportunity of pointing out that they did not see fit to commit themselves to any specific community service because the best service a young man could render to the community was to make himself responsible and experienced in his own profession or craft. He was presented with a plaque. In the evening there was a banquet and ball. It was after all the twenty-first birthday not only of Norwich Table no. 1 but of Round Table as a movement.

A banquet, no doubt supplied by Langford's, was in order for an occasion such as this, but in 1948 there was a considerable shortage of food in Britain. This occasioned the most remarkable gesture on the part of Britain's friends in Canada, Land of Plenty, who mounted an enormous 'Food Parcels for Britain' exercise. The Kinsmen Clubs were responsible for these, and distribution of the first consignment from the Overseas Gifts Allocation Centre was undertaken by members of the Women's Voluntary Service (WVS) – the Ministry of Food paid for delivery to a local authority. Round Table took over distribution after that, with the aid of WVS.

Apex of Australia also sent food parcels to British Round Tables direct, for them to distribute to whomever they saw fit; 20-30 dispatched five tons of clothing and food in October 1949 which Round Table members distributed in four big British towns. By the end of 1949 Kinsmen had sent 36,600 parcels which Round Table had distributed to a hundred towns. London Table organised a special distribution by the Lord Mayor who handed over an illuminated scroll to commemorate Canada's generosity, which was repaid in 1950 when Round Table opened a Relief Fund to help members of Kinsmen Clubs who had been made homeless by the flooding of the Red River in Manitoba. A cheque for £2,000 was sent to Canada at once without waiting for the money which Tables then set themselves to collect by garden parties, balls, torchlight processions, bonfire parties, jumble sales, carnivals and fêtes. Donations to the fund soon reached more than £10,000 most of which was spent on shipping livestock to Canada in conjunction with the Commonwealth Relations Office and providing equipment for the much damaged Princess Elizabeth Hospital in Winnipeg. The stringent exchange regulations of the day prevented the sending of any more money. Hubert Praat practically handled the national aspect of this appeal single-handed, and the subsequent administration of the fund. Round Table's gift to stricken Winnipeg was second only in size to that of the British Government.

Fund raising of the kind undertaken for the Manitoba Relief Fund had been a feature of Table life from the start. When Britain had a flood disaster in Lynmouth in 1952, not only British Round Table but Round Table South Africa, Kinsmen and Apex contributed to a relief fund. To have achieved immediate reaction to natural misfortunes in the territories of World Council members was itself a matter of some moment. The response to the appeal to relieve the Hungarians who fled to Britain after their short-lived revolution in 1956 which raised £8,000 was also commendable. This was Round Table fund-raising in its most justifiable form. What was frowned on from on high was agreeing to raise money for charities which were neither Round Table nor World Council orientated, and came to Round Table because of the reputation of its members for hearty, aggressive, and therefore successful, attacks upon the public pocket. The invitation was invariably accepted because of the fun it gave – and anyway did it not promote 'fellowship'?

Such group projects, as opposed to individual action, was never part of the Round Table programme, nor was group voluntary *action*. But the latter was considered more consistent with what it was hoped the type of people selected to join the clubs had to offer.

After the East Coast Floods of 1953 Area 5 Tables mobilised a convoy of 120 vehicles to take cooking equipment, china, clothing, stoves, rubber boots and torches, as well as 50,000 garments, to the inundated areas. Without the spur of a natural disaster of this magnitude, other Tables took the trouble to explore possible areas in which they could best perform a voluntary service, and then acted. Basingstoke Table, for instance, undertook to do social welfare work at the plastic surgery unit at Rooksdown House attached to Prewett Hospital, and members made themselves responsible for helping discharged patients to find a job and places of training. Members of Tables up and down Britain were visiting old people, reading to the blind, collecting clothing for the poor, chopping up and delivering wood, teaching handicrafts to the physically disabled, entertaining orphans, collecting books and repairing toys for children, transporting cripples, talking to boys at approved schools, as well as engaging in work more suited to business and professional men like membership of a Youth Club Management Committee, a Marriage Guidance Council, a Vocational Advisory Panel to assist a Juvenile Employment Bureau, a Town Planning or Safety First Council. Leicester undertook to furnish an old-people's home; Hull Table instituted a fine scheme for guiding school leavers on careers by organising visits to local factories.

Overseas Tables were even more ambitious. The East London Table in South Africa which received its charter from RTBI in February 1950 planned to raise £18,000 to build a settlement in Fort Grey Forest Reserve to fight TB. Tables which were formed outside Europe in South Africa, Rhodesia, Kenya* and Malaya did not at first join RTI which by 1950 consisted of 250 Tables in Britain, thirty-one in Denmark, twenty-seven in Holland, fifteen in Sweden, four in Finland, three in Norway, one in France (the Paris Table founded on 11 August 1950) and one in Belgium. In 1950 Holland and Denmark suggested that RTI and not RTBI should be the member of the World Council of YMSCs. Each association in RTI was equal; not, like Rotary, a number of 'branches' looking to a head. But in fact RTI did not come to replace RTBI on the World Council until 1956. From this date Tables in countries other than Britain and Ireland had representation on it for the first time. RTI in its turn was dissolved in 1962.

Before the war the pursuit of international understanding and goodwill was motivated by the belief that its achievement would contribute to the factors which led nations away from armed conflict and towards the settling of their differences by peaceful negotiation and the more civilised methods of diplomacy. After six years of war, when immediate prospects of further hostilities seemed remote, international understanding and goodwill became a desirable end for another reason, apart from maintaining the spirit of the wartime East and West alliance. This was the acceptance of the erstwhile enemy into the company of those who had suffered at her hands, and the quickening of the pace by which Time would, eventually, heal the wounded spirits and reduce the heat of antagonism. There was no denying the depth of these wounds and the vividness with which the inflicting of them was still remembered. But the English who had never known Occupation and did not find it

* Keith Pascall and an ex-member of Leicester Table launched Round Table in East Africa in May 1952 and his Nairobi Table was the nucleus of what became the Association of Round Tables of East Africa (ARTEA). In 1976 he is still in Nairobi – the second senior surviving past president (1930/31)?

easy to imagine what it, or anything else, could be like unless they had experienced it, thought the continuing continental sensitivity on the matter misplaced. But obviously to press for the opening of a Table in Germany in 1948 was a misjudgement, as the Harrogate Conference of 1947 revealed.

Hermann van Bruggen, a member of a Table in Holland, described his reactions when he heard British members blithely discussing the proposition in the plush setting of the comfortable North of England spa.

'We Danes and Dutch in the room looked at each other and knew exactly what we were thinking about – these good British people must be told something because they do not understand.' He and others stood up and tried to explain how, if they wanted to live in peace, they did not trust the Germans. In the magazine he expounded his views further. Englishmen were too sporty, he wrote. They would fight in a third world war started by the Germans and once more take it all as a kind of cricket match, taking the former enemy with them to the club-house to enjoy a nice cup of tea and a cigarette. 'But you must *never* take the German people for a losing cricket team. . . . One never learns a man better than when he is in a position which permits him to handle you just as he likes. And how they treated us the whole world knows.' (*News & Views*, September 1948)

It was to the great credit of Round Table that it managed firmly but tactfully to overcome this understandable reluctance to mix socially with the erstwhile 'enemy'. Round Table became a regenerative chamber in which wartime tensions unwound. It gave Swedes, Dutch, Germans, Norwegians, Danes, French and English an excuse to meet on the common ground of human affinity, and, by uninhibited, friendly inter-club meetings, it provided the one touch of nature that has always helped to make the whole world kin.

And it was not just a gesture, a one-off token meeting here and there, but a sustained campaign. As Laurence Sterne remarked, 'Any one may do a casual act of good nature, but a

continuation of them shews it is part of the temperature'. It became part of the temperature of the Round Table of the 1950s.

Round Tables outside Britain adopted the King Arthur's
Table emblem, generally with their own national colours and
other variations. There was no legislating for these, but in 1950
British Round Table rather belatedly decided to standardise the
badge (designed by Neville Heaton of Manchester) for the use
of its own clubs. With rising 300 Tables, efficient administration of the national organisation through the Areas, increased
from eighteen to twenty-nine in 1949, had become too much
for the honorary, annually elected president and secretary, and
in the summer of 1950 Council decided to appoint a full-time,
paid General Secretary. From several hundred applications they
chose V. M. Collins DFC, a member of Oxford Table with a
diploma in public administration and a distinguished war
record who took up office on 1 January 1951. It was just in time,
for there was an upsurge in new Tables which by 31 May 1951
numbered 330 representing 8,600 members. The average number of members resigning each year on reaching the age of forty
was around 1,000; but in 1950/1 there were more than double
that number of new members. By May the following year there
were 374 Tables with 9,740 members. Five years before there
had been only 120.

In the decade since VE Day Round Table had been taken over
by a new generation of young men, with fewer inhibitions than
their pre-war predecessors. They were being given positions of
responsibility in management at a much earlier age. Television,
jet air travel, instantaneous communication by telephone and
teleprinter had made it One World beyond the wildest dreams
of the schemers of Langford's Smoke Room in 1927. Society had
both loosened up through a much greater mobility from one
'class' to another, and tightened up through higher standards of
education which made understanding between all sections of
the community very much less of a problem than hitherto.
Moreover abandoned merrymaking *à la* Chelsea Arts Ball was
no longer the monopoly of Society debs and the young bloods

who escorted them. The final Tramps Ball of 1951 led the following year to what has become traditional ever since, the new-style 'Farewell Party' with which to end the annual conference – fancy dress and fancy free. Horseplay and practical jokes were the order of the evening; hilarity reigned unconfined.

The Welfare State, built on the foundations of the 'political' Beveridge Report, was now firmly entrenched in spite of the fall of the Labour Government in 1951, who had managed to introduce an element of compassion into social legislation which was there to stay. Much of what had been considered the realm of 'charity' had been absorbed by the State. As Sir Lionel Heald, attorney general in Sir Winston Churchill's new Tory Government, said in his speech as guest of honour at the Round Table Silver Jubilee Banquet at London's Grosvenor House on 16 October 1953 – Coronation Year – the problem of the future with the Welfare State was how to retain the idea of personal service. Justly proud of his 410 British Tables, Louis Marchesi looked back on the twenty-five years during which the movement had grown to this size with pardonable nostalgia. In the expansion of Round Table overseas it had given him particular pleasure to hear of the formation of the first German Table at Hamburg in October 1952. He hoped the previous summer's experiment under which fifty-five British children from twenty-two Areas were exchanged for fifty-three Danish children for a fortnight's holiday would take a permanent part in Round Table's avowed intent to stimulate international understanding. It did. Many Tables marked the beginning of the new reign of Queen Elizabeth II with a specially large community service exercise – Wolverhampton presented the town with a fully equipped children's playground on Warstones estate.

To mark the silver jubilee, the National Association published John Creasey's book *Round Table: the first twenty-five years*. His last chapter was headed 'The Future'. He wished he could see where a member first joining in 1953 was going to take Round Table.

Twenty-five years from now, of course, many things will be the same. It is even possible that there will be arguments on the proper nature and title of Community Service! ... I wonder if any will try to explain just where the Movement is going. It is remarkable that no one has tried yet. In fact most have been extraordinarily careful not to hazard a guess.

We know, of course, that there will be more great moments, more great causes. In Great Britain and those countries where Round Table is already strong in numbers, it will grow much stronger; countries which have no Tables now will get them as the years go by. It requires no great effort to imagine 50,000 Tablers, or even twice or thrice that number. The more men in the Movement, the greater aggregate good is likely to be done – and, much more important, the greater will be the chance of enlisting members who prove to have the vision and the desire to lead Round Table to greater heights than it has yet climbed; or even sighted.

Such leaders are needed; it might almost be said that they are badly needed.

It is true, I think, that no one has any clear idea of where Round Table is going; as true that no one has really discovered exactly what it is; where it wants to go; or how high it wants to climb. I don't think anyone yet realises its great potential strength. They do not really understand what has happened in the past twenty-five years. They have been too close to the event to realise that for *the first time in history, towns, cities and nations have felt the impact of young men moved only by the impulse of goodwill.*

These young men have been stirred to take an interest in local problems, and to solve them. They have seen these problems through fresh eyes and tackled them with the vigour which only youth possesses.

It was dangerous, he said, to try and reach some objective,

good in itself, which however was disruptive of the movement. It was dangerous too to listen too readily to the voice of caution. But he believed that it was simply a matter of time before some great cause gripped the mind and heart of Round Table and brought its members to swift, decisive, concerted action. He could not foresee the nature of this impact, but he believed it would come – from a member somewhere in the world – and transform the movement into an irresistible power for good. This leader of the future would suddenly realise that the movement had not yet done everything it could. 'Then I believe he will inspire a boldness which will make Round Table a vital force carrying its great power for good to all the people the world over . . . I find myself wondering whether it is Round Table's destiny to lead the youth of the world into the splendours of peace and understanding among all nations.'

Unfortunately Tabler Creasey, author of the still widely read 'Toff' and other detective stories, is no longer alive to tell how well he thinks his Churchillian forecast has stood the test of time. He died in 1975.

As for a cause, the World Council of YMSCs set the pace with a plan to support the foundation of a chair of Race Relations at Salisbury University in Rhodesia, a project which failed in its early stages to attract the attention it deserved, but was finally carried to a conclusion in 1973, to a large extent due to the dogged support of British Round Table.

With its 512 Tables and 13,700 members, British Round Table was by far the largest unit in either Round Table International or the World Council. Head office space had once again become cramped, and in February 1956 the freehold of a fine house 'of architectural interest' in Regents Park off Baker Street, London – no. 15 Park Road – was acquired for £10,000, half of which was subscribed by members through an Appeal Fund. It was opened by Louis Marchesi on 24 March 1956 and subsequently named 'Marchesi House'. It was an occasion for reviewing the whole administrative machine. Council agreed that the honorary secretary should have a capacity for administrative and secretarial procedure, and the honorary treasurer should be an accountant. They were accountable to the Executive Committee and Council. There was a General Secretary, but 'it is in the interests of the movement that the principal officers be not changed too quickly so as to produce officers who are solely dependent on his guidance, for it is in that way that movements tend to be directed by their General Secretaries'. (Minutes of National Council meeting of 10 January 1956.)

Round Table was never directed by its General Secretary; but guidance inevitably meant influence. Given the personality and dedication of the movement's perceptive choice for this key position – or, what was more pervading, the affection he showered on it (he called it a love affair) – that influence was never other than benign. So far as the public and Table members were concerned Round Table was never 'run' by Vic Collins, in the way that Stenson Cooke ran the AA or James Findlay the Baltic Exchange. But to many he became 'Mr Round Table' in the way the media always like to latch on to a single individual as a focal point. Sitting in the seat he occupied he influenced those who *did* run Round Table, and in a way few would have had otherwise. Whether those that ran it affected the rank and file's enjoyment of their membership is questionable. Speeches were delivered and messages promulgated, showing the hand of the *éminence grise* of Park Road at work, postulating an ideal organisation called Round Table and building a much more sophisticated image of its founder than he merited. It was an effort that cannot but be admired, but since few thought it was part of the enjoyment of being a member to tune in to the pronouncements of the leaders and the philosophy-builders at the remote top, it was unlikely to have had much effect. Vic Collins's brave attempt to give the movement a philosophy and a modicum of intellectual content came too late. Few needed that sort of motivation to make their membership worthwhile and fulfilling. If Leonard Hines, Rutherford Lindsay or Vic Collins had formed the mould from which Round Table had been cast, things might have been different. But by the 1950s the character of British Round Table had set, with the main ingredient the pursuit of fellowship – and if that ended in a capture who cared about the whys and wherefores?

Louis Marchesi sold Langford's Restaurant in 1954, which left him free to roam the world with Dolly at his side to see how his idea had fared in strange environments. But he had no need to go to Holland to learn of its reception there. Was it to be in continental Europe rather than provincial Britain that pure Marchesian Round Table would flourish?

In an article in *News & Views*, H. N. Wakkie the Dutchman who had been president of Round Table International stated he still had the impression that the movement could not agree on the usefulness and necessity of community service. He reminded his readers that Round Table was founded to bring young businessmen and professional men round the table. 'There is no objection if young men who meet regularly feel a need to do something for the community and take up some task which arises, but the history of Round Table so far and the original aims point in another direction. The intention of Round Table will be de-natured if too predominant a place is given to community service. If this is accepted it implies that more attention must be paid to quality than quantity, and that extension will not proceed so quickly in the future. We must take care that we do not form Tables which are going to regard community service as the only possibility.'

He pointed out the differences in mentality between the Anglo-Saxon world and Europe. The mental attitude on the continent was more abstract, a wish to improve matters by discussion and a study of conditions. In Britain activity aimed at alleviating local wants, mainly material, which was useful yet not helping to attain the *difficult* aim of Round Table, the creation of better understanding and better relations. On the continent this was held to be the essence of Round Table and it was chiefly to these objectives that they wished to devote their energies. They saw 'community service' as more of an intellectual exercise, attainable only by means of discussion and achieving a better attitude to, and a more aware assessment of, social problems. Continental Tables tended to have meetings in the evening to give more time for discussion, with speakers from their own membership. They only invited guest speakers if they had something to contribute germane to what the Table was studying and trying to achieve.

Round Table's organisation was casual and unco-ordinated. Britain and others maintained the age limit of forty; Finland and Sweden had forty-five; some had 'part active' members, others not. RTI was merely a group of separate, national organisations linked by aims only loosely similar. Hubert Praat of RTBI had suggested that the Round Table movement would benefit if it became an integrated international organisation with a single constitution observed by everyone who joined wherever they were. All RT associations could then become sprigs of a real Round Table international movement in much the same way as Rotary International. Tablers in Sweden, France and Britain were not members of the same organisation; RTI was merely a liaison body with no administrative power.

When he·went to South Africa and Rhodesia in 1956 Louis Marchesi took the opportunity of preaching the Marchesi/Marsh/Wakkie version of his idea – the Ur-Round Table. It had nothing to do with the Arthurian legend, he assured his listeners in Africa, and it was not a junior Rotary. As the Mufulira correspondent of *Northern News* of Rhodesia reported on 9 March 1957, 'Mr Marchesi stressed that Round Table was not a society which was got together to raise big sums of money for charity. "I may get put on the rack for saying this here and in the Union, but there is nothing in the aims and objects to provide a lot of money for charitable purposes".'

South Africa's first Table had been founded in East London in 1948 and the second in 1950 in Durban, the town he had last 'visited' after his troopship had sunk in February 1917. In 1956 there were fifty-four Tables in the Union of South Africa and South-West Africa. What impressed Marchesi most was the contribution which the movement was making to the creation of better understanding between the younger Afrikander of Boer origin and the British South African. At Table meetings they both could meet and talk without bringing in politics or religion. It was gratifying too that the Chair of Race Relations Appeal started by the Salisbury Table stood at £12,500 and collecting was still in progress.

It was a gruelling fourteen-week tour alleviated by meeting old Norwich friends like Dick Culley, once chairman of Norwich Table, and Clifford Hindle, but the pace of the nightly feasting and speech-making and the toll of the heavy social drinking which was expected of him in temperatures to which he was not accustomed played havoc with his health which never fully recovered. In four months he was guest of honour sixty-one times! He and Dolly had thoroughly earned the long sea journey home in the *Athlone Castle*.

In his absence the Special Purposes Committee had been analysing the state of the movement at home, and produced a report, 'What of the Future?', for discussion at the 1958 Conference in Bournemouth. It attempted to answer the question, Was the current British Round Table organisation the right one in its latest stage of evolution? [the right one to do what?] The committee found that the spectacular growth of Round Table in Britain (580 Tables in thirty-seven Areas with 16,000 members) was, in the main, attributable to the service, enjoyment and fellowship which young businessmen and professional men found in association with like-minded men. There had to be a balance between efficiency and democratic control and that meant a sensitive mechanism. Greater efficiency could no doubt be achieved, but at the expense of the fellowship which was the basis of the movement. They estimated that in the next ten years (by 1968) there would be 750 Tables and 25,000 members. Their putative scheme for complicating the hierarchical administrative structure even more by the creation of four 'Regions', each with a council elected by Areas meeting twice yearly, was not acceptable to the members who came to the Bournemouth annual general meeting. There was a healthy surplus of £3,800 for 1957 and, now the Association's finances were at last on a sounder basis, this was no time to start experimenting.

The National Association had just rescued itself from a near-crisis. The anticipated deficit for 1956 had been £1,600. Up to 30 June expenditure had exceeded income by £1,000. The honorary treasurer said the problem was too big to be remedied by small economies. The Executive Committee reported that the loss was the largest and most serious in the history of the movement; in two years they had lost more than half of the Reserve Fund built up over twenty-five years. If the same amount was lost next year there would be no liquid funds to carry on. Plans were afoot to form a Round Table Benevolent Fund – it was estimated a shilling a year from 13,500 members would bring in £675 a year – and, renamed the Round Table Fellowship Fund, it was put before the next annual general meeting to give their views on it, though it was obviously not too happy a moment for a scheme of this sort. But in the event 1956 showed a deficit of only £684, and there was a reassuring HQ building fund of £6,900. The liquid position was righted by having ·Tables pay £10 each in advance of their capitation fees, which brought in an immediate £4,000 with which to pay pressing debtors. It had been a near thing. The honorary treasurer bid his fellow-officers 'think very seriously about the status of our association'. Realistic budgeting was the key. Expenditure for 1957 was estimated at £17,660, as compared with actual expenditure of £13,360 in 1956. The 'Travel Pool' from which money was drawn to pay the expenses of Table delegates travelling to the annual conference was to be 2s 1d a head – it had been only 1s 2d in 1955. But with 551 Tables – 15,118 members – income was substantial.

And it was going up each year. The capitation fee was raised to £1. Five hundred new members were enrolled in 1956. In towns where the only Table had a waiting list because the classifications were all full, a second Table was opened. There seemed to be plenty of money about: £9,220 was subscribed to the Round Table Hungarian Relief Fund, and £8,430 for the Chair of Race Relations Fund. Capitation fees brought in £17,850 in 1957 which, with expenditure being only £15,160, gave the Association a surplus and restored it to a strong liquid position.

But the movement's bank balance was not the only measure of its success. At Norwich an independent observer who, of anyone in Britain, had reason to be well disposed towards the movement, was at loss to assess Round Table's achievement. At Norwich Table's annual dinner on 19 March 1958 Tom Eaton, Lord Mayor of Norwich, boldly asked what had been its impact since it was founded, and answered by saying it had done little more than collect money for charity occasionally and organise lotteries. 'In 31 years there seems to have been no impact made here.' He asked them what they were doing about the Chamber of Commerce which a number of leading firms of Norwich had refused to join? What were they doing about the Norwich Publicity Association? There was considerable difficulty in getting people to stand as mayor – what was Round Table doing about that? He suggested that members of the Norwich club might turn their attention to four matters of interest to the town: education; the need for a sense of partnership between Trade, Commerce and the City Hall; problems of the young and the aged; the Arts.

Obviously the high note sounded by Archie Rice in his peroration at Norwich Table's first annual dinner no longer rang in the ears of the members of 1958. Whatever animated them it was not the spirit of Bignold, Rice and Marchesi.

5

Maturity
1958–1969

Gaining Self-confidence — and Respect of the Community

In 1927 when Round Table was founded voluntary bodies seeking to serve the community were comparatively few. The YMCA, founded in 1844, was still very operative and was to remain so. The first Guild of Help, started in Bradford in 1904 – motto 'Not alms but a friend' – led, under the inspiration of Edward Birchall, to the formation in 1911 of the National Association of Guilds of Help which assisted the National Council of Social Service (formed 1919) to set up urban councils of social service throughout Britain. The famous City of Birmingham Aid Society (founded 1906) and the Liverpool Council of Voluntary Aid (founded 1907) were still making their influence felt. In 1925 the Charities Department of the NCSS distributed £40,000 and recovered £6,000 in tax. In 1927 the Prince of Wales became Patron of the NCSS.

But thirty years later the ground was more thickly covered. And the thinking was deeper: not so much alleviating distress as preventing it. The Church of England Board for Social Responsibility was formed in 1958. Semi-government agencies were also entering the field in greater numbers like Voluntary Services Overseas (VSO), started in the same year to give opportunities to young men between eighteen and twenty to give service in developing countries. Inter-Church Aid, Save the Children Fund, the British Section of The World Council of Churches and others concentrated their efforts on problems thrown up by World Refugee Year 1959/60. In particular the Oxford Committee for Famine Relief, which had been born to help European war refugees fleeing from the Germans and was registered under the War Charities Act of 1940, mobilised its well organised resources. In 1957 it distributed help worth £300,000 to destitute, sick and homeless children and the aged. World Refugee Year also gave birth in 1961 to Amnesty International, a humanitarian movement designed to stimulate public opinion for the release of political and religious prisoners. When it came to Round Table contemplating the particular niche it could carve for itself in the World Refugee Year exercise, which would distinguish it by reason of its particular membership from contributions made by others, Robin Langdon-Davies could only pronounce, 'Round Table are masters of the art of raising money for good causes and could provide a real stimulus to World Refugee Year'. Prompted by one of their members who had returned from a business trip, Area 17 formulated an ambitious plan to build a village in Hong Kong for Chinese refugees at a cost of £100 a cottage, but there seems to have been no concerted Round Table contribution such as, for instance, providing information in a variety of languages about the conditions under which the various professions in Britain were prepared to recognise aliens, qualified in their own countries, as capable of practising their skills – accountancy, surveying, medicine, architecture, engineering etc. – in the UK, and the attitude of British trade associations, professional institutions and trade unions to their taking up positions in Britain. This, one would have thought, would have been a service which young business and professional men would have been more suited to provide than fund raising for food and clothing which

Oxfam, Christian Aid and the rest were geared to do more efficiently.

R. A. Butler MP, Deputy Prime Minister, certainly believed Round Table to be high in the league of the nation's influential bodies. At a dinner to celebrate the chartering of a Table in his Saffron Walden constituency, he commended Round Table in fulsome terms. There were not sufficient organisations for younger men, he said, which gave them an opportunity of getting together to help their fellow human beings and getting inspiration from each other.

It will have been on the strength of Round Table being praised by so high a personage in the realm that someone even higher agreed to associate himself with the movement's aspirations. In the summer of 1958 HRH The Prince Philip, Duke of Edinburgh, became Patron of British Round Table. The gesture inspired Dr Peter Bush, retiring president 1958/9, to declare, 'We can be the spokesman of our generation if we so desire', but he laid no plan before members for achieving that admirable end. As other presidents had done before him he was content to ask Can Round Table any longer be divorced from the main issues of our day? without giving the answer, let alone the detailed answer, for which members had been waiting since William Lincolne Sutton, who died at the end of 1958 aged ninety-one, had set the ball rolling in the 1920s.

Council certainly had the movement's possible wider role on its conscience, and added a significant question to the 'What Of The Future?' report discussed at the plenary session at Bournemouth.

'Experience indicates,' ran this addendum dated 29 March 1958, 'that at Table and Area level certain non-political matters of national policy are discussed, and it is anticipated that more frequent requests may arise for the National Association as such to make formal representation to the Prime Minister, Cabinet Ministers and Government Departments. It is possible to interpret our aims and objects as indicating that the National Association should make its views known on such matters as

Capital Punishment and Nuclear Warfare, etc. There may indeed be a majority opinion throughout the Movement that, with a membership of over 16,000, the time is now ripe for the Association's views on such important matters to be made known at each annual general meeting. In recent years the business on the agenda for an annual general meeting has been restricted to matters affecting the domestic operations of the movement. Is any change desired?'

The answer given at Bournemouth would seem to have been No, but the *News & Views* correspondent did not think it worth reporting when there were weightier matters to review such as capitation fees, a sub-committee's powers to co-opt experts, the election of tellers at AGMs, the allocation of banquet tickets – the persistent pre-occupation with the means and so little concern for the end. Over the next few years however the Executive Committee's Aims and Objects Sub-Committee continually had an item in their report headed 'Matters of Public Interest'. At a meeting in October 1959 they revealed 'consultations still proceed with Her Majesty's Minister' and in March 1960 that they were completed.

In the September 1960 issue of the Round Table journal, a new anonymous writer calling himself John Candid wrote: 'To hell with flag days, tombola, balloon races and raffles! Let's have a year's respite from this chicanery! Community service chairmen will have to sell this idea and sell it hard. They will have to convince members that the real point of community service is not the odd twice-a-year effort raising funds, but the monthly or even weekly donation of a few hours of their leisure time to an appointed purpose.' But Peter Newman was probably voicing the opinion of the majority when he wrote to say he was a Round Tabler because he liked its friendship. 'I like a noggin at the bar and a natter with the boys. If by chance this friendship motivates a feeling that we might be able to help people less fortunate than ourselves, that is all well and good. But don't tell me to do good for the sake of do-gooding, don't tell me to attend meetings as an obligation . . . don't waste my

time trying to explain to me what Round Table is and is not.'
He seemed to be of the kind that regarded a railway as something to take a ride on and resented the idea that it might actually take him somewhere.

It seemed a long way from the days of J. Rutherford Lindsay,
the barrister who also died in 1958 and had emphasised, during
his 1932/3 presidency, that the service a member rendered
his community or society at large *through his occupation* was the
most accurate standard by which to measure him as a member of Round Table. 'If you decide to do a piece of community
service work,' he had said, 'preparation is absolutely essential.
There must be investigation before activity and an intelligent
application of the results of the survey to the problem at
hand.'

David Parry-Maddocks could not think of a single instance in
1960 when Round Table had worked as a body wholeheartedly
to adopt, adapt or improve anything. It was the natural outcome of government from beneath. 'Round Table as an entity
does not and cannot exist under its present constitution. I say
simply that we must put our house in order or adopt a less pre-
tentious motto before the closer integration of World Council
provides wider scope for failure.'

But outside Britain, as Wakkie had shown, young men had a
keener appreciation of Round Table's potential. 'In Round
Table,' Per Sjogren, Swedish president of RTI, told the Ostend
conference of 1960, 'we have the opportunity to accept responsibility, to experiment in speaking and organising, to develop
our personalities and our characters. It is the only university
many of us will ever know. And its principal faculty is the hu-
manities . . . The thing which makes Round Table unique, the
thing which makes it different, is that it utilises practical men
and taxes their strength in hopes and causes larger than their
own private interests and concerns.'

It was a concept which Vic Collins, in his unique position as
general secretary, was trying, discreetly and politely as fitted his
behind-the-scenes role, to bring before all those with whom he

came into contact on his travels round Britain and across the world.

It was a point of view echoed too by Arthur Tiley MP, once a member of Bradford Table, when in 1960 he said, 'Round Table was to me, and I am sure must have been to thousands of other young chaps, the common room of the university. . . . Cheek by jowl we talked together. We knocked the humbug out of each other, the pomposity, the swank, and the conceit, bitterness and prejudice – or at least most of us did. We were not supposed to carry out social welfare work. As a Table it was not one of our aims, but we found ourselves doing it because it followed naturally from the things we talked about together.'

There was a suggestion at this time that Tables might be formed within universities among young dons, post-graduate research students and any interested undergraduates who, on leaving the university, would join Tables in the towns where they took up appointments. As more and more clubs had a leavening of university men in their make-up, it was hoped that the intellectual level of Round Table would rise.

Round Table had always encouraged members to join their trade associations and professional institutions, and at times had insisted on it. This was the mark of the well-intentioned Tabler. Through membership of such a body, he could be seen to be working for Round Table's aim of making business and professional services serve *the community*, because the *raison d'être* of these associations was the maintenance of high professional and ethical standards. It was better for the movement that members should infiltrate these bodies as individuals than that groups should be formed within them, as in universities, and this was never advocated. But the principle of forming Tables other than in geographical units could profitably be applied, it was thought, to groupings like Government Departments, the Court of St James's, public authorities and maybe HM Services. A Foreign Office Table and a Treasury Table of young civil servants, a Table of young army officers or young diplomats could not do other, they thought, than raise the prestige of Round

Table as a national group worthy of the nation's attention. But none of these ideas found favour.

If they had they might have provided a welcome diversion from the 'unfortunate press publicity' to which the president, Jim Cooke, drew the attention of Council members on 19 March 1960. He told them he believed the movement was chosen by the Duke of Edinburgh for royal patronage because it was a mature organisation, uniquely representative of its generation and because the past had indicated the kind of contribution Round Table had and could make both in Britain and abroad within its local communities. They must guard the name of Round Table jealously and be careful not to gain an unfortunate reputation. Round Tablers were responsible men and they would not do anything wittingly to harm the movement. During the last thirty years or more they and their predecessors had worked hard to establish Round Table as a responsible organisation, representative of the best of their generation and worthy of a position of honour in the community. None of them would deliberately discredit the Association in the eyes of the general public, but lately there had been a risk of their giving themselves a bad name. 'Sometimes the trouble has been boorish or over-boisterous behaviour at charter nights or on other occasions when the public is present. On other occasions there has not been enough discretion at our private parties, forgetting that unexpected publicity might cause something which appears harmless at the time to appear as though we have behaved disgracefully. No one has a wish to spoil the fun which is an essential part of Round Table Fellowship. At the same time a bad reputation easily earned would be difficult to lose. If our good name disappears, so will our friends with whom our name is now proudly associated.'

In December Council took note of 'regrettable incidents indicative of a decline in standards in recent months particularly on public occasions which, if continued, would have a cumulatively deleterious effect and in the course of time not only injure the standing of the movement in the community, but cast its future in an impoverished quality of membership at variance with Round Table's well established traditions.'

Quality apart, world growth had certainly been phenomenal. At the 1959 Round Table International annual general meeting at Leyden it was reported that there were 25,280 members in 1,040 Tables in twenty-one countries. At the 1957 meeting in Stavanger a move had been made to merge all young men who belonged to any of the clubs of the World Council of Young Men's Service Clubs into a new single body under a new name with its own new constitution. Individual names like Apex, Round Table, 20-30 would disappear and their subscribers become members of 'Young World', or whatever it would be called. The British delegation were unhappy at the thought of 'Round Table' disappearing as a name, and the representatives of other associations took the same line. The idea was dropped. Instead Canadians, Australians and Americans got together with Europeans at Hamburg the following year to agree a new World Council constitution. At Salzburg in 1960 everyone met for the first time under the new structure by which each Round Table association including RTBI became a member with equal status, and Round Table International was wound up – Denmark's jibe that the new World Council was a Commonwealth Bulldozer with RTBI at the wheel notwithstanding.

When the new constitution was formally adopted at the Wo-Co conference in Brighton in 1960, the body was said to have a membership of 53,970,* with the Round Table element amounting to 29,340 in 1,183 clubs – well over half the total. Peter Myers of British Round Table was elected World Council President, and at once embarked on a world tour.

Many resented the dismissal of Round Table International; others looked to the World Council to succeed where RTI had failed to produce a single project to command the support of

---

* In 1963 the International Association of Lions Clubs had 700,000 members in 17,500 clubs organised in 700 districts covering the whole world. There were ninety clubs in the British Isles. The Lions were governed by an elected Board of twenty-eight directors sitting at Chicago, headed by an International President.

member associations. Peter Bush however saw a great future in the new body. 'Within this organisation of Canadian and Cypriot, Frenchman and Finn, Jew and Arab, black, white, red, yellow, brown can all sit down together, chat, discuss, argue and fight with words, yet retain that fellowship and friendship we all cherish. We will be demonstrating that unity of mind and thought which embraces men of goodwill throughout the world. If we, the young men of the world, in some practical measure can demonstrate while we are young the brotherhood of man, the unity of nations, classes and creeds, then, as we grow older, we shall live the same tradition. The spirit of Round Table will be with us, will pervade our communities and our nations, and individually again we shall be able to have contributed toward the peace of mankind.'

A manifestation of this spirit was the Children's Holiday Exchange Scheme begun in 1950 which had steadily grown in popularity so that by 1960, 100 children were being exchanged each way through London (thirty with Sweden, thirty with Germany and forty with Denmark) and fifty-five each way to and from Scotland. At this stage the organisation of the scheme passed from a single volunteer member to a sub-committee of Council's International Committee.

For the World Council of Young Men's Service Clubs Dr Bush had dreams of a more dramatic role. It may be, he said, that it 'should directly approach the United Nations offering the services of 60,000 young men in some project – perhaps educational, perhaps exploratory, or an independent investigation of some world problem'.

If the UN took the WCYMSC up on this it was unlikely, in the view of 'John Candid', that the British Round Table element would ever be able to rise to the occasion. Explaining why *News & Views* never carried articles on vital national or international topics, John Candid said space had to be found for the boisterous revels of Tables with their obstacle races, blow football and ring hockey. 'A lad with philosophic and intellectual aspirations must find *News & Views* hard to stomach. So far the

Cyril Marsh at the Hastings Conference of 1948. He kept RTBI in being throughout World War II.

The round seat in London Street presented to the City of Norwich by Table no. 1 as a memorial to Louis Marchesi who died in December 1968 – the handing over to the Lord Mayor on 6 March 1971.

No. 15 Park Road, Re[...] Park, London, the [...] quarters of Round [...] Great Britain and Ir[...] since 1956 and later [...] 'Marchesi House'.

The Duke of Edinburgh, Patron of RTBI, is guest of honour at the fortieth anniversary luncheon in London on 25 October 1967. He is flanked by Louis Marchesi, the founder (left), and Cyril Marsh, JP, Honorary Member.

V. M. Collins, DFC, General Secretary
from 1951 to 1969.

Denis Tizard, appointed General Secretary in 1969.

movement has had little time for "namby pamby" pursuits, and a more earthy, animal vigour has characterised Round Table. We seem to be an overspill for antiquated rugger players and young farmers.' What the writer of the previous piece had not realised, said John Candid, was that intellectualism in Round Table was a dormant force – even perhaps extinct. In all his years of service he had met only one intellectual, a somewhat jaundiced solicitor who joined Round Table in a fit of temper on being refused admission to the local Fabian Society.

For the Special Purposes Committee which reported in January 1961 on the Future of the National Conference such jibes were irrelevant. The *raison d'être* of Round Table, stated Denis Reid, David Tatlow, Bob Almy and John Robson, was fellowship – at Table, Area, National and International level. 'Challenge that and the meaning and purpose of Round Table becomes a matter of personal interpretation, individual argument, contemporary conjecture. Acknowledge and apply it and few, if any, conceivable circumstances or situations arise within a Round Table context incapable of clarification and evaluation. Looked at in this way one can say of Round Table in general that to the extent that fellowship is facilitated on any occasion the movement succeeds; to the extent that fellowship at any level at any time is impeded, impaired or imperilled, it fails. Postulated thus we have ready to hand at once a basic principle, a true yardstick with which to measure the success of the movement's activities.'

For Wolverhampton Table no. 17, which there is reason to think is as typical a club as any in Britain, Fellowship meant 'getting to know the other man'. There is no better way of seeing how the principle of Fellowship was being put into action in the field at this time than by taking a look at the summary of Wolverhampton's activities for 1957/8 (apart from their weekly meetings of course) given by Arthur Johnson in his history of the Table's first forty years, 1929–69.

Organised inter-Table visits were arranged with Cannock,

Ludlow, Bilston, Brierley Hill and Stourbridge – with parties of 12–15 Tablers on each occasion; cricket matches were played with Stafford and Wednesbury; 2 football matches with Tettenhall; Skittles with Wednesbury; John Thorne Mug Competitions with Halesowen and Stourbridge; a party attended the 25th Anniversary Meeting of Walsall Table; Area Sports fixtures at Golf, Tennis and Table Tennis – incidentally the Area Bellamy Cup Golf Trophy came to Wolverhampton for the third year running; parties, 8 to 14 strong, attended every Area Council Meeting; parties from Wolverhampton attended 2 preliminary Meetings and the Inaugural Meeting of the new Bridgnorth Table (sponsored successfully at last by Ludlow, with help from Stourbridge, Wolverhampton and other Tables). Inaugural Meetings at Droitwich and Welshpool and a Charter Night at Rowley Regis; a party of 27 Tablers and Ladies attended the National Conference at Bournemouth; and 14 Wolverhampton members went to the 1-day Area Rally held at Wrekin. For good measure, ordinary Table Meetings during the year were attended by no fewer than 32 visiting Tablers from 12 different Tables as far apart as Bristol, Derby and Grays.

Even all this inter-Table fellowship, however, seems to fade into insignificance as compared with the International highlights. It all started with a suggestion that perhaps a few Tablers might attend the Brussels International Exhibition in September. It finished with one quarter of Wolverhampton Table No. 17 (a party of 18 in all) piling into 4 cars, and in a period of 5 days completing a round of inter-Table visiting which had never previously been envisaged. What better opening could there have been than a visit to Luton Brewery followed by an Evening Meeting as guests of Bletchley and Luton Round Tables? Thence to Southend and across to Belgium by air. A special Meeting organised by Hal Table No. 17 of Belgium, with other visitors from Brussels No. 1 La Louviere and Mons Tables. A continental Charter Night at Courtrai Table, and a visit to Ghent Table No. 3 (where

Wolverhampton Tabler Vernon Mills was the Speaker – in French!) Thus was the banner of Wolverhampton Table carried high into the field of Round Table International – and incidentally the party did take a liberal supply of bannerettes to distribute on their travels – and collected not a few in return!

A sequel lay in a return visit of 18 continental guests from Belgian Tables who attended Wolverhampton Table Ladies' Night held this year at the Civic Hall, Wolverhampton.

The breadth and depth of Fellowship could well be said to be a measure of Round Table's success; so also could size. Those who looked to Round Table's growth as a yardstick could point to the movement's 718 Tables and 21,095 members at January 1961 compared with 518 Tables and 13,760 members in 1956. At this rate the 1957 forecast of 750 Tables and 25,000 members by 1968 would be achieved well ahead of time. With an average increase of thirty-nine Tables a year there would be 750 by 1962. In fact 1960 had seen an addition of forty-seven – 1,845 members. Reckoned in terms of fellowship and numbers, Round Table was being an undoubted success.

Top jobs were now being held by men between thirty and forty-five which was something of a revolution in Britain, and Round Table membership should have been enriched by the young leaders who attained these high positions. When in a discussion between British Rotary and British Round Table on relations between the two bodies Roger Levy, editor of *Rotary*, said top men in industry had always found they had no time for Rotary, Colin Firth, a past president, thought the new young leaders *would* have time for Round Table. Mr Diefenbaker, the Canadian Prime Minister and Richard Nixon, Vice-President of the United States, were in a movement to which Round Table was affiliated. 'They were active participants in their clubs in Canada and in California, and we say that if we can develop the movement throughout the world so that men who knew each other when they were young and who inspired each other when they were young men and who came into positions of political power later – if these men had a common association, in the past, then we could change the world.'

Others' spirits were raised by such a dream, like Bill Thomas of Carmarthen who saw Round Table's role in the world as 'something like a Peace Corps peddling the cause of humanity, a supplementary Red Cross, a universal conscience-prodding organisation'. Chris Band, Area 34 press officer, had no illusions that the public regarded Round Table as anything other than 'just another charity-helping organisation-cum-beer-drinkers'. He did not think people looked on it as an organisation which aimed at the encouragement of high ethical standards in commercial life even though the strength of Round Table had once lain in the fact that members encouraged and stood by the ideal of fairness, uprightness and integrity in the business and professional life of the country. John Cardozo thought over 20,000 young men, full of energy, all professing the highest ideals, should impart a tremendous drive to public life. 'This splendid movement to which we belong deserves a better public image than that of a slightly older students' union.'

Those at 'National' noted such speculation and often took part in it, but at the same time were continually satisfying themselves that Round Table's machinery was still of the right design and in full working order. In April 1961 a sub-committee appointed to report on the Administrative Structure of Round Table concluded that the current basis of organisation had not outlived its usefulness. 'Remoteness in the process of decision must never be allowed to lead to unbridled authoritarianism and unwished-for bureaucratic control from the centre. We must be very careful to preserve the most visibly direct link and the most effective personal and collective control over the organisation by the members who constitute it.'

But the end product could not be affected by adjusting or redesigning the administrative machine; only by changing the nature of the raw material – people. And that was not as easy. President Bryan Coker was receiving 'disturbing reports' of members' bad behaviour at official functions in front of guests. He hoped Area Chairmen would take steps to end 'this menace', even to the extent of ejecting boorish troublemakers and so remove a stigma. Hurling bread rolls about and tying tablecloths together might enliven a choirboys' treat, but it revealed a somewhat immature lack of a sense of occasion when they happened while a Round Table guest was doing his best to respond to the toast of the Visitors.

It reached a new low with an outbreak of 'trophy-hunting', the euphemism (on the lines of the army 'winning') for stealing other Tables' crested mugs, tankards and pennants when one Table visited another for an Area meeting. It was excused as only a boisterous form of inter-Table 'fellowship' (the robbed Table would have to visit the robber Table to recover the lost bauble), but not by all. 'Hindsight' felt he had to send a protest. 'For undergrads, rugger types and oarsmen, selective looting of premises is an accepted tradition providing less mature males with some sense of achievement . . . It is bad form at any time for guests to witness the boorish activities of their hosts. But this has occured at functions attended by some of the leading citizens of local communities, when a mild fracas has developed over a prized possession of the host table in danger of making an unscheduled journey to another place. Oafish, graceless behaviour, discourtesy to guests and misappropriation of another's property is intolerable; among Tablers it is also inexcusable. Although confined to a tiny minority of members, such behaviour must be eradicated as it is incompatible with the spirit and dignity of Round Table.'

Every young man who saw nothing censurable about behaving in this way had been quizzed by club members sitting in judgement as a Membership Committee or, if they were sponsoring a new Table, an Extension Committee. Obviously much Extension work was being taken too lightheartedly and superficially, or with due intensity but little idea of what they were looking for other than 'a good fellow' who would add to the 'fellowship'. To get the movement's Extension policy right –

and known – was now top priority.

In the spring of 1961 Council issued an Extension Manual which stressed 'the vital importance of ensuring the persons they seek to introduce as Founder Members already possess the very highest qualities of character, intellect and personality'. Character and personality could take a variety of forms, but there should be no mistaking intellect.

The greatest disservice to existing members, stated the Manual, would be to form a new Table of individuals who had little to offer their fellow men and were unlikely to have a sufficient sense of responsibility to carry out the simple obligations of membership. A number of Interviewing Don'ts were given 'which experience has shown should not be ignored if trouble is to be avoided at a later stage': (1) don't understate the obligations of membership; (2) don't question him on his financial position; (3) don't delve too deeply into his private and business affairs; (4) don't be afraid to dissuade unsuitable people; (5) don't forget that you alone are responsible to the movement for the maintenance of the highest standards of membership in a new Table – a poor legacy in this respect will take many years to overcome.

Fifteen potential members had to be found before a new Table could be formed, and the temptation had to be resisted to find *any* fifteen young men in order to get the Table launched. The responsibility was that of the Sponsor Table which made a list of first contacts whom they invited to a Primary Meeting at which they were told what Round Table was all about. This was followed by half a dozen or so preliminary sessions culminating in an Inaugural Meeting, often a dinner with members of neighbouring Tables as guests and presided over by the chairman of the Round Table Area to which the new Table belonged. A resolution to form the Table was passed and it was given a number. The Area Chairman inducted each founder member with a lapel badge, and then declared:

You have been chosen for membership of Round Table

because you are believed to be worthy representatives of your vocations, possessed of qualities which can be of service to our movement and your fellow men. Your acceptance of membership implies that you will carry into your public and private lives the aims and objects for which this movement stands. Your membership will involve you in an obligation to make regular attendances at meetings and to support in every way possible the various activities of your Table. Wear your badge at all times and remember as you wear it that you carry the good repute of Round Table into all your affairs, for the movement is judged by those who recognise you as members.

He then called on the other members present to drink a toast to their newly joined brothers. The new Table's officers were elected – chairman, vice-chairman, treasurer and secretary – and the members of the executive committee (council) which would run it with the aid of several sub-committees dealing with such matters as recruiting new members, community service and social activities, and probably the production of a Table bulletin. The new chairman then took over and thanked the Sponsor Table for giving birth to the latest Round Table cell.

'It is the responsibility of the Area Chairman and the Table Chairman,' stated the Extension Manual, 'to see that boisterous behaviour is kept in check, notwithstanding the legitimate desire of all to celebrate enthusiastically, so that boorish behaviour is not allowed to impair the enjoyment by all of what should be a memorable occasion, nor the public image of Round Table damaged in the eyes of the guests present'.

Six months later, provided the new Table had met at least twelve times, it could apply to be affiliated to the National Association of Round Tables and receive a charter. In this time it had had to show willingness not only to run its own activities but to take full part in those organised by its Area, sending representatives to Area Meetings and attending social as well as business functions in the Area. Many Tables prided themselves, observed the Manual, on their indifference to both the Area and the National organisations. 'But they lack the essential humility and true sense of responsibility for which the movement stands and can only be considered under these circumstances as Dinner Club Members who may from time to time engage in a little local community service.

'Tables who conduct their affairs in this way are failing the movement, and the chairman and officers of Tables who permit and encourage such behaviour are scarcely worthy of consideration as good Round Tablers. Table chairmen are best advised to put the well being of the movement first in importance and always before the individual and short term needs of their own Table where these are running contrary to the movement's ideals.

'Table members should at all times conduct themselves as responsible and mature persons accepting that membership implies a privilege which is denied to many and only accorded to those considered worthy to represent the aims, the objects and the ideals of the movement. They should use their influence in their business and private lives to uphold these ideals and should in their own Table activities make every effort to attend and actively participate in all properly constituted Table meetings fostering Table fellowship to the best of their ability not only at Table meetings but at social events also.'

A charter night would almost certainly be a dinner, attended by eminent civic and local dignitaries, and possibly the president of the National Association or his representative. The climax came with the Area Chairman's speech ending with his presentation of the Charter of Affiliation to the new Table's chairman. 'It is always wise to schedule the conclusion of the evening early enough to avoid the restlessness and often unintended discourtesy occasioned by the high spirits of Tablers present, which can be aggravated by long, dull speeches and the lateness of the hour.'

The leaders of Round Table at this time might well have returned to Louis Marchesi's first principles by trying to *understand* the behaviour of those much younger than themselves instead of merely deploring it. If they had, they might have found it was an unconscious protest against a stylised framework, borrowed second hand from the Rotary of 1911, which they considered both tedious and meaningless. Non-Rotarian Bernard Durrant had twice appealed to members to stop calling each other by formal titles as long ago as 1927, but the attractions of pomposity had been a long time a-dying. In a looser, more friendly, spontaneous ambience, forced heartiness of the robust kind these young men had no inhibitions about demonstrating, might have been entirely foreign, and those who indulged in it laughed out of court. *They* would have been the ones to feel ashamed and out of place.

In 1962, for the first time since the capitation fee was fixed at £1, income growth levelled off for British Round Table. A certain amount of additional income was now being raised by the sale of a range of Round Table goods like key fobs, silk scarves, ties, pennants, lapel badges, car stickers. The 1959 turnover of £7,600 from this rose to £16,000 in 1961. But the following year the gross profit fell by £1,200, in spite of membership growing from 19,000 in 1959 to 23,000 in 1962. The 1959 annual general meeting authorised the building up of a General Reserve Fund of £15,000 from the 1962 balance of only £1,500. It would take seven years.

More important however was the building up of morale, giving members a reason for joining more than the 'fellowship' they could get with the Lions, the British Legion, the Jaycees, the Community Service Volunteers, Toc H, the County Club, the Young Liberals.

At home there were the annual film and film script competitions for members who were amateur ciné enthusiasts; those who looked to the international aspect of Round Table found an outlet for their energy in interchange visits with European Tables which bore their Table number. All Tables no. 15 met for a weekend in England: Dutch no. 15 of Arnhem, Belgian no. 15 of Couvin, French no. 15 of Sarreguemines, German no. 15 of Wuppertal, and British no. 15 of Newport, Mon. A Union of Tables no. 26 was formed: Louvain (Belgium), Roubaix (France), Nykobing Falster (Denmark), Kalmar (Sweden), Hyrinkas (Finland) and Walcheren (Holland). Britain's Table no. 26 at Cardiff declined to join, but paid visits to some of the continental 26s. Tables in Britain now numbered from 1 to 800 so it was only those in the lower register who were able to play this game; but of course those with the bigger numbers found other excuses for paying visits, or followed the example of Doncaster who corresponded with Springs (South Africa) Table by recording messages on magnetic tape, or of Area 28 which held the imaginative International Weekend of African Students.

The most dramatic overseas 'visit' made in 1963 was by the six caravans which set out on the 1,600-mile, ninety-six-hour journey from Hounslow to the earthquake shattered town of Skopje in Yugoslavia, after BBC television cameraman Peter Beggin, a member of Hounslow Table, had returned from the scene to report on the need for temporary homes. The idea spread, and soon more empty caravans were leaving London, Bristol, Devon and Cornwall and the Midlands. Eventually eight motor convoys took to the road towing ninety-seven caravans. They were met and helped by local Round Tables en route.

With news of these fine acts of mercy still fresh in their memories it was not unexpected that the members who crowded in to the Debate in the Brighton Royal Pavilion on the third day of the 1963 annual conference overwhelmingly defeated the motion 'that this house accepts that modern youth has no regard for society'. 'Youth' of course was not 'Young Men' and the debaters were not upholding themselves but the teenagers they had ceased to be a decade before. Declining interest in politics and ethics? Obsession with sex? Declining moral standards? The house would have none of it.

It was these debates, plus the International Luncheon, which justified calling the annual four-day, Wednesday to Saturday, gatherings of the 1960s (in 1963 it ran through 1, 2, 3 and 4 May) 'conferences' and not annual general meetings with supporting social junketing. Often the subject of debate was of internal interest only – in 1960 it was the Area System which everyone considered still to be 'a good thing'. In 1962 the motion 'Service to the community should be local to be logical' was carried by seventy-eight to fifty-six.

In March 1961 Council had adopted the recommendations of its Special Purposes Committee on Future Conference Policy which set out a model programme as follows:

Wednesday: meeting of Executive Committee, followed by informal welcome party.

Thursday: meeting of Council and open sessions of executive sub-committees; civic reception in the evening.

Friday: 'Official Conference Opening' with address by the mayor, a review by the out-going president followed by a discussion on international matters – open to members and wives; the 'International Luncheon'; 'General Assembly' in the afternoon, and 'Presidential Buffet Ball and Cabaret' in the evening.

Saturday: AGM start in morning; AGM delegates' luncheon; AGM continue in afternoon; 'Farewell Party' in the evening.

At Brighton in 1963 the organisers took liberties with this prototype, as they were entitled to do, and the Wednesday closed with a new style 'President's Banquet' attended by 430 members, wives and guests. The evening Civic Reception on the Thursday began as a cocktail party but ended with 1,900 people dancing to two orchestras and watching a cabaret mounted by Bexhill Table. Friday opened with the debate in the morning, proceeded to the showing of films by Table amateurs, and ended with the Friday Night Ball ('President's Buffet Ball') with a professional cabaret, an act by Hastings Table and Richard Hearne dancing his one-man Lancers as Mr Pastry. The annual general meeting took place on the Saturday morning and afternoon, and the four days were rounded off with a riotous Farewell Party with dancers in fancy dress and a parade of Table tableaux – floats decorated to a given theme. This had to end at midnight, but fellowship continued to the early hours of Sunday in places other than the official ballrooms – one Area hired its own floor and band for a Farewell Again Party. Somewhere along the line the idea of an official conference opening and the Friday afternoon General Assembly had become mislaid, but the conference achieved Round Table's main objective by providing a setting for so many to meet together (if only a small proportion of the total membership), make new acquaintances and renew old ones.

The vast majority of members were unable or unwilling to attend the national conference, but in the gatherings of their own clubs and Areas they found that Round Table fulfilled, in the words of Malcolm Hurwitt, the need for something warm, human and immediate in a society where there was too much cynical self-seeking. That was why fellowship had been Round Table's prime purpose, and community service something which had grown out of it. Hurwitt wanted Round Table to resist any attempt to propagate the idea that it had a special mission. There were organisations designed to set the world to rights, but Round Table was not one of them. John Goldsbrough who became president in 1964 on the other hand saw Round Table as possessing a community of interest, an acceptance of responsibility, a degree of intelligence and knowledge, which qualified the movement, beyond any body he knew, to offer the help of the younger business and professional men in tackling a whole range of matters, 'but by and large we close our eyes and an opportunity is lost'.

Round Table was represented on only twenty of the 147 Councils of Social Service, whereas Rotary was represented on all of them and had helped to found twenty new ones. Governments were still reluctant to give Round Table statutory recognition and invite representatives to sit on royal commissions, enquiries and committees.

But to some, like Geoffrey Wheatley of Royston, it was an asset that Round Table should not be regarded as a professional elite. It was not a place for young men to make friends with others of similar backgrounds. The idea that artisans had no contribution to make and no service to offer was both restrictive and ridiculous. A classless group of young men were now playing an important role in society. They were mainly from the red-brick universities and had jobs in the technical fields. They were no less fellowship-conscious and service-conscious than the established middle-class 'callings' of dentist, doctor, solicitor, accountant. 'Let us once and for all drop this class barrier that would seem to surround our movement and let us judge a man for his fellowship.'

Undoubtedly, in the minds of some, the term 'businessman' had acquired a new, wider connotation; there were now more young men in a host of occupations peculiar to the post-war era for whom there was no new generic term like 'the workers' or 'businessmen'. No one could say that they were 'entitled' to membership of Round Table; it was up to any group to define its area of membership and refuse to move outside it without being accused of failing to move with the times or having 'elite' applied to it as a word of abuse. But probably most members *wanted* to admit them – or certainly did not want to exclude them because of some old-fashioned, doctrinaire interpretation of the word 'businessman'. But the same members would probably have liked to have seen the line drawn *somewhere* – above, that is, those to whom Geoffrey Wheatley gave the label 'artisan' – though loth to admit it. But it was only realistic, and not snobbish, to believe that those who were at home in the ambience of the Ancient Order of Buffaloes would have felt ill at ease in Round Table, and vice versa. For many Tablers, making the qualification for membership a man's potential for 'fellowship', and leaving it at that, would have watered down the mix to an extent that would have robbed Round Table of whatever remained to distinguish it (apart from the age limit) from any other social club. Those in the anti-elite camp considered the catholicity of a movement that embraced *all* sections of the community a worthy distinguishing mark, and one to be proud of.

It was a difficult subject, and in the view of many one best left well alone. Others considered it was just the kind of social change to which the Prince of Wales had said men of industry and business should adapt. Being 'with it' was an expressive phrase, born of the 1950s and 60s, indicating awareness of what there was to adapt to, of the kind that Louis Marchesi was trying to inculcate when he drafted the original Objects. Try and live on a broad front as opposed to a narrow front bounded by your own little world, he was trying to say, particularly in relation to those who are above you and below you in intelligence, experience and age. Try and understand what it can be like to be older; and when you are yourself older, remember what it was like to be younger. That it was still a social issue in the 1960s was underlined by someone giving it a name – the generation gap.

Insofar as Round Table, like Rotary, was an attitude of mind, an outlook, and insofar as it had succeeded in making young men more aware than they would otherwise have been, the next problem was how to harness this concentration of awareness and apply it to Round Table's other Objects. Taking their cue from John Goldsbrough's conference speech, Council determined to see what positive steps could be taken by a movement maturing in years to realise something of their president's conception of Round Table's place in a responsible society. 'An informed Round Table membership is an essential prerequisite and objective in such a conception nationally as well as locally.' They wanted to see a conference programme providing for national speakers on important issues (Iain Macleod who had refused to serve in the new Tory ministry of 1963 spoke at Bognor). 'Meantime Tables are recommended to give their attention to matters of local consequence of a non-political and non-sectarian nature, to acquaint themselves of the facts, to develop contact with those concerned with such facts and by thought about them (be they problems of local traffic, community needs, planning) to establish their Tables at local level as vital elements, of a responsible movement concerned with the public well-being.' (Agenda, 23 January 1965, para 14.)

The kind of subjects which come to mind are Opinion Polls, Packaging, Alcoholism, Commercial Radio, Inertia Selling, News Values, Comprehensive Education, Censorship, Trading Stamps, Industrial Espionage.

In taking over the baton of presidency from John Goldsbrough in 1965, Duncan Lawton expanded on the same theme of Round Table's role in a quickly changing world. 'Round Table,' he told members at the Bognor conference, 'is an opportunity to express our potential in society in a contemporary way. It is not an encumbered inheritance preventing us from living in our times and age.' It was a deeper change he was asking for than an adaptation of methods to meet the needs of the day. He was putting it to members that they might like to contemplate changing gear after forty years from Neutral to Drive. Was it too late to substitute Action for Inaction?

A week before the conference he had been granted an audience with Round Table's royal patron who since his acceptance of the role had been content to bide his time and let the movement prove itself worthy of his active participation.

A statement in the 1965 annual report read: 'Arising from correspondence initiated by the president with the private secretary to HRH The Prince Philip, Duke of Edinburgh, KG, KT, the Patron graciously received on 4th May 1965 a party from the Association consisting of President John Goldsbrough, Vice-President Duncan Lawton, Executive Member Stewart Hunter and Mr V. M. Collins. During the course of a stimulating hour's meeting views were exchanged upon, and suggestions made as to, the present and possible roles of British Round

Table, from which developed an awareness of the opportunities for corporate action by the Association in fields of thought wider than those hitherto adopted. An assurance was conveyed to the Patron of the honour felt by the Association on his appointment and of the sincere desire of the Association to welcome its Patron at a suitable function on an appropriate occasion.'

John Goldsbrough told members who attended the annual general meeting at Bognor he had gone into the interview with a feeling of buoyancy and left with one of inadequacy. Prince Philip was a Man of This Day, a man of his age. Had they any right to expect him to be proud of them? They claimed to be unique, but what distinction had they to such a claim? Did they use it or dissipate it? What corporate action or lead had they given in the last five years to justify their claim to distinction? Could not others less fortunately endowed undertake what they did equally successfully? The time had come when they could no longer content themselves with local good works but accept national and international responsibilities. 'At the moment the National Association of Round Tables of Britain and Ireland is just going round and round. Its power of good must now begin to drive it forward in a positive direction.'

Anyone looking for Round Table's justification in terms of the sums of money it was raising for charity, apart from whether others less fortunately endowed could have done so with equal success, would have had an easy task. Very large amounts were being raised by Tables in 1964/5: £825 from a car raffle; £700 from one carnival, £2,500 from another; £200 from a mock auction; £600, £925 and £595 from donkey derbys; £2,500 from a May Fayre; £325 from a piano smashing contest; £250 from a food and wine festival; £350 from a barbecue; £500 from a rummage sale; £750 from a white elephant shop; £730 from a charity football match; a Whit Monday fête with Miss World as the attraction raised £1,083. And the money went to providing radio, television and mobile telephone sets for hospitals; irrigation pumps for

Oxfam; a motorised wheel chair for Kampala; drugs for an Ethiopian leper colony; an ambulance for a Leonard Cheshire Home; endowing a berth in the Sail Training Association's new schooner; the purchase of an in-shore rescue craft for the Royal National Lifeboat Institution; a Russian electrical impulse limb for the Lady Hoare Thalidomide Appeal; a van for Meals on Wheels; a guide dog for the blind; establishing a scholarship for a Rhodesian child's secondary education; sending staff and pupils of a Handicapped Children's Home on holiday; providing children's playground; sending elderly folk to a holiday camp; installing 'visual help signals' in the windows of old people's homes. Pontypridd and Rhondda Table raised some £4,000 over a period to relieve distress caused by thirty-one miners being killed in the Tonypandy pit disaster.

Gordon Liversidge of Erdington reckoned that Round Tables in Britain raised at least £250,000 every year, and it was this continuing effort with special exercises like setting up the Chair of Race Relations at Salisbury University in Rhodesia, and the driving caravans to Skopje operation, which reflected the true spirit of Round Table and established its worthwhileness. If this was not enough to demolish Duncan Lawton's sense of inadequacy, surely the 'fellowship' displayed at the Farewell Party at Bognor would have given the final blow?

But someone at this hour of need should have been thinking of a word to describe the purpose of Round Table which did not need to be put apologetically between inverted commas (by those outside the movement, that is to say); for a word less cold, for one which hinted less of the cloister and sinister design. Good-fellowship, as already suggested, was what everyone really meant; jolly good companee, companionship or comradeship.

As G. K. Chesterton remarked (in *What's Wrong With the World?* 1910), in the mere observation of 'a fine day' there was the whole great human idea of comradeship. Pure comradeship, he went on, was one of those broad yet bewildering things. Everyone enjoyed it, yet when they came to talk about it they almost always talked nonsense, chiefly because they supposed it to be a simpler affair than it was. It was simple to conduct, but by no means simple to analyse. Women stood for the dignity of love, and men for the dignity of comradeship, which would hardly be respected if the males of the tribe did not mount guard over it. The affections in which women excelled had so much more authority and intensity that pure comradeship would be washed away if it were not rallied and guarded in clubs, corps, colleges, banquets and regiments.

'No one has ever begun to understand comradeship who does not accept with it a certain hearty eagerness in eating, drinking and smoking, an uproarious materialism which to many women appears only hoggish. You may call the thing an orgy or a sacrament; it is certainly an essential. It is at root a resistance to the superciliousness of the individual. Nay, its very swaggering and howling are humble. In the heart of its rowdiness there is a sort of male modesty; a desire to melt the separate soul into the mass of unpretentious masculinity. It is a clamorous confession of the weakness of all flesh.'

The purpose of Round Table was once again in the melting pot, and many were eager to re-cast it in a different mould. The General Purposes Committee were invited to consider a Re-appraisal of the Aims and Objects; in April 1966 they submitted their report which had been the subject of comment by Council and Tables so that in its final form it was thought to represent a fairly wide consensus of opinion. It was the outcome, said the committee, of the views of John Goldsbrough and Duncan Lawton, and of more than thirty years uncertainty. Over this time there had been a feeling that the movement should exert its potentially powerful influence over the community by putting the weight of its membership behind any national policy which emerged from members' meetings, though in the 1960s feeling was less extreme; the movement should develop its potential by a natural growth in corporate action. Over the years too there had been criticism that the Objects failed to reflect 'the true spirit' of Round Table – by which the committee presumably meant the spirit as it was, not what someone considered it should be, or what the founder had intended it to be.

Only sixty members found their way into the Children's Theatre at Butlin's Bognor Holiday Camp during the 1965 conference to speak for or against the view 'that the Objects are obscure, out-dated and inexpressive of the purpose and spirit of Round Table'. But the General Purposes Committee considered that the debate, though badly attended, had shown that the Objects were not sacrosanct, were not accepted unconditionally as absolute for evermore. Duncan Lawton had urged the movement to be earnest in self-examination, truthful in self-criticism and courageous enough to accept changes. But someone had to decide the premiss on which to base the argument. Were they going to say that Round Table had never been 'right' from the start, and that the sooner it became what they considered to be 'right' the better? Or were they saying that Round Table had strayed from its original Objects through the carelessness of its early managers, which they deplored, but that in 1965 it was too late to haul it back on its base; that they must be realistic, publicly admit the shift and re-write the purpose of Round Table to conform to what, willy-nilly, it had become? Or were they going to say that in their view the fundamental motivation of the movement had never changed and should not now be changed, but they should build on the foundation in a way which would bring contemporary members greater satisfaction and the country greater benefit?

In trying to discover whether the Objects were a 'true' statement of the principles of Round Table in 1965 the committee acquainted themselves with how they came to be written, and found that they were 'adapted by a handful of Tablers from the Objects of Rotary'. Their predecessors however had rightly wished to shift the emphasis from service to fellowship – 'rightly', that is, according to the committee's way of thinking.

What had Round Table's principles become in 1965, the committee asked themselves, and were they still reflected in the Objects formulated in 1927? They had become fellowship, community service, personal integrity, citizenship and internationalism. The committee took exception to the 1927 Objects on the grounds that they did not express the 'true' meaning of 'our fellowship', nor recognise that Round Table was a service organisation for individual and corporate action.

They appreciated that fellowship might have its beginnings in business and professional contacts but felt the real meaning of an expression of that fellowship was achieved through the activities and membership of Round Table. 'We would like to make this clear in our first Aim and since we mean to insert the reference to business and professional men and to our age group in the preamble, we suggest that any further reference is unnecessary. Indeed we are inclined to think that to underline any suggestion of differences between business and the professions is not in keeping with modern thought and certainly not in keeping with the spirit of Round Table.'

The meaning of the last sentence is obscure, but the intention expressed in the whole Fellowship paragraph of the report seemed to be to shift Round Table away from its 'narrow' attachment to young men in a particular section of society, namely the world of business and professional life. Their reason was either because membership had, by default, been opened to a wider section of the community, or because in their view it should be – probably the latter.

They were also anxious to strip Round Table of Louis Marchesi's basic idea that a young man could serve his community best by being efficient at his job. 'The present Aims and Objects reflect the one Rotary Object which deals with vocational service. Rotary however develops the theme into a much wider concept of service as an individual responsibility, as a business responsibility and as an international responsibility. Round Table does not.'

This time the dogmatic 'does not' would seem to be reporting what they consider a historic fact, not expressing their view on what *should* be – though the two coincided, as the remainder of the paragraph showed.

'Round Table does not. Not because it does not believe in such service for it patently does, but because we took one Rotarian object and used it out of context when the Aims and Objects were devised all those years ago – the sort of mistake one makes when manipulating established work. We can do better now!'

Use of words like 'mistake' and 'better' in reference to Louis Marchesi's Objects indicate a desire to pass judgement on them as 'wrong' from the start, not merely to record a current state of affairs on which an opinion is then expressed. They were entitled to do what they liked of course, but it would have been helpful if they had shown what *their* Objects would have been designed to produce – more fun? richer companionship? more satisfying voluntary service? greater respect from the outside world? more likelihood of statutory recognition from the Government? greater chance of survival into the 1970s and '80s? more members joining in greater numbers? more Tables being formed? more money coming in? a greater sense of identification as against all the other clubs and organisations in the field? greater possibilities for members to train themselves for taking a place in the life of the community?

In other words, what was the target?

The idea that Round Table should be a medium for the active *promotion* of high standards of business ethics and of the conduct of professional and civic life, was retained, though in the weaker phrase, 'to encourage personal integrity in public and private life'.

Were the Objects acceptable as written and spoken words? To the committee it seemed 'they are written in a style so wordy, so cumbersome and repetitive that the point of the message is blunted; that the individual Aims and Objects appear to lose their identities and that the whole thing is difficult to learn and almost impossible to memorise. Nor can the language escape criticism. Many of the phrases used have unfortunate overtones. For example "legitimate occupations" has a rather ominous ring to it, and "peace and goodwill" when applied to international relationships grossly resembles an ideological cliché and suggests something rather different from the activities of our internationalists.'

Many members had expressed the view, they said, that had a reading of the Objects been their only knowledge of Round Table the thought of joining it would not have occurred to them. The committee did not think the Objects read well when repeated in the presence of strangers. 'Indeed such readings may induce feelings of embarrassment both in members and non-members. All in all we think that most, if not all, the weaknesses in our Aims and Objects can be traced to their Rotarian origin. The "Object of Rotary" is service, and our paraphrase does not do Round Table justice. The "Object of Rotary" is not as a rule read aloud at meetings and our paraphrase is just as unsuitable for such a practice.'

The committee's recommendations were:

1. that, when a preamble to Round Table Aims and Objects is appropriate, it be:

   "Round Table is a non-party political and non-sectarian organisation of men between the ages of eighteen and forty, of varied occupations whose objects are"

2. that the new Aims and Objects be:

   to promote fellowship through the medium of Round Table.

   to serve the community both individually and collectively.

   to encourage personal integrity in public and private life.

   to stimulate individual interest in matters of public concern.

to improve international friendship and understanding.

John Goldsbrough and Duncan Lawton who had inspired the
exercise accepted the committee's recommendations for submission to the annual general meeting, except that they wanted
'non-political, non-sectarian' removed from the preamble and
from the letterhead and all literature. They did not wish to remove the rule, only undue emphasis on it.

So, if they had had their way, Round Table would have
become 'an organisation of men between the ages of eighteen
and forty of varied occupations'.

The reformers no longer wanted Round Table to be 'just' an
Association of Young Business Men. They found this too re-
stricting. They wished to take it out of its context and release it
from commitment to the world of industry and commerce,
the professional and civic life. They wished to 'improve' it by
widening Marchesi's terms of reference in the belief that to do
so was 'moving with the times'. It was an assumption of people
who had not done their homework. If they had really moved
with the times they would have been more aware, as those who
had *studied* such matters at St George's House, Windsor Castle,
were, of the part which Business and Industry had come to play
across the whole spectrum of contemporary living; and that an
Association of Young Business Men had a very much more significant role to play in 1977 than in 1927.

'From all the consultations,' states a St George's House
report* 'we have come to see that industry is no longer just the
method of providing most of our material and some of our
social needs; it is also, and increasingly, the determining factor
on the way we live. Our whole style of life has become business
centred and in a situation where we can make more and more,
the market for more and more has to be created and maintained.
Without the profit of industry there can be no social services,

* *Exploring the Business Ethic* by Kenneth Adams, Director of Studies, St George's
House, Windsor Castle, January 1971.

and without the increase in this profit the whole social structure of the state would stagnate. . . . In such a business centred society businessmen, industrialists and trade union leaders have very great influence; indeed it is probably true to say that they form the most influential group in the nation. This influence, for good or ill, spreads far beyond what people normally see as the area of industry. Through the markets they create, through the products or services which they supply, through advertising, through the sort of people they require to work for them, through the relationships in the work situation which they encourage, through their attitude to the suppliers of raw materials, their influence affects every life and enters every home in the land. Seen in this way this influence is the most powerful single influence on the whole style of our national and international life.'

The would-be reformers of Round Table who saw Business as restrictive wanted to divert the movement officially into the more general field into which it had already strayed, the Relief of Human Suffering, for which state and voluntary organisations were working in their hundreds, if not thousands. But by sticking to Marchesi's original terms of reference and fulfilling the promise seen in it by those who witnessed its birth in the 1920s, they would have made Round Table more not less potent. The narrower a purpose, the more pointed and effective. The smaller the definition of the common bond, the richer the sense of companionship.

The reformers were working on opposite assumptions, which probably accounted for the fact that their proposals were rejected by the 1966 Bournemouth annual general meeting.

It took them eight hours and the way they did it aroused the ire of at least one young member. 'No efficient or progressive body,' wrote David Bell in the magazine, 'would tolerate its vital annual business to be transacted in such a manner and have nothing to show for it other than a string of negatives on any issue that even hinted at importance. It is a criticism of our movement that we fail both to make an impact on society and to

attract the leaders of society to our ranks. Are we to be condemned as a "second class movement"?'

On the contrary, declared Duncan Lawton, the out-going
president, in response to the toast of the Duke of Devonshire
who was guest of honour at the Bournemouth conference banquet. Round Table represented an ideal full of fire and inspiration. It was never intended to be a movement for grey-beards, a
meeting of elders, or an annual outing for barrack-room lawyers. Members should apply energy in Round Table terms, not
personal terms. Some might regard that as immaturity, but to
him it added up to the pulsating movement that was the Round
Table of 1966.

If the organisation failed to attract leaders of society to its
ranks, some of them like His Grace at least regarded it as worth
giving time to, if only as guests at its social gatherings. It is true
that only a handful attended the conference dinner and few took
heed of what went on at 'National', as they called it, but it
cannot but have steadied a body in need of reassurance to have
had a leading politician assert in public that where high principles were at a premium Round Table was a movement from
which anyone anxious about the future of the country should
take encouragement.

If the base was shifting in the country of origin, the European
offspring determined on conservation. In 1965 every Round
Table no. 1 decided to meet together every year 'to ensure that
as the movement spreads to new countries its purpose and tradition is unchanged'. It was a good idea, though of course Norwich Table had no special status or paternalistic influence in
Britain, as some of the first Tables had elsewhere. The first of
these gatherings was held in Brussels, and the second on 25
March 1966 in Norwich when the Lord Mayor held a civic
reception for Louis Marchesi and members of Norwich Table
no. 1, and representatives of the first Round Table clubs in Belgium, Holland, Italy, Germany, France and Luxembourg. The

following month, at the first charter night to be held in Norwich, a second Table was inaugurated, Norwich, Wensum and
Yare no. 892 – Table no. 1 had never had a charter. In spite
of bad health Louis Marchesi attended this dinner and was given
a standing ovation by the 450 guests who included members of
nearly a hundred Tables as far apart as Aberdeen and Bath.

'Mark', as Marchesi had now for long been affectionately
known throughout the movement, was no longer in a state to
enunciate Round Table's first principles as he had tried to do
with such limited success. His wife Dolly had died aged fifty-
nine on 12 July 1965 – a Dolly Marchesi bed was endowed in
Norwich YMCA as a memorial – and the shock of this added to
the physical decline which had been evident since his South
African tour. He had to leave the development of Round Table
as he saw it entirely in the hands of others. He was not able to
give his views on the Goldsbrough-Lawton reforms – which
was a pity. For his authority as founder, given firmly for or
against the proposals, might well have encouraged Duncan
Lawton to have taken a stronger line when members asked him
how he intended to put into action the inspiring sentiments he
had expressed at Bognor. 'This is really up to you,' he told
them, like so many of his predecessors. It was his duty to outline
policy and lay its foundations. The decision whether to build on
it and implement it was theirs. He was of course only acting by
the constitution. British Rotary had a more autocratic form of
government, but neither the Council nor the Executive Committee of British Round Table, let alone the president on his
own, could say to members You Will, only We Recommend.
As president, David Tatlow was only able to 'call members' attention to' the kind of service which came from an enquiring
mind, the wish to study the other man's problems – but in doing
so he was echoing the movement's original purpose. He appealed to members to widen their horizons and accept the fact that
the other chap might not share their point of view. Real friendship meant a sense of awareness, of mutual achievement accomplished by working together through community service. To

agree to disagree, that was the challenge. He did not want a Round Table View, but he would like to see 26,000 individual young men better informed and better equipped through their membership of Round Table to deal with the problems of the day. He wanted a member of Round Table to be recognised as a young man of integrity, not afraid to study controversial subjects and able to give a considered and unbiased view.

The spur to action had to come from inside the movement. When in March 1967 at the first meeting to be held in Scotland (at Glasgow University), Council considered Alan Young's invitation to associate Round Table with a City of Edinburgh scheme called Project John Bull Junior, they declined. It was an attempt to refute the same feeling that 'Britain was done for' expressed by speakers at the 1927 BIF. 'As a nation we under-sell Britain socially and industrially at home and this unfortunately reflects abroad,' declared John Bull Junior. 'That we lack confidence in ourselves is obvious in the recurring crises. It is time the people of this country endeavoured to make a contribution towards reversing this line of thought – think progressively, not depressively, and this will go a long way towards reaffirming pride and faith in Great Britain. . . . For many years John Bull has been a symbol of this country – solid, dependable, likeable and determined but possibly a trifle slow and contented. Now is the time the new generation emerged in "John Bull Junior" – progressive, active, dynamic, resourceful.'

It was a good idea, but Edinburgh had thought of it first. In any event the rules specified that no direct appeal should be made to Council on projects of this nature, only after they had been debated and submitted by an Area.

There was no side-tracking the constitutional machinery, but in November 1968 an attempt was made by a so-called Ad Hoc Committee to loosen it. In their report, circulated to Tables in the autumn of 1969, they recommended streamlining Council's committee system and separating management and policy-making. Council approved almost all the changes suggested with only minor amendments. They agreed Council was too unwieldy – there were fifty-eight of them round the table that day – and that they met too infrequently to discharge day-to-day management functions. They vested the delegated powers of their committees in the convener of each. They abolished the Rules and Headquarters Committees entirely.

It was a bold clearing of the lines, but carried out the more easily to effect – what? Not the spreading of any 'message' if Stuart Macpherson, president for 1967/8, had anything to do with it. For him Round Table was no kind of evangelical crusade. He was deeply committed to the view that Round Table was meant to be fun, was based primarily on deep fellowship between members, and should not be seen purely as a service club.

It was in pursuit of fellowship that Council decided, but not without much heart-searching, to accept the offer of John Player & Son, the cigarette manufacturers, to sponsor a Speaking Competition with £1,750 in prize money, 'The Doncella Speakers Award', to go to the 'charity accounts' of the winning Tables. At a long discussion Council debated the merits and demerits of sponsorship and of allowing Round Table to be exploited by a commercial company trading in products which many regarded as injurious to health. Theirs was a permissive society, contended David Tatlow, a society experimenting in new freedoms, many of them arguable. It was vital for Round Table to be seen to act responsibly in those sectors of choice where it was open to give a lead, particularly where that lead, taken on indubitable evidence, could influence the young. But others could see no moral issue involved and invited Council to put aside old-fashioned prejudices. 'Can anyone doubt that a great deal of fellowship will be the result?' They voted to give it a trial year and then review it again.

Seen at Table level it was a question of keeping the pursuit of fellowship in proper perspective. 'Fellowship is not an end in itself, nor is community service,' wrote Maurice Horspool at this time, summing up the history of the first thirty-four years of Scarborough Table no. 88. 'They are mutually complementary.

Should either dominate the other, they are dangers. There were dangers twenty years ago, in the five immediate post-war years, when fellowship dominated everything else. Since then the pendulum has swung, with growing momentum, until it has almost reached the opposite end of its swing. Not fully, perhaps, but quite near. Round Table was never, nor was it ever intended to be, *per se* a charitable organisation. It has however no set terms of reference, as most charitable organisations have. It has no governing Rule or Object. Its decisions are not wantonly capricious but they are governed by a curious set of factors – views, energy, ambitions, and personality of successive Community Service chairmen, current Table opinion, feasibility of execution, conflicting needs, emotional feelings and Table support.'

To Ron Huggins (not to be confused with Rodney Higgins of Reading) recollecting the imbalance which overtook Scarborough Table in 1958 when he was chairman, it seemed that at that time some members were becoming very intense about the Table's activities and functions. It was most important to remember, he reflected in 1968, that Round Table was a spare-time social occupation. It was not a full-time job, nor was it a religion. 'There have been to my knowledge occasions in the past when certain members of Table have insisted that everyone should put into a particular activity, either social or community service, their whole energies, both physical and mental, to the exclusion of their family life, and indeed in some cases to the detriment of their work. This is, quite obviously, wrong.'

There was little danger that frenzy of this sort would become an epidemic, but for any over-obsessed member in need of a sedative the knowledge that Round Table was not alone in its chosen field, and Britain was not dependent on it, might have had a steadying influence. Awareness of this fact was kept alive by the president attending the Annual Meeting of the Heads of Service Organisations – British Rotary, British Round Table, Lions International, Toc H Men's Section, Toc H Women's Section, Inner Wheel (Ladies Rotary), Ladies Circle (Ladies

Round Table), Soroptimists (women's clubs with membership on a job classification basis like Round Table), Royal Women's Voluntary Service – and later ALTRUSA, an American-based women's organisation. In 1967 British Rotary suggested, and Round Table agreed, that this co-operation should be extended by the clubs, whose heads met in this way, holding regular meetings to co-ordinate activities in each local authority area.

There was no doubt about Round Table being in the Big League, and confirmation of its status, if any was needed, came with HRH Prince Philip agreeing to be the guest of honour at the movement's 40th Anniversary Luncheon at the Hilton Hotel, London, on 31 October 1967 attended by 1,200. It was the patron's first public engagement on behalf of Round Table. It was a proud moment for Mark when he was presented to the royal duke, and at the end of the dinner, at which he was escorted by John Watson, the Norwich friend who had been president in 1952, when Stuart Macpherson handed him a silver salver with the badges around the edge of the twenty-eight countries where there were then Round Tables. In Britain and Ireland alone at the last count there were 1,200 Tables and 34,000 members.

Not unnaturally, as patron of a national association, Prince Philip made it an occasion for enjoining Round Table to act nationally, and who was Stuart Macpherson to say him nay? The Prince hoped Round Table would throw into the pond not a stone but a boulder, to show they were capable of *doing* something really effective in the face of the apathy and muddle everywhere around them. 'I don't think for one moment Round Table can change things over-night on their own, but it's got to start somewhere and like a stone thrown into a pond, the ripples eventually reach the furthest shore. I hope Round Table will heave a ruddy great boulder.' He challenged the movement to *examine* some of the problems which bedevilled modern society '– education, industrial relations, local government. He did not expect Round Table to find over-night solutions, but he thought the movement capable of making a constructive contribution to the discussion of these topics.

For the man who had thrown the stone in the pond forty years before without it yet having made any ripples on the national shore (in the sense the Duke of Edinburgh was meaning, and in the way the Prince of Wales who became the Duke of Windsor had urged in 1927), it was his last public appearance. Louis Marchesi died on 10 December 1968, aged seventy, and was buried beside his beloved Dolly in Norwich. On his tombstone were inscribed part of Rudyard Kipling's *If* which he had kept in a frame above his bed: 'If you can talk with crowds and keep your virtue, Or walk with kings nor lose the common touch'.

If he had lived a few months longer he would have been able to witness as fine a demonstration yet of the extent to which his idea was making the whole world kin when British Round Table were the hosts to some 400 young men of every nationality who gathered in Eastbourne for the 1969 Wo-Co Conference from 29 September to 5 October. There was a Get-Together-Party at Michelham Priory, an opening ceremony at the Congress Theatre, a President's Ball and Banquet in the Winter Garden and Pavilion. At London's Guildhall on 15 September British Round Table President Derrick Mason presided over an International Luncheon with Sir Alec Rose, the round-the-world-singlehanded yachtsman, as guest of honour.

But an even greater international assembly of Round Tablers took place in Westminster Roman Catholic Cathedral in London on 14 February 1969 for the founder's memorial service. Those who came to mourn included ten of the members who had responded to the call of the twenty-nine-year-old confectioner in 1927 and had lived to see the movement grow to the world-wide association of 1969: J. B. Hanly, T. V. Howes, E. G. Cooper, W. A. Copeman, A. C. Thirtle, A. L. Bunn, N. D. Woodrow, C. D. Leveton, F. O. Winter, A. George. Mark's son Peter came with his Danish wife; and Mark's three brothers and two sisters who had married Englishmen, Mrs M. C. Morgan and Mrs R. C. Long. As Canon F. J. Bartlett who gave the address pointed out, they and the 2,000 Tablers present were witnesses of Mark's ideal of brotherhood and love. Mark himself spoke five languages and had visited thirty-eight countries in the course of stimulating the formation of more and more clubs. In a tribute at the Invitation Dinner at the Naval and Military Club in Piccadilly that evening, Cyril Marsh said the chubby, genial Mark represented the section of society that he wanted Round Table to serve. He had always been full of hope and confident of success. The aim of the Norwich club and, so far as he was concerned, of all subsequent clubs was the development of the individual. But he was no starry-eyed idealist. He could join in all the fun with the best. He remembered him at one conference borrowing a cap, coat and broom from a pier attendant and standing leaning on the broom at the entrance to the pier with members and their ladies arriving for a function. No one recognised him, and he greatly enjoyed the joke.

'Mark served his own generation in a manner permitted to few. It is for those who follow his trust to take Round Table through successive generations; to ensure that young business and professional men in company with one another can learn of their responsibilities to the community which are part of their heritage; and through their Table activities encourage the individual members to develop the friendliness, understanding, abilities and talents that Round Table has brought to the fore. And in it all to do as adversaries do in law — strive mightily but eat and drink as friends.'

Table no. 1 presented to the City of Norwich as a memorial of their famous son a round wooden seat on which shoppers could rest in the shadow of Langford's restaurant (now Moss Bros) where it all began in London Street (now a footway). Its teak seat, six feet in diameter, encircled a tree, and it was set in a base of black and white concrete slabs in the design of the Round Table badge. John Jarrold, Lord Mayor of Norwich, accepted it on behalf of the city on 6 March 1971. The headquarters of the National Association at 15 Park Road, London, which had been modernised at the end of 1968, was named

Blackpool Opera House is filled to capacity once again for a Round Table annual general meeting – the scene in 1976.

Every annual conference ends with a jubilant Farewell Party which ushers out the Round Table year and welcomes a new National President.

Round Table raises money for a variety of good causes including the elderly, the disabled, the mentally handicapped, hospitals, by means of fêtes, carnivals, competitions, races, garden parties and sports days. RTBI also donates funds overseas. £20,000 worth of irrigation equipment went to drought-stricken Ethiopia in 1975 (*above*).

Peter Marchesi, (extreme right) son of the founder of Round Table, drinks a toast at the opening in August 1976 of the 'Louis Marchesi' public house in Norwich, named after his father.

Roderick Burtt, National President for the Golden Jubilee Year (left), and Rodney Huggins, National President 1975/6, greet Canon Graham Foley, a principal speaker at the Presidents Banquet at Blackpool 1976.

'Marchesi House' in 1970; in it was placed a bust of Mark by an Ilfracombe member's wife, Avril Vellacott. January the Nineteenth, Mark's birthday, was designated 'Founder's Day' on which all Tables were asked to hold meetings for discussing the State of the Movement as a whole.

Mark had dreamed of members establishing a Travel Fund as a memorial to him when he died. In March 1967, the 40th anniversary year, Council recommended that the AGM be asked to approve the raising of funds for a 'RTBI Founder's Travel Fund for Overseas Travel', but the resolution was lost for lack of the required two-thirds majority – 497 for and 328 against.

When Mark died, knowing of the founder's wishes regarding a travel fund memorial, but with no rules to guide him, President Paul Perry immediately took steps to honour them. He admitted to Council on 15 March 1969 that the idea had not originated with him and that Council would have to approve and the AGM endorse the scheme. But Council were not to be hurried. While agreeing to the principle of setting up a memorial fund, they considered the AGM should determine its nature. But Stuart Macpherson gave Paul Perry full support. He felt an initial travel fund of £27,500 would at least put RTBI alongside other national associations in being able to entertain members from abroad, which they were not able to do at present. International Convener Jim Kenroy said they were trustees for the future not only for British Round Table but for other national associations who looked to Mark as their founder; they should prize Mark's wish highly and endorse the president's lead. Peter Marchesi, Mark's son, was invited to address the meeting and confirmed that, in doing what he had, Paul Perry had only been trying to honour his father's wish. But Council were split down the middle. They virtually shelved it by referring it to a sub-committee, and as an idea for a Marchesi Memorial it was never heard of again.

But in 1971 some seventy members and their wives made a three-week, 35,000-mile journey to Hong Kong (where they saw the three Round Table villages in full operation), New

Zealand and Australia, led by Vice-President John Watts, in order to attend the annual meeting of Wo-Co (the World Council of Young Men's Service Clubs), of which Paul Perry of RTBI was president that year. It was the occasion on which Wo-Co admitted as an associate member the new Junior Executive Clubs of Japan organisation. To the travelling members from Britain the benefits of international travel were made so apparent that at Darwin Airport on their return home they vowed to establish an International Fellowship Travel Fund by hook or by crook; but by then opinion in Britain had moved towards a Louis Marchesi Award Scheme, backed by a fund of £100,000 (£100 from each Table?) from which awards could be made to a Table for a project it could not finance from its own funds.

The Travel Fund idea however was not allowed to lapse and three years later John Watts raised it at the Bournemouth AGM which voted enthusiastically for the creation of a trust deed although no formal vote was taken. Raising the money was taken over by Ray Gabriel, the 1974/5 president. 'Its prime objective' he said, 'will be to further international understanding through the benefits of travel, be it the sponsoring of one of our members, or even a group of them, travelling abroad, or an overseas guest or guests being invited over here.' The fund only stood at £2,200 at the end of 1976, but endeavours were subsequently made to extend its scope. It was not conceived as a memorial to Mark nor as a fund to celebrate the Golden Jubilee Year. Therefore through the passage of time the Award Scheme had been discarded and all plans to establish a Marchesi Memorial Fund had been abandoned. But like Elizabeth Fry, one of the Gurneys of Norwich, Louis Marchesi of Norwich could not have any better memorial than the living evidence of his life's work – the chain of clubs spread and ever spreading across Britain and lands far away.

Mark's death was followed in the summer of 1969 by the

retirement of the man who next to Mark and Cyril Marsh had done more for Round Table than any other, Vic Collins, who had held the position of General Secretary since 1 January 1951. He was made British Round Table's second Honorary Member. WCYMSC gave him a silver salver at their meeting in Nice, for he was of course General Secretary of that body too – and, for the greater part of its life, of the now defunct Round Table International. His beneficial influence on the whole Round Table movement in Britain and throughout the world during his long term of office had been incalculable.

'From the outset,' wrote Hubert Praat, 'Vic set himself the highest standards and expected these to be maintained by all those with whom he was in contact. In manner urbane, in argument stubborn, in action he was decisive. In 18 years the association which Vic and his staff served so well multiplied four-fold. That his powers of organisation are outstanding was apparent to the thousand members present at the Hilton luncheon in 1967 and again to the congregation of twice that number at the memorial service in Westminster Cathedral, each occasion enriched by meticulous forethought and preparation. But though he has done his job so supremely well over these years, it is as a man of rare and complex character that those who have known and worked with Vic will always cherish him.

'A compulsive reader, widely travelled, he has invariably had a positive point of view on controversial topics of the day. Yet none was more self-effacing and purposely inconspicuous on public occasions.

'For Vic believed the permanent official should remain in the background, get on with his job and leave the platform to the elected representatives and those bearing the responsibility of office. Every president has had this wealth of experience and advice at his elbow – though he hasn't always agreed to use it.

'But the captains and the kings depart – and there must always be the niggling thought that a long spell of years at the centre of a great association's affairs, especially one with a rapid turnover of membership, could result in a dangerous concentration of power and influence. But not with this man. As Mr Collins became known as "Vic" and later "The Old Vic", his transparent integrity and love of Round Table were plain for all to see.'

So Round Table entered the 1970s without the man who had laid the plates, and without the helmsman who had had his hand so firmly but unobtrusively on the tiller for almost a half of the movement's life to date.

Vic Collins was succeeded as General Secretary by forty-four-year-old Denis Tizard, a Conservative Party agent who for a time had been in the Isle of Thanet and since 1954 had been agent to the Dorking division of the Surrey County Conservative Association. With Miss G. N. Rolfe as his personal assistant and L. J. Preece as office manager, he headed a hard-working team at Park Road dedicated to serving Round Table in a way every member whose turn it came to hold office at Table, Area or National level came instantly to appreciate. Their capable hands were going to be fuller than ever.

After Fifty Years

6

Fulfilment
1969-1977

35,000 Tablers Find Fellowship –
and Raise £1 Million A Year

Before 1969 was out the thousandth Table had been inaugurated
– at Sandy in Bedfordshire. Within another five years there
were to be 174 more. The species Round Table Man was breed-
ing fast. The population of Britain had risen from under
46,000,000 in 1927 to more than 55,000,000 in 1970, and Round
Table Man had multiplied in proportion, and a bit more, at a
time when rival claims on his leisure time had greatly increased
in variety and extent. Round Table Man, seeking in some vague
way to devote part of his out-of-office hours to 'serving the
community' for no return other than the satisfaction of feeling
he was trying to be as full a citizen as he could, had a choice of
voluntary activity which varied according to whether he lived
in a town or the country. He could throw in his lot with local
amenity societies like the Ratepayers Association, the Rail
Season Ticket Holders Association, and the Civic Society, with
the local hospital's League of Friends, the Church of England's
Children's Society, Toc H, the Child Poverty Action Group,
the International Friendship League, Shelter, Christian Aid,

War on Want. He could work for Oxfam, Help the Aged and Action in Distress under the wing of Voluntary and Christian Service, the creation of Jackson Cole who in the 1930s gathered together a small team of businessmen in the estate agency world to use business skills for human needs.

Apart from the call of family life which came first (the typical Round Table Man of over thirty had a wife and young family*), there was the call of business life – from the employer whose image of him as a clock watcher never available out of hours must not be allowed to harden, from the local branch of the trade association or professional institution with its programme of meetings and lectures, from the local Junior Chamber of Commerce.† Jaycees aimed to 'improve ourselves and our environment without losing our capacity for self-enjoyment'. 'Unlike other organisations such as Round Table, Rotary or Lions etc., Junior Chamber offers a unique opportunity of combining personal development, fellowship and community involvement, and is an organisation for people who wish to develop their own abilities and/or play a part in the affairs of their local community,' stated their introductory brochure at this time, though for the second edition the words 'Unlike other organisations such as Round Table, Rotary or Lions etc.' were deleted, and 'outstanding' substituted for 'unique'. Apart from providing opportunities to gain experience of leadership and management techniques, and playing an active role in community affairs, Jaycees aimed to participate in projects involving young people, to investigate and prepare reports on topics of economic local, national and international concern, and to provide a forum for furthering their knowledge

* Roderick Burtt, 1976–7, is only the second bachelor ever to become national president of British Round Table. Eric Bliss was the first (1956–7).

† From 1 January 1976 British Junior Chambers of Commerce, whose secretariat is at Lutterworth, Leicestershire, changed its name to 'British Junior Chamber' – 120 Chambers in the British Isles with some 5,500 members between the ages of eighteen and forty, a large proportion in the North and North-East. It is affiliated to Jaycees International Inc. whose secretariat is in Coral Gables, Florida, USA. Throughout the world there are some 10,000 Chambers with about half a million members.

of industry and commerce. 'By encouraging exchange visits and other links with JCs in other countries, and by attending the international conferences, the aim of promoting goodwill and co-operation amongst all people is achieved.'

When Derrick Mason, president in 1969, suggested Round Table offered a service to the business community of a town by arranging business seminars on basic matters such as tax planning and security, he was right in thinking that this was something Round Table was competent to do, though of course in the fewer towns where there were also Junior Chambers it was not unique in this. He appealed to Round Table to give a lead by developing a spirit of good citizenship; it was second to none in charitable deeds, but had little influence in communities. There is no evidence of his words being taken to heart, though probably in the North of the country, where significantly Junior Chamber had a greater hold, more attention was given to Round Table's role in this respect than in the South.

There was the call too of the open air and the demands of keeping fit – the squash club, the rugger club, the golf and the sailing and the motor rallies, with their attendant indoor social events. There was the call of Further Education – learning another language or a new hobby at evening classes; the call of political involvement through the local branch of the Labour Party, the Young Conservatives, the Young Liberals, through the United Nations Association, the European Movement, Amnesty International, or membership of a parish, district, borough or county council. Not only these avowedly political bodies contributed towards what PEP called Active Democracy. All autonomous, self-supporting groups did so, including Round Table, while at the same time being Recreation in the fullest meaning of the term.

The character of leisure-time activities had changed, and their range extended very considerably since 1927 in response to the decline of religious observance, the rise of living standards, universal use of the motor car (increasingly available to the young executive as a business 'perk'), the loosening of social convention, the raising of educational standards, the shortening of working hours, the eroding of class barriers, and above all by what central government had come to assume as its proper role in the well-being of every section of the community from cradle to grave. Round Table may have ignored the Beveridge Report but the Welfare State did not fail to have its effect on Round Table, as on all voluntary organisations.

The years leading up to the First World War – between 1906 and 1912 – had seen unparalleled advance of state functions in social security and well being. The Great War extended the organisation and controls of the state, and World War 2 extended them even further. But with this expansion of the state's role came a remarkable development of the voluntary organisations in Britain. At one time it seemed that the statutory bodies would do away with the need for voluntary action, but in fact state action encouraged and used the resources of voluntary organisations to an unprecedented extent. The vision of community life with co-operation between the state and voluntary effort as a central feature stimulated a wide range of initiative and activity by well-disposed individuals of whom Round Table Man was typical. As Dr W. G. S. Adams, chairman of the National Council of Social Service from 1919 to 1949, pointed out in his introduction to the 1948 edition of *Voluntary Social Services Handbook*, the good life was an activity not a receptivity, a doing of things spontaneously for the good of the community and for the satisfaction of the social instincts of man. Self help and state aid were complementary. 'Destroy instincts for self-expression and self-realisation which freedom of speech and freedom of association can alone make possible, and we sap the very lifestream of the community. It is in the freedom of the spirit that the real energy source lies, an energy which can transform the material world as a means to the end of the good community.'

The average Table member was unlikely to be conscious of any such deep-seated motivations. The reason for joining, particularly the under-thirties, was mostly subjective. As a PEP broadsheet (no. 263) put it, 'the personal satisfaction – the amount of sheer enjoyment that the associations provide – is something which the members regard as very important. . . . Any attempt to take away the carefree pleasurable character of the independent associations by over-weighing them with formalities or forced education, weakens their prime function – the provision of a setting which, though stimulating, does not impose constant strain. The associations supplement the re-creation, generally of the spectator type, provided commercially for the increased leisure of to-day.'

Voluntary action, away from the making-a-living environment, was an escape which fed back however into the character of the earner/volunteer and helped to develop him in the way Louis Marchesi saw his movement helping those who joined a Table. 'Nothing has a *more* powerful effect upon character than the kind of work men have to do; the qualities that are constantly demanded by daily work are bound to be developed to the best of our capacity; those that are useless on the job which occupies the major part of our time tend to atrophy, unless we have ample resources for leisure. The qualities of maturity in judgement and responsibility, of sympathy and balance, of drive and tenacity of purpose, are strongly developed in some kinds of work and not in others.' (Reaveley and Winnington, *Democracy and Industry,* 1947.)'

'In general,' observes PEP in commenting of this, 'when members of an association are at one of their meetings they are doing something – pursuing some kind of creative work – themselves. They grow in social stature because they find an outlet for capacities which have been neglected in the work-aday life.'

This could not apply more aptly than to the membership of Round Table, nor PEP's remarks on the role which voluntary organisations play in the development of team work and social confidence. 'Absence of opportunities for making any more than superficial contacts at work increases the need to do this in free time. Shyness, inability (rather than unwillingness) to make contacts outside a small, familiar circle is a very real difficulty, particularly to many women. It is one of the reasons they most frequently give why they take no part in the life of the local community. Incidentally, it is also a factor in perpetuating class barriers. Urban civilisation, making for speed, has encouraged the decay of some of the qualities that make for easy personal contacts — graciousness, patience etc. Some ability to make social contacts readily, even if they are only superficial ones, is particularly important at a time when large numbers of people will have to live in new localities, and when mobility of labour generally is becoming more necessary. The independent associations play an important part in this kind of education with their continually changing circle of new members, their inter-club visiting, their area conferences and their matches.'

The black and white lapel badge was the passport that by-passed conventional introductions. Common membership of Round Table opened strangers' doors in strange towns and villages as nothing else would do. The hospitality of one Tabler to another who was setting foot in an unfamiliar part of Britain could always be relied upon — and the certainty that both would 'get on' with one another. A telephone call was all that was needed. Outside Britain Round Table was even more greatly prized as the password to instant acquaintance.

It would seem that the climate was right not only for existing voluntary organisations to flourish but for the launching of new ones; and indeed in 1970 British Rotary added to the agencies which might be said to compete with British Round Table by starting what they called 'Rotaract' for young men and women of between seventeen and a half and twenty-five. At the Round Table Council meeting of July 1971 'concern was expressed at the activities of Rotaract and at the number of members lost on removal'. They were discussing the recruitment of under-thirties. Relations with British Rotary however were firm — and becoming firmer.

Since 1970 a Liaison Committee had been meeting regularly
to co-ordinate the activities of British Rotary, British Round
Table, and the National Association of Boys Clubs; and for
many years the officers of Rotary and Round Table had met in-
formally just before Christmas to discuss matters of mutual interest. Mick Thorpe who was president of Round Table in 1972
institutionalised these casual joint meetings into a committee of
four, the two presidents and the two secretaries. This was the
first concept of 'Rotable'.

'We now hope that what has been done at "national" level
can be repeated locally,' said John Savage, president of British
Rotary. 'This is not to ensure that superannuated Tablers have
automatic rights of entry into Rotary Clubs. That is not what
most Tablers nor indeed most Rotarians would want. But in
terms of the new situation which we are faced with it is the hope
of the Rotable Committee that these two movements of business
and professional men can set an example by working together
to reduce overlapping in the Community Service field, and to
increase by Heaven knows how much their individual value by
working together on a planned basis.'

There were times, agreed Savage, when Rotary and Round
Table looked at each other askance; but in slightly differing
ways they were aiming for the same ends. Anything that enabled at least two of the bigger voluntary agencies to work together must be on the credit side. Perhaps they could go jointly
to the Director of Social Services in an area and ask what more
there was for them to do.

Rotary had for long had a reputation as a do-er and not just a
fund raiser in the field of social service, and it did much for
Round Tables when in 1972 president John Watts was asked to
represent the Association at the biennial meeting of the Duke of
Edinburgh's Award Schemes with Prince Philip in the chair.

But of all the agencies already in the field, and of the new
organisations straining at the leash to be let loose on the problems ahead, would Round Table, founded 1927, have the kind
of members very much longer who were willing and able to

play their parts? David Berriman, a member of Council, was not at all sure. 'Round Table as a movement must offer something of an intellectual challenge if it is to continue to attract the right type of new member,' he said. 'The old two-sided concept of Table as being only interested in fellowship and community service is now somewhat out of date, and if adhered to for too long will see, with the inevitable development of the Welfare State, Round Table developing into a drinking club; and when this happens the death knell will have been sounded.'

The development which took the state's role in the field of community service a step further was the creation in July 1973 of a Voluntary Services Unit within central government. Its purpose was to co-ordinate the government's efforts to support and encourage voluntary service, to help voluntary organisation and to increase opportunities for them. The unit was established in the Civil Service Department under the Lord Privy Seal, but later moved to the Home Office. Lord Windlesham, Lord Privy Seal, speaking on Government and the Voluntary Movement to the annual general meeting of the National Council of Social Service in December 1973, assured his listeners that the new Unit would see that organisations who obtained financial support from the government did so without risking government interference.

At the beginning of 1973 also there took place what John Savage of British Rotary called 'a quiet revolution in the field of voluntary service' requiring a new attitude to that part of their activities by both Rotary and Round Table. 'The standard bearers of that revolution are the directors of the new social service departments of local authorities. These men bear a heavy load; they have big staffs learning the need for and the importance of co-ordination and co-operation as they go. They are faced as they evolve with human cries for help which certainly do not diminish because the potential helpers are in their own personal maelstrom of re-organisation. On the edges of this somewhat turbulent situation stand the volunteers. What is their role to be? The same as before or utterly different? Will they need more training or can they go peacefully on with their Christmas parcels and their summer outings, with the warm feeling of a noble job well and truly done. This present generation of Rotarians and Tablers must decide, since they are involved in the making of a sizeable area of social history. For the next generation the war against distress and inhumanity [which he assumed to be Round Table's *métier*] will be waged in a different way. We must prepare ourselves and those who will follow us.' (*News & Views* April 1973.)

Three years later one of the more imaginative of these Directors of Social Services, Rev. Nicholas Stacey of Kent County Council, introduced a plan which showed only too clearly the kind of change which John Savage was hinting at and to which Round Table would need to adapt its thinking. It was for the payment of people of up to £35 a week to take care of old people living alone – cooking their meals, walking their dogs or just providing a little companionship. The cost, some £50,000 a year, would be less than keeping them in council old people's homes where they did not want to go.

The National Council of Social Service also sensed a turbulence – to the extent which set them seeking to change their name to 'Voluntary Action'. Those who attended the Extraordinary General Meeting called for this purpose in July 1973 were told that pressure had been put on the council's executive committee because the implementation of the Social Services Act in 1970 had caused increasing confusion between the voluntary and the statutory bodies at local and national levels. Furthermore the interpretation of the term 'social service' had changed over the years and was now a narrow definition of the work of the NCSS. But members would have nothing of it and threw the motion out.

No doubt some of the highly qualified, hand-picked young businessmen and professional men who, in spite of its having little to do with Round Table, continued to rely on Community Service as the serious activity which justified the junketing which took up most of Table time, regarded with apprehension the overcrowding in their chosen field, not least through the entry of two types of non-volunteers, the professional fund-raiser and the convicted felon, which should have made them question whether this was any longer the area in which their qualifications could best be employed.

'It is not the role of the professional to eliminate the volunteer,' was the reassuring message in the promotional brochure of a typical fund raising consultant. 'The role of a firm of fund raising consultants is to enhance the financial strength of the voluntary movement and to make the goodwill of those who value it more productive.' Nonetheless the entry of the professional on to the charity scene pointed to the need for a scientific approach to fund raising to meet the demands of the more complicated structure of society than existed, say, in 1927. It is not without significance that in July 1971 Council discussed a proposal, designed to give Tables quasi-professional status, that they should deduct a percentage from monies raised for charitable purposes as a standing administrative charge. But this was 'regarded as highly undesirable and of doubtful legality'. Charging for the service of course did not make it any less 'amateur' in execution.

The Criminal Justice Act of 1972 empowered courts to give anyone over the age of seventeen, convicted of theft, burglary, assault, receiving stolen goods, and serious traffic offences, a sentence of 'Community Service'. Like Probation, this could be offered by the judge, if he saw fit, as an alternative to prison or a fine, though the prisoner could reject it in favour of the latter. The bench could impose a sentence of community service of from 40 to 240 hours' duration, the work to be completed within twelve months. The form the service would take was for the probation officer to decide; in the five years since this form of punishment, completely new to British law, was introduced, offenders so sentenced have helped handicapped children and elderly people in their homes, the sick in hospital, undertaken decorating and gardening, and the building of playgrounds.

Further semi-government agencies joined the Community

Service ranks in 1974 in the form of Community Health Councils composed in part of members of voluntary organisations. Round Table accepted an invitation to participate, but at Table level there was little response. 'Too often,' reported *News & Views*, 'the uncharacteristic cries of "We don't want to get involved" or "It's not for us" have been heard. I believe we do ourselves less than justice when we fail to make available on a wide scale the talent, enthusiasm and personal involvement which has given our Association the undoubted success it enjoys to-day.'

Perhaps at last there was a sense of being out of their depth. In fifty years, voluntary action had steadily grown in volume and spread into every field of social need. The year 1976 was declared 'Age Action Year' and no fewer than *eighty* organisations, voluntary and professional, supported it. Special groups have been formed to *study* and aid particular circumstances – Apex Trust and New Bridge to find jobs for the ex-convict on release from jail, Shelter for the homeless, the Multiple Scelerosis Society for MS victims etc., etc. Round Table had strayed into an overcrowded field. It looked as if the need for more people to help relieve suffering had receded and the greater need was for more people to bring their minds to bear on creating understanding in industry and commerce. It seemed to many in 1977 that Round Table had backed the wrong horse (mainly because it was the easier one). To disengage from Charity would not expose Round Table to accusations of changing horses in midstream, because Business and Industry was the horse on which Round Table was first seated. It would merely be a question of getting back in the saddle, back to where it belonged.

Though in comparison with professional giants like the Imperial Cancer Research Fund British Round Table's impact on the fund raising scene had been on a smaller scale, that was not to say that its annual effort had not been considerable. Moreover, unlike the professionals with their paid staffs and high rents, *all* the money collected went to the cause without the retention of

223

any of it for 'admin'. In 1972/3 it was estimated that 333 Tables raised £300,664, and in 1973/4 481 Tables raised £454,641. These figures are conservative and incomplete, and it is probably truer to say that at the time of the Golden Jubilee British Round Table was raising about a million pounds a year.

The ranks of the fund raisers may be swelled, but for the receivers of course the more the merrier. A hospital which received from the government only half the money required to build a new wing appealed to the mayor to appeal to local voluntary groups to raise the other half. Though the size of the public from whom the money was to come remained constant, there was a feeling that the more agencies collecting it the more quickly would it become available – and the more merriment for members of groups like Round Table and the Lions. No matter the local Table was one of twenty voluntary agencies contributing to the mayor's appeal; the satisfaction – and fun – came from organising the event (carnival, barbecue, fireworks, dance, raffle), not from collecting money or giving it, or from any direct association with the cause benefiting from it, which demanded interest in social problems and taking time off to *study* them. For most at least it was for a cause in their community, though of course enormous effort was put into raising £14,000 for the victims of an earthquake in Nicaragua and £15,000 for drought and famine relief in Ethiopia. Many would-be givers to this kind of fund would probably send their contribution to The Disasters Emergency Committee, comprising the British Red Cross Society, Christian Aid/ CAFOD, Oxfam, the Save the Children Fund, and War on Want, created for the purpose. But the intimate nature of Round Table's worldwide structure had created the tradition of mutual help in time of need which was at the heart of the Round Table mystique.

On occasion too a Table found itself being asked to send money to *another Table's* fund, as those who undertook, with the approval of Council,* to subscribe to Table no. 50 for the build-

* In March 1972 Council approved for submission to the AGM the resolution 'That

ing of a school for autistic children in Birmingham.

City of Birmingham Table *did* study the problem they had chosen to solve. They spent six months examining the situation in the Midlands and discovered there were 400 registered cases of autism and no building designed for the purpose to which they could be sent for their education. Members of Table no. 50 spent another eighteen months finding a suitable site, having a school designed and receiving estimates. They then set themselves the task of raising £65,000 by writing to the thousands of industrial and commercial firms around Birmingham, and to charities and trusts. It soon became clear however that the amount was not going to come from the Birmingham district alone, and letters were sent to all Round Tables in Area 35 (twenty-three Tables, 700 members) and beyond. This was the nearest approach to a 'national' appeal Round Table had ever mounted, though undertaken not by the National Association but by one Table. Two Tables in every Area in the UK including five in Ireland and thirty-seven in Scotland contributed to raising £65,000 over a period of two years, as well as British Rotary, Ladies Circles and many charitable trusts. In the spring of 1975 it was realised that another £30,000 would be required. Building began and the first pupils occupied the Round Table School for Autistic Children at Northfield in January 1976; on the strength of a generous gift of £25,000 from Midland industrialist Douglas Turner, the second part of the building programme was completed in March of that year. But City of Birmingham Table did not see their responsibility ending there; they ensured that one of their members represented the Table on the school's board of management. Table no. 50 incidentally was one of the few that held lunch-time meetings. Another was Table no. 19 Kingston upon Thames which met *weekly* for lunch and in 1976 claimed to have held more official Table meetings than any other Table in the world, well over 2,250.

---

a general circulation of Tables by other Tables for the purpose of raising funds should not take place unless prior approval has been obtained from the Aims and Objects Committee.'

Fund raising followed on by the employment of members' business skills in the running of the project for which the money was being donated was widespread. After Weymouth Table for instance collected £17,500 to build an Old People's Home their members became its Committee of Management. Reading Valley Table established a good precedent in 1974 and 1975 by raising £18,000 through two large-scale sponsored swims involving, and teaching the techniques to, the Girl Guides Association of Berkshire – and then withdrawing from the project. Round Table might have taken a feather out of the National Council of Social Service's cap by encouraging members to establish management advisory bureaux for voluntary organisations in their district. Indeed when several Industrial Training Boards approached Round Table in 1975 for ideas the Association submitted a pilot scheme for apprentices and students to carry out local activities such as adapting the house of a bed-ridden widow with materials supplied by Round Table and under the supervision of members qualified to do so.

Included in the annual million pounds raised every year of course were the amounts collected not for Charity but to meet an unexpected emergency. Round Table saw itself as one of the bodies required to make a response whenever disaster struck. Mendip Table's reaction to the plane crash at Basle in Switzerland in April 1973 involving the deaths of so many from that part of Somerset was to set up, with other voluntary organisations in the area, a round-the-clock information centre at the Oak House Hotel, and to make themselves responsible for weeks afterwards for helping with the rebuilding of the lives of the families affected, towards which a sum of £30,000 was collected. Scunthorpe Table formed a joint committee with Rotary and the Lions to mount relief operations in June 1974 when Nypro's chemical plant at Flixborough exploded, killing twenty-eight and damaging 2,000 homes. Peter Clark, chairman of Area 30, headed the committee which saw to the manning of information centres and provided transport, financial assistance, food, consolation and advice for the victims. Letters of thanks came from Nypro and the National Coal Board, joint owners of the plant. In 1975 £13,000 was raised by City of Birmingham Table, no. 50, led by chairman Richard Temple Cox, in addition to giving practical aid, to succour the victims of the bomb outrage in the city by members of the Irish Republican 'Army' of urban guerillas. In the same year direct assistance was given by members of Islington Table under chairman Phillip Howells, in conjunction with other organisations, at the time of the tube train crash at London's Moorgate.

It was a fine record but it was not the one by which everyone thought Round Table should be judged. 'This is not a fair criterion,' wrote Michael Hollingsworth in the Winter 1975 *News & Views*, 'nor is it right that, in the context of our second Aim and Object, there should be so much emphasis on fund raising. Too often it seems one hears it said by a Table that it has so much in its charity account and does not know what to spend it on. . . . Surely the stress lies on the word "service". *Help without cash* – the giving of one's time. *Doing* something for someone less fortunate; using the skills one has developed through one's own occupation to the benefit of others outside the sphere of one's work; taking a place, however lowly, in the life of the community.' He was the latest of a long line of young men to make the same plea. In 1976 the case for listening to it and taking it to heart was never stronger.

But for the most part, Table members who found it easy to bare their arms as blood donors found it difficult to open their minds to any fields of operation other than those conventionally associated with Charity. The imagination which Archie Rice had asked for at the launching of the movement, and he knew was sadly at a premium in the business and industrial circles of 1927, seemed to be singularly lacking also in the 1970s. The idea of an Institute for Community Studies in Northern Ireland (at Magee University College in Londonderry) did not occur to Round Table, but to its credit those who attended the hastily organised Birmingham Conference in 1972 (after one at Dublin had been abandoned because of the disturbances) 'carried handsomely' a resolution to sponsor it. Here was a worthy project though necessarily its implementation had to be left to the qualified staff of the new University of Ulster; the only way was financial support. It was something for Ralph James, honorary editor of *News & Views*, whose post also included the appointment of Press and Public Relations Officer for the first time in 1972, to tell the world about.

In 1972, for the first time, the Press were invited to cover a Round Table annual conference. A *Birmingham Post* reporter attended the Birmingham conference and was duly impressed; but when it was considered asking reporters to be at the next conference at Blackpool many thought their presence would 'restrain the good-humoured interruption'. Indeed the main reason for not asking the Press before had been a fear of exposing the movement to ridicule through reports which drew attention to the minority who indulged in excesses of behaviour or speech. A few perhaps were ready to behave as a member of Round Table at conference in a way they would never have contemplated as a father at home or a member of middle management in the office. But most believed that membership of Round Table and attendance at a conference away from the home ground (which to many gave life a temporary unreality) demanded conduct if anything a little above the norm; and felt that the undue prominence likely to be given to a single, newsy happening would unjustifiably add to an already not too savoury public image.

When Prince Philip, the movement's patron, was invited to attend a Pre-Conference Luncheon at the Hilton Hotel in London in 1974 he thought better of giving Round Table serious advice after the manner of his inspiring throwing-a-boulder-in-the-pond speech of 1971, but pitched his remarks this time to the flippant key which no doubt he sensed was more in tune with Round Table at the grass roots. In proposing the Duke's toast, president Dick Chapman claimed that Round Table was a great leveller as it knew no barriers; the answer to the question 'And who is my neighbour?' was certainly 'A

Round Tabler'. But for the most part he kept it light, and the guest of honour, while hinting that the highest ideals in business which he took to be the object of Round Table to cultivate, were thrift, industry, enterprise, charity, gentleness and integrity, quickly turned to propound ten 'more realistic' (and cynically orientated) Ten Commandments.

Ralph James's appointment as PRO in addition to being National Editor was the result of Council discussing Round Table's image in July 1971. Some councillors thought it was regarded as a junior form of Rotary, others as an expensive supper club, a debating society, charity collectors or 'a frivolous group'. 'A bad image reduced recruitment,' stated the minute, 'limited our activities through lack of support and affected internal morale. The answer was more effective use of local and national media of publicity and a high standard of conduct among ourselves. Possibly a national councillor might be appointed PRO.'

Unfortunately the 1973 conference marked the return of horseplay in a way that had not been seen at a Round Table conference for many a year.

'At times during the Blackpool Conference there were incidents which to most Tablers would have seemed emanations of high spirits but to most non-Tablers would have seemed to be the acts of hooligans,' reported Ralph James. Was this meant to imply that Round Table operated on a lower level than civilised society as a whole? Did it mean he thought members regarded the movement as a Closed Order which was a law unto itself, and were pleased to keep it that way?

Was it all a jolly lark and not worth wasting official breath on? Take it in your stride, smooth it over and learn to live with it as endemic in a certain type of Round Table Man? Or should the nettle be grasped in public and be disposed of once and for all? In his message to members on taking over as president in 1973 Dick Chapman saw fit to remark that 'the question of conduct is unfortunately to the fore again following a number of regrettable incidents, particularly during the conference'.

On assuming the presidency in 1975 Rodney Huggins took the common sense line that Round Table's public image had been slightly tarnished on rare occasions by a very small minority, but the key to diminishing unruly behaviour lay in good planning and organisation. 'Round Table improves responsibility of the individual and makes him more aware of his surroundings. A Tabler is therefore assured of becoming more mature by his membership provided he participates fully.' The 1975 conference at Torbay was a happy one in every respect; the Press were admitted to the AGM and nothing but good came of it.

It was at this 40th conference, attended by 5,000 Tablers who congregated under the largest stretch of canvas in Europe, that consideration was given to re-structuring the Association and the Presidency in the light of thirty years' rapid expansion – from ninety Tables with 1,376 members in 1945 to 1,174 Tables with 33,737 members in 1975, by which year however overall membership had begun to show a backward trend. Early in 1975 the opinions of the movement were canvassed through a booklet called 'What Do You Think?' and following discussion of it at Torbay and elsewhere a Special Purposes Report was produced in December 1975 outlining schemes for giving members of Council, who willy-nilly had become involved in administration, more time to act as the representatives of their Areas. They had to attend three full Council meetings a year – in July, November and March – as well as two short ones at the beginning and end of the annual conference. 'After we have taken action on communication and consolidation,' announced the new president who came riding into office on the Biggest Plaster Hippo in the World, 'we shall be able to enter our Golden Jubilee Year celebrations with freshness and renewed vigour.'

The burden of being president had become extremely heavy. During his year of office from May to April Rodney Huggins reckoned he wrote a thousand letters, visited every one of the fifty Areas of RTBI and, with his overseas visits, travelled 85,000 miles. He attended Inaugural Meetings, Charter Nights (including Malta no. 1 in November 1975), Area Rallies, 10th, 21st, 25th and 40th Anniversary Nights, and of course the Ladies Nights which most Tables considered the most important event on their calendar. He was away from home every week-end of the year except at Christmas; he usually began travelling on Thursday and returned on Sunday. On the average he spent thirty hours a week in his office as senior partner of a firm of Reading solicitors with a staff of fifty. The strain of travel was often relieved by members of his Area (Thames Valley) driving him in his car – registration no. RTB 1, handed from president to president. As the movement's social figurehead he replied to the toast of RTBI at every function he attended. He represented Round Table at the annual conferences of British Rotary, the National Association of ex-Tablers' Clubs and the 40th anniversary luncheon in London of the National Association of Ladies Circles.

Viewed from below the visit of the national president was An Occasion which merited at least a page in the Area Magazine.

A MEETING WITH GOD

Once upon a time, there were two easily impressed young men on the Area Executive. Then the Chief Disciple (Uncle Geoff) said – "Hey you two – if you come to Wrexham next week – you can meet the boss himself – a fellow called Henry Higgins". When we explained that Henry Higgins was a bullfighter in Spain, he looked again and confirmed that the Boss's name was Rodney Huggins and so we said we would go.

Allan grew a beard for the occasion, but Bethan wouldn't let him wear the candlestick bedspread, so he had to wear his old Beatles jacket instead. I just wore a suit, but made sure that my underpants were "St. Michael".

And so the great day arrived, and the traumatic experience

of how to address him. Should it be Sir or Your Highness?

The roll call of Tables went without mishap, although I did feel sorry for that chap from Reading Valley who came on his own – I do hope somebody spoke to him. . . .

Chief Steward Ron Davies rushing around like the proverbial blue ***** fly – Oh – it was all too much. Roger Waters – remember him? – is still waiting for the local Ruthin dry cleaners to have their Annual Sale of uncollected cleaning so he can get a new suit, and instead advertising some Indian Restaurant specialising in Curries. . . .

Congratulations to the Wrexham Tablers whose expertise at waiting at Table (no pun implied) seemed to be better than that of the regular staff. Didn't enjoy the food though (neither did Allan) – all a bit too greasy for my delicate Southern stomach.

Apart from Wee Squirrel Jones Evans boasting about his sexual prowess again (I understand that Pwllheli Table's next fund raising event is to get enough cash for Cyril to have the operation) I couldn't really understand the rest of his speech, apart from his presentation of a rabbit skin to the Boss. I presume it was some sort of ancient sacrifice or other. So – what of the boss?

Not as funny as Ray Gabriel, but then a change is as good as a rest. All of what he said made sense, and if anything showed to me another facet of Table life. I'm not too sure – at least at this stage – of the real content of the Presidential Address, as it seemed somewhat radical to me. Perhaps I'm wrong, but I felt that it was reckoned that with 33 thousand members, Table was a force to be reckoned with, maybe in a para-political way. Hopefully I'm wrong in my assumption, and no doubt someone will soon be putting me right.

In all – a nice night, and the nine-hundred-odd tablers who missed it should be ashamed of themselves. (*Bell Buoy*, the magazine of RTBI Area 36, North Wales and Wirral, November 1975.)

How to lighten the president's burden? Give the movement another layer, the Regions, on top of the Areas, so the President need only visit six of the former instead of fifty of the latter? Appoint a second vice-president to share the duties? Make the overseas tour as Immediate Past President the year following the presidential year? None of these ideas met with approval – after all there was no lack of candidates for the post – and the Presidency remained the same.

At Torbay, after a slight hesitation, members did agree to raising the capitation fee which a Table was obliged to pay to the Association for each member from £2.65 to £3.25. The cost of living had doubled since 1970, and so had the National Association's income which was £69,771 in the twelve months ending 31 May 1971 and £112,247 in 1975. Surplus for 1970/1 was £1,160; for 1974/5 £7,230. Capitation fees produced £48,900 in 1970/1 and £77,540 in 1974/5, when £15,780 had been paid in entrance fees and there was a profit of £10,800 on 'sales' – of jewels, badges, car accessories, clothing, ashtrays, tankards, diaries, wallets, knives, key fobs, sleeve links, ties and the rest (there was a list of seventy-four items). The president received an allowance of £2,000; £15,000 was spent on reimbursing delegates with the cost of travelling to the AGM; £17,800 on head office salaries; an annual capitation fee of £10,500 was paid to the World Council of Young Men's Ser-

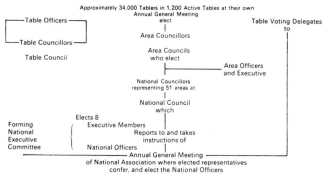

The organisation of Round Tables in 1976.

vice Clubs. The president's world tour cost around £1,500 and
sending members of the Executive Committee to overseas
meetings about the same. Every year the Association managed
to put a sum into reserve, and at 31 May 1975 the Balance Sheet
balanced at £104,974, with investments at a healthy £99,538
and current assets of £142,903.

A more determined effort to re-structure the Association was
made at the 1976 conference at Blackpool, after which Council
found themselves no longer able to censor resolutions submitted
by Areas for the approval of the annual general meeting.
Moreover Council was kept compact. In spite of there now
being fifty-one Areas they resolved to maintain the number of
national councillors at thirty-five – the number of Areas in
1950. One Conference Committee, they decided, should run all
annual conferences. But, most important of all, delegates
accepted the new Rule Book drafted by a sub-committee
headed by Roger Webb. This meant that for the first time every
Table had the same, standard rules and no longer had to spend
the time and money on having their own approved and printed.
Each continued to determine its own procedure at meetings and
the way it was administered. Area Councils received standard
standing orders too. The Draft Rule Book contained a fresh set
of Aims and Objects but Council decided to postpone voting on
these until the 1977 AGM at Great Yarmouth. They were:

    (i)   to promote fellowship
    (ii)   to serve the community
    (iii) to encourage personal integrity
    (iv) to improve international friendship and understanding.

At Blackpool they elected Richard Bangor-Jones, Liverpool
chartered accountant, vice-president, which meant that at Great
Yarmouth he took over as president from Roderick Burtt for
the remainder of Golden Jubilee Year. A national fund-raising
project – the movement's first – was launched to buy a lifeboat
for the RNLI to mark the jubilee.

Fulfilment

When Hal Rogers, founder of the Kinsmen Clubs of Canada, with objects similar to Round Table and exposed to the same hazards, asked himself at that movement's 50th anniversary in 1970 who his members were, he replied they were 'the significant generation'. 'Active in their business or professional responsibilities, they contribute time and talents in community activities; in local, provincial and national governments; in their church and fraternal groups; and with "those less fortunate than themselves". In all this these young men and women of to-day (and yesterday) share in the rewarding satisfaction of their home and family, and the friendships, the fellowship they know in their own Club and with other young men and women throughout the nation who also are "the young people doing things NOW"! They are *not* the present fringe generation, benefactors of a too permissive society, seeking and attracting the publicity that effectively promotes a relatively small minority of vocalists and exhibitionists more popularly referred to as "the youth of to-day" – including the so-called "hippies", "yippies" et al.'

No more could it be said that the RTBI members of the 1970s were the much hounded Youth of To-day on which so much blame was always being heaped. Wearing their Round Table hat they were necessarily caught in a moment of throwing off the cares of business in an often frenetic, frequently crude, group activity of the kind that was not everyone's cup of tea, but attracted – well who?

The 1,045 members of the thirty-six Tables in Area 36 stretching from Birkenhead in the east to Holyhead in the west, Llandudno in the north to Newton in the south, described themselves (on their 1976 Area letter-head) as 'young businessmen between the ages of 18 and 40 embracing representatives of nearly every profession and trade. Its objects are the encouragement of high ethical standards in commercial life, the promotion of social intercourse and fellowship among young professionals and businessmen, and the quickening of individual interest in everything affecting the public welfare.'

Area 5 (West Midlands) made an analysis of their membership in 1972 which there is no reason to believe has changed to
any great extent in five years. The classification with the most
members in it was 'building and civil engineer' – sixty. There
were fifty-seven in banking, fifty-two in insurance, forty-five
in accountancy, forty-five solicitors, forty-four in retail
trade, thirty-eight in the motor industry, thirty-six in surveying, thirty-one sales representatives, twenty-eight teachers,
twenty-three in architecture, twenty-two in agriculture,
twenty-two auctioneers, fifteen in dentistry, eighteen in medicine.

Round Table also attracted young men who saw in the movement a great potential force for international goodwill, a role
which was emphasised by Britain's bid to join the European
Economic Community. Several Tables held meetings and debates on the issues at stake, and in the summer of 1973, when he
was Prime Minister, Edward Heath MP, who had been in the
forefront of the negotiations on Britain's behalf for so long, was
guest of honour at a dinner held by Area 26 (Thames and South-
East) in which his constituency lay. 'We have some interests in
common,' he told his hosts, 'and one is internationalism, and
our interest in the rest of the world, our interest in the relationship between Britain and other countries. In this sphere
on 1 January Britain took an historic step forward in becoming
a member of the European Community and I know that Tablers up and down the country have studied these problems and
you have your contacts – which are not only European but
world-wide. These are invaluable.'

It was a flattering appraisal of Round Table's role in the EEC
national debate which never took the form of any concerted
effort to formulate a Round Table opinion, which could have
been a valuable European one embracing the always articulate
Tables on the continent. Apart from being a chance to take a
part on the national scene in a way that its development over
the years had peculiarly fitted it, it would have established machinery for sounding out the movement and propagating the

findings to the nations as the voice of the Young Business Men of Britain.

The structure was already well established. Each Table had its International Relations Officer; British Round Table always sent a representative to the annual general meetings of Europe's national Round Table associations; there were the International Hospitality Week-ends on the continent; the Wo-Co conferences – in Britain again in 1974 at Edinburgh – which brought all the old RTI associations to the Mother Country; the tradition of one Table helping another across the world when disaster struck. For long European, and indeed World, Round Table had been a mutual benefit society demonstrating a very practical sense of inter-national goodwill which transcended commercial, political and religious considerations. The link which bound a Table in Hinckley with a Table in Helsinki was stronger than any treaty or contract or moral obligation or political faith. It was inexplicable – and indestructible.

Communication was an aspect of Round Table in which president Rodney Huggins took a particular interest throughout 1975. Tablers All Communicate – TAC – he urged; streamline reports so major issues could be discussed properly and with clarity. By these means Round Table could become more efficient and more effective. It was essential too to extend contacts between individual clubs and Tables, and he hoped that Ray Gabriel's promotion of the Travel Fund would gain support. Personal contact and exchange was the best medium for fulfilling Round Table's fifth Object.

As president, Huggins, like his predecessors, practised what he preached by travelling widely during his term of office. In the spring of 1975 he visited the Channel Islands, Belgium and France. In August he set off with his wife and young son on a world tour culminating in the Wo-Co conference in Hong Kong where he was joined by ninety British Round Table members accompanied by their wives, mostly 'Circlers', paying £290 a head for ten days. Another 100 took the twenty-one-day excursion to Hong Kong via India at £440 a time, most of them also with their ladies. Every British Round Table president attended Wo-Co Conference; in 1976 it was in Germany, in 1977 in Canada.

But fulfilling Object 5 was not the monopoly of the man at the top. Twinning with an overseas Table was more popular than ever, the Same Number link still being a useful introduction. British contingents attended the charter celebrations of every new continental Table – a solemn presentation ceremony in the afternoon and a not-so-solemn dinner and dance at night. All sorts of other excuses for making contact with Tables abroad were provided by the Inter-Club Contact and Twinning Officer of British Round Table. The annual Round Table ski meeting was a stimulating occasion – in 1976 it was held from 29 February to 7 March at Flaine in France. The Children's Holiday Exchange scheme continued to flourish, and then Home Exchange for adults as well – a straight swap of houses between British and continental members. A growing traffic of letters, club magazines, tapes, slides and films developed between British Tables and members of World Council clubs in India, Africa, Canada and USA.*

Though Round Table International had died, the creation of the European Community restored cohesion to Round Table associations and individual clubs in Europe. But the concept of business and professional men using their skills for any purpose other than earning a living – in voluntary service to the community during leisure hours, for instance – was alien to the continental mind. It had never been part of their way of life as it had been in Britain and in the countries to which English, Scots, Welsh and Irish had brought this and other traditions as colonisers. For this reason no one had ever been moved to form a Table in Portugal and the attempt to do so in Madrid had not been fully successful.

To compensate for the absence of RTI, European and Mediterranean Presidents Meetings were held each summer at a dif-

* An attempt to establish Round Tables in Boston and Washington in 1973 had been discouraged by Active-20/30.

ferent centre to discuss mutual problems. A bi-lingual co-ordinator was appointed to give them a sense of continuity and consolidate *entente*. In June 1975 a British Round Table party of eleven flew to Rabat in Morocco. The hospitality and friend-ship displayed by Moroccan Tablers deeply impressed vice-president Roderick Burtt, president in 1977, for whom it was a startling insight into the meaning of international fellowship. In 1976 the EMPM took place in Finland, and in 1977, the Golden Jubilee Year, it was fittingly held in Britain at the historic city of Bath.

Each year there was Nordic Summit Meeting of the Scandin-avian Round Table associations in one of the member countries. In 1976 British Round Table's executive committee were guests of the Nordic Summit in Oslo. Each year during his term of office the president tried to visit at least two Round Table as-sociations outside Britain. In addition there were joint National Executive Meetings with the French association, with 225 Tables, the second largest association after RTBI.

To make up for the cancellation of the annual conference planned for Dublin in 1972 (theme 'Alive Alive-O'), Council held a meeting in the capital of the Irish Republic in July 1975 – Round Table Britain and Ireland (RTBI), it will be remem-bered, had from the beginning been the organisation for Eng-land, Scotland, Wales and the whole of the Emerald Isle, north and south. It was a mark of the esteem in which Round Table was held in the Republic that during the three-day visit Rodney Huggins was received by the President of Ireland at his resi-dence Arus an Uchtarcien.

In the English-speaking world, serving the community for no financial reward could be undertaken without fear of ridicule or the taunt of being a prig or a prude. Mostly started by British ex-patriates, the Tables in India, Africa, New Zealand, Malta, Gibraltar and Hong Kong, were soon infiltrated, and then run, by members of the indigenous population. But every now and again there was an invasion from the home country, as when in September 1975 ten members of Area 5 (West Midlands) flew to Zambia to rebuild a dam and bridge which had collapsed in a remote part of the bush near Lake Victoria.

The growth of the multi-national corporation gave Round Table with its world-wide infrastructure good reason for bringing back into play, in the overseas field, its dormant industrial role. To quote Kenneth Adams's *Exploring the Business Ethic* once again, 'Business management is increasingly international in character. This is the product of a shrinking world in terms of transportation and communication which encourages the development of large international corporations based in one country but operating in many. In this way management transcends national frontiers and business begins to reveal the fact of our world-wide economic interdependence. The decisions of our industrial leaders will affect the whole of our world society and not just our own national society. These men and women will determine by their decisions the way of life of a large percentage of the population of the planet. The most important point is for this power and this responsibility to be recognised by those who hold it, and from that recognition to appreciate that they must be concerned with values as much as with economic factors. They are increasingly responsible for the quality of our lives as well as for our standard of living. The young tend to see this responsibility more clearly perhaps because they have grown up in a world which had already shrunk.'

As this story has shown, in the course of fifty years many saw exploring the business ethic as a role more suited to Round Table than any other – and not only exploring it but championing it without embarrassment. Few however saw fit to tackle this lonely and difficult assignment. Taking its cue from Rotary, British Round Table prepared itself to face the issues and wrote the intention into its Objects. But in the event it took the path of least resistance, made a few token gestures, and then rushed headlong into the crowd of those who collected money not for causes but 'charity accounts'.

Neither 'social accountability' nor 'the unacceptable face of capitalism' had been coined in the 1920s, and company law disclosed no awareness, for instance, of what is now called insider trading as anything other than a commendable display of business acumen. The general climate changed for the better after World War 2, and because the overall standard was higher exposure of the few who, if they had been operating in the 1920s, would have got away with it, hit the headlines and rightly caused alarm. New tricks of the trade for the Business is Business brigade emerged in the 1960s and '70s – warehousing, asset-stripping, window dressing, expense padding – and there were plenty to play them for all they were worth, which was hundreds of thousands of pounds.

'There is no such thing as an English gentleman any more,' despaired Singapore's prime minister when yet another scandal broke in the 1970s. In some ways, observed Patrick Sergeant, City Editor of the *Daily Mail*, it was the best commodity we had to offer – 'it's a pity it's gone'. Social responsibility was a dimension of business which could not be ignored just because quantitative analysis could not be stringently applied to it, said a *Times* leader of 30 January 1973. 'There is a great urgency for the business community to build this dimension into its thinking and practice. Increasingly the subscribers to the doctrine of the Chicago economist who has denounced social responsibility in business as "a fundamentally subversive doctrine" are being relegated to the lunatic fringe. What has really been lacking is action on the part of business. There seems to be a wide gap between altruistic statements of good will on the part of business leaders and events that follow after.' (*Times*, 30 January 1973.)

The pressures and incentives on those in local government – euphemisms for bribes – have never relaxed: payments for showing favour in relation to planning applications, for granting licences and the rest to smooth the way through the forest of legislation produced by governments who considered they were 'running the economy'. The case of

architect John Poulson, sentenced to seven years' impris-
onment for corruption, revealed practices in local government which while commonplace on the continent, in the
USA and in much of the Third World was not normally associated with civic life in Britain, though it existed to a far
larger extent than generally believed. 'We cannot afford to rely
on the continued benefit of the ethical standards established by
our grandfathers. We shall have to supply a greater vigilance
ourselves.' ('The Changing British Ethic', leader in the *Times*,
25 May 1973.)

Very many less were standing watch over this scene, let alone
positively working to bring about a longed-for 'fundamental
shift in the invisible contract between business and society', than
were operating in the field of Social Service. There were a
lonely few. Justice, the British section of the International Commission of Jurists, issued a report on insider trading; the Foundation for Business Responsibilities published John Humble's
Social Responsibility Audit; the Christian Association of Business
Executives published a booklet *Towards a Code of Business Ethics*;
the Institute of Directors published *Guidelines for Directors*, giving its views on the use of inside information in share dealings,
the ethical implications of take-overs, business expenses, etc; the
General Synod's Board for Social Responsibility, as its name
implies, was set up for this sole purpose; the Billy Graham
Evangelistic Association has always made the maintenance of
high business and civic standards a pillar of its programme.

For Round Table, geared to fun and fellowship, to enter the
lists in such company and in such a 'priggish' cause would to
many seem laughable. In any event, they would say, it was a
London matter of no concern to the essentially provincial
Round Table and too 'left wing'. But it was the concern not just
of those in the metropolis or of any one political party, but of
the whole citizenry. And for a group of *young* men *not* associated
with the City of London but aware of its effect on them to be
enlightened, imaginative and disciplined enough to elect to take
the matter under their wing – left, right and centre – and make

their movement the reference point on a matter which they had taken the trouble (at Table level) to *study* and become local experts on, would seem to be doing a service to the community more exciting and more fun for those engaged in it, and more valuable for those who benefited from it, than any activity the movement had managed to undertake in the whole of its life to date.

On being appointed at forty-one, the youngest chairman of the Stock Exchange, Nicholas Goodison told the *Sunday Times* in January 1976, 'My views are well known; insider trading should be made a criminal offence'. It would have been a useful contribution to the dialogue if a new-look Round Table could have let it be known that it supported or opposed Goodison's point of view and was able to make constructive comment based on its independent study of the subject; or better still had sponsored a conference at which Goodison was principal speaker, along with others of his generation, to thrash out the problem in the form of a Teach-In and let the voice of Britain's young businessmen be heard on a matter of national importance.

Joining the select band of vigilants over the standards of business, professional and civic life in furtherance of Object no. 3 would give substance to the claim of wanting to be regarded as performing a continuing Community Service (apart from reacting along with a host of others to disasters as they arose) which to many in 1977 seemed to be more mythical than real.

Moreover it might spread beyond the confines of the British Isles and, through the Tables in so many different parts of the world, have a beneficial influence (however small) on the conduct of business where bribery and corruption are the deeply entrenched habits of commercial life, untouched by any changes in the climate of public opinion of a kind which have taken place in Britain.

Staging events which are fun to organise and take part in, through which money can be collected and put into charity accounts, is far removed from Community Service. Voluntary social action has a place in the Welfare State where the volunteers, unlike the state, are moved to action by their *concern*, and can communicate their concern to those on the receiving end directly and *personally*. Those who deplore the spread of state charity do so on the grounds of its impersonality. Voluntary Service must have a heart as well as heartiness behind it. To have any meaning it must be undertaken in a spirit not of paying lip-service to something reassuringly referred to as 'the Community', let alone even more vaguely 'Charity', but in *serving* old Freda Canning five streets away and Joe Hurst in the next village. If Round Table is to undertake Fund Raising Without Concern, it would be as well not to dissipate its effort but amass the money its members collect into *one* Round Table Charity Account which can be dispensed only in large sums and to meet a national need inside Britain and Ireland for which no state aid is forthcoming. If, on the other hand, Round Table wants to be identified with conventional Community Service, it should recruit young men who are likely to have concern for aspects of the contemporary social scene to an extent that they are prepared to *study* them at the level of their own community and, having consulted their own Social Service Council, seek ways of remedying them by voluntary action.

There is no fear of diminishing the intensity of the conviviality. Stemming from the common, identifiable activity (and not vice versa) it would acquire a new richness. There is nothing cheerless or solemn about having serious intent. It would mean a shift of emphasis in the way the movement purported to serve the community however. It would mean Round Table would start attracting a different type of young man – or rather a preponderance of a type of which there are already large numbers. But it would not shift the movement away from its primary purpose, which is not Community Service, but maturing the young man with no natural attributes, enabling him to co-operate with, yet out-perform, his peers in a way he will never find himself able to do in the cut and thrust of business in which opportunity is seldom equal, or in the world of sport for which one has to be born with a talent. It would not stop membership of Round Table helping young men in the difficult process of becoming adult social animals, easing them out of adolescence among young acquaintances who become friends and enjoying the social activities they generate. It would not affect Round Table's role as an experimental training centre where young men can discover the best way to use their gifts to the benefit of the community and practice the art of serving it.

It may help to justify the move from business and industrial life into Life with a capital 'L' to say that it is more consistent with the mood of the times, though in fact it is a *non-sequitur*. But having done so probably accounts more than anything else for the increased membership figures – particularly the tremendous growth of the last fifteen years – which for many is the yardstick of Round Table's success. But moods and hidden forces do not change organisations; people do. Movements do not 'develop'; people change them. If the young men who have been running Round Table in an unbroken relay race over the years have hit on a formula which they prefer to Marchesi's, they can substitute theirs for his because that is what they want. It is their will which has brought about the changes, not 'pressures' which dictate that Marchesi's idea needs 'bringing up to date'.

Be that as it may, the standing of Round Table in the guise it has chosen to present itself in the 1970s has never been higher. In May 1976 Rodney Huggins represented the movement as one of the thirty-five leading groups attending the four-day conference at St George's House, Windsor Castle, at the invitation of the Archbishops of Canterbury and York to consider the further implications of their 'Call to the Nation' of October 1975. Past President Mick Thorpe attended a Royal Garden Party in 1972, and Richard Temple Cox of Birmingham Table in 1976. Harold Wilson addressed a Round Table meeting as Prime Minister and his successor in 1976, James Callaghan, agreed to become an honorary member of Maidstone

Table. In local communities everywhere Round Table is held in high esteem, particularly as the group to turn to for the organisation of fêtes and carnivals, to help out with the celebrations of a special year – Blackpool North ran the main event in 1976 to mark Blackpool's centenary as a borough. The Lord Mayor of Bristol is always an honorary member of Table no 9.

But national standing played a small part at the level where 'Tabling' all happened – the local Table where a member proved himself in the company of others and accepted his potential and limitations within a bond of friendship. But the movement to which he belonged being treated by Authority as an association able to make a contribution to modern social problems might have given him added satisfaction, if not pride. It should have given a new edge to the fencing at Table, Area and National meetings, in the sub-committees and committees where the confidence-building and character-training took place. Field manoeuvres would become a fight over real issues; the closed circuit would plug itself in to real life – and what an exhilarating, transforming experience that might prove! But the 'democratic' structure insured against any hasty scene changes of that sort. In the meantime, for the average member his furthest Round Table horizon stretched as far as his Area. In time he would become one of the two members chosen to represent his Table at an Area committee (council) meeting which sometimes involved a stag dinner – though of course there was no knowing what, or who, might step out of that big box which the lads carried in with such hilarity after the coffee, and no one would have risked being torn off a strip by protesting at an incursion into what till then had been a strictly male occasion. The Area Banquets, Area Balls with anything from 150 to 500 guests were mixed, and wives and girl friends always attended the Area Rallies and Outings. They were mainly Area Teams who took part in outdoor events like the National Sailing Regatta, the National Sporting Week-end, the National Caravan Rally. The seven Scottish Areas had a massive

Rally every year at Aviemore.

Forty-six out of fifty Areas nominated members for the Round Table team which raced a National Association of Boys Clubs team from Calais (Cape Gris Nez) to Folkestone in the great Cross-Channel Swim on 2 August 1975. It was a relay race with each swimmer taking a twenty-minute stint, the last laps to Folkestone beach being swum by boxers Joe Bugner (Boys Clubs) and Henry Cooper (Round Table). Round Table lost the race but it was well publicised, and it was the first time RTBI had been involved in a nationally participating event. There was criticism by some Tables of the lack of liaison over the raffle organised by S.P.A.R.K.S. (the charity through which sportsmen show their appreciation of their fitness by helping the handicapped). £10,000 was raised out of a target of £100,000 – but those who took part had a great day.

Any Area was entitled to apply to the National Conference Committee to be the hosts of a national conference and to undertake the planning of one which took between three and four years – though the core of the occasion was the one-day annual general meeting, numerous social events were organised, as had always been the tradition, 'to increase the attraction' of the meeting. The NCC considered all the applications and selected the site suggested by one particular Area, mainly on the grounds of its accessibility and the adequacy of its hotel, banqueting and conference facilities. Over the years the number of places able to accommodate the Round Table Annual Conference had contracted. By the middle of the 1970s some 7,000 were attending the conference's peak days – it had become the largest conference of any voluntary movement in Europe. The time came when there were no hotels, public halls, assembly rooms or conference centres large enough to accommodate the numbers, and resort was had to tenting over football grounds. Where to hold the actual annual general meeting also created a problem. It first became acute at Bournemouth in 1974 when the doors had to be shut with some 2,500 crammed inside. In 1976 at Blackpool the Opera House in the Winter Gardens had every one of its 3,200 seats filled, and several hundreds were unable to gain admittance to the observers' galleries.

Most Areas had an Area Bulletin with information and a pep talk from the Area Chairman. 'Already the Table year is half over, my word how time does go so quickly. In spite of the many unhappinesses that face us all these difficult days, Round Tables in Area 16 [Kent] seem as usual to surmount the difficulties of general apathy both without and within our movement. Many of you have done wonders for bettering fellowship in your own Tables, and in so doing have rendered much money and service to the community at large. All of which is greatly appreciated, and furthers the good name and enjoyment of Tabling . . . So far this year, matters in Area 16 have gone along without too much of an explosive nature being thrown up, and now the season of Ladies Nights, Civic Nights etc is upon us may I wish all success to your every venture.'

But there was a word of warning too.* In a piece headed 'Area Council Meetings Business or Pleasure?', the chairman said he hoped the answer was Both. During the previous eight years attendance at Area Council Meetings had increased to the point where one fifth of the total Area membership was present.

'How encouraging this is, since it is surely an expression of general awareness of the importance of Area as a forum for individual Tables and Tablers where opinions can be exchanged and new thought put forward. It is also the link between individual Tablers and Tables with other individuals and Tables, both in Area and, via National, elsewhere in RTBI Area Council Meetings also provide an opportunity for fellowship, enabling old friends to meet and new friends to be made. The nett result is an opportunity on four occasions each year, for the aims and objects of Table to be given a wider meaning than can be obtained in an individual Table.

---

* This is an Area Bulletin taken at random without any claim that it is representative of any other Area's, but it is genuine; the mood it reflects may, or may not, be widespread.

'Round Table being made up of young, intelligent, lively and hard working men is naturally an exuberant organisation and this exuberance is never more manifest than when several Tables gather together. It has always been accepted by the majority, however, that a certain amount of self discipline must be exercised and that the Chairman of any meeting shall be extended the courtesy of being allowed to run his meeting, whether it be a Table, Area or National meeting, in accordance with the adopted rules and procedures. In return it is incumbent upon the Chairman to run the meeting fairly and (in the old fashioned sense of the word) democratically within the framework of those rules and procedures.

'Patently at Area Council Meetings at the moment there is a tendency for these considerations, in both directions, to fall short of a reasonable standard. At S—— recently there were several extraneous interruptions, very funny at the beginning of the meeting but less funny as the meeting went on. There were examples of officers usurping the Chairman's function, there were several instances of procedure which were blatantly "out of order". The result of this is that relatively little business is absorbing a lot of time to the detriment of all. Several people at S—— used the phrase "boring discussions". Why? An Area Council Meeting is the place for discussions and Tables have the right to have their views expressed and commented on. Some items for discussion might not have the excitement and impact of – of what? – can you think of many subjects discussed at Area which cannot be described by someone as boring. To those Tables that wish to speak on any given subject that subject is not boring.

'It is vitally important to accept that Area Council Meetings are a necessary and essential link in the communications between Tables and other Tables as well as between Tables and National, and it is incumbent upon every Tabler attending to listen and discuss matters which he might consider have little relevance to him individually or to his Table individually.

'Harking back to S—— there were, from an early part of the

249

evening, between twenty and thirty Tablers absent in the Bar. There were constant "comings and goings" and a constant hum of conversation from little groups dotted around the hall. These people weren't really interested in the business of the evening. So let us streamline operations, get the business done and done properly and then all have the opportunity of fellowship. Otherwise Area will fall into disrepute.'

It was unfair to be expected to take an interest in the business of the evening after a hard day's work sorting out insurance problems, dealing with the wine orders, walking round the harbour on a survey, coping with a class of unruly schoolboys, inspecting the apple trees, drafting the minutes of yesterday's housing meeting, calling in the taxi company's loan, telling Farmer Ellis his sheep had foot rot, giving police evidence in court all afternoon – after a hard day's work wrestling with other people's problems. These young men were in no mood to weigh the pros and cons of raising the capitation fee or amending Standing Orders, let alone to set the world to rights. They wanted to let their hair down every other Tuesday when they came to a Table meeting – and for the vast majority Round Table life began and ended with the local club.

It was a rural Table and they had driven in from their homes in nearby villages to which they had gone from work for a quick bath and a change into something less formal – or more formal – and a quick good-night to seven-year-old Tessa and jokes with little Jeremy, and a promise to darling to drive carefully and not be back too late.

The regular rendezvous is the Folderol Arms Hotel, one time mansion up the end of a long drive, where local firms hold their Christmas parties and entertain their foreign customers. From 7.15 to 7.45 they stand in the lounge bar and drink pints of beer in glass tankards, the few residents with their women folk outnumbered at the two tables in the corner. For most the talk is badinage and taking the mickey out of Rupert and Arthur for their lapses at the last meeting; but a trio by the door, which includes a moustachioed young man wearing his chairman's chain with the rows of bars bearing past chairmen's names which shows the Table's antiquity, are deploring the increasingly high cost of Tabling – the new charge for dinner, up a pound in the last twelve months to £2.50, petrol at 76p a gallon, bitter beer at 25p a pint, the higher subscriptions. The price of fellowship Round-Table-style, was becoming a serious drain on the family budget. Many a member with higher gas, electricity, clothes and telephone bills was reviewing his priorities and wondering for how much longer he was going to be able to afford it. At least there was a tendency to spend less on drink. The risk of incurring the severe penalties of being found driving with too much alcohol in the blood was not to be taken light-heartedly; they could seriously affect a man's earning capacity. In spite of these the temptation to go on drinking at the end of the evening in the post-prandial glow – the landlord was always very flexible with his licensing hours – was very real.

Strictly on time they drift into the wood-panelled 'Tudor' dining-room arranged formally with a top table and three tongues. On one of the walls is the board giving the names and dates of the chairmen since the Table's inauguration. In front of it is the high-backed wooden chair for the chairman, the gift of a couple of members who left the fold many years before on reaching the age of forty. In front of the high table in a central place of honour is a fine porcelain water closet, the gift of who knows who? On the white table cloth among the knives and forks laid for the dinner that is to come stand the embroidered banners presented by visiting Tables.

There are more members than usual as the occasion is a quarter-finals round of the knock-out Area Debating Contest. The Table is acting as host to two other Tables in the Area, one of whose teams of three speakers will be judged the winner of the round and go on to the next. At the tables are seated some sixty young men in lounge suits or sports jackets (dinner-jackets are reserved for the more formal Charter Nights and anniversaries).

They talk with loud voices and swill the beer they have brought in with them from the bar, to which every now and again they return for fresh supplies. The din subsides as the chairman bangs his gavel and invites a member to say the Round Table grace, for which everyone rises:

> May we, O Lord, adopt thy creed
> Adapt our ways to serve thy need
> And we, who on thy bounty feed,
> Improve in thought, in word, and deed.

The hubbub resumes as the company sits down and another member is invited to read to the assembly the Objects of Round Table (cries of 'Shame! he ought to know them off by heart!'). Another member is asked to read the list of apologies for absence. This done, the chairman introduces the guests amid sporadic interjections and handclaps, each stranger rising in his seat so all can see him. 'A warm welcome to Eric Fuller who. . . . Eric nice to see you here this evening ('can't hear you!'). . . . And Arthur Silversides who will be transferring to us from Pashley ('provided he pays his sub!'), and Miles Dashworthy who has transferred to us from Mornington Table. . . . Welcome to Tipiton Table!' At this the chairman announces that each member of the Table present – some eighteen out of the complement of twenty-four – will perform the usual ritual of standing and giving his name and occupation clockwise round the room so the new member can see just who his fellow-members are. Barracking accompanies this set-piece as members identify themselves – 'Jonathan Stitt, teacher; Tony Lumpkin, public servant; Joe Fluke, apple grower; Marmaduke Pelling, something in property . . .' ending with the chairman who describes himself as a Bleeding Old Man to the shouted observation 'Your flies are undone!' from a distant corner.

'Business' is the next item on the agenda. A sub-committee head rises to recount how the Table still has to find £1,200 for the ambulance they are presenting to Bumbleby Hospital; the book sale, the bonfire night and the barbecue only raised £730. A loan from another Table? ('Not bloody likely!') Whether they were going to be able to avoid paying VAT was dodgy ('Oooh!').

That concludes the Business and an elderly uniformed wait-ress brings on the soup, followed by the lamb chop and the dishes of leeks and brussels sprouts and roast potatoes. Members leave the tables from time to time and return with tankards re-brimming with bitter. Comes the vanilla ice and fruit salad, and the chairman calls members to their feet to drink the toast of Her Majesty the Queen, after which he declares a half-hour break. Pipes and cigarettes are lit and the mellow light from the chan-delier becomes even mellower with the haze of rising smoke.

One of the rules of the debating contest is that the chairman must read them all out to the meeting, and this he proceeds to do. The host Table are the judges and have set the motion which by custom gives little opportunity for serious debate but plenty for sexy *double entendre* and the maximum rudery. It is not for judges to say who has 'won' the motion – it is never thrown open to the house – but every member of the host Table allots marks for Posture and Delivery, Continuity and Development of Argument and General Impression. Each of the six speakers speak for their allotted eight or five minutes in turn. Alistair begins by going to the wooden reading-desk at the top table and placing on it a hand-written script which he then begins to read as best he can, the fruits of much time-consuming drafting and re-drafting. There is nothing near-the-knuckle about the stor-ies, they are all thoroughly *on* the knuckle; no innuendos but the most direct of references, long and tortuous, evoking little response other than good-humoured groans and puzzled frowns. But on he ploughs undaunted, every now and again a jovial outburst taking him by surprise at a point in the script not designed for laughter. His opponent, next at the lectern, calls it speaking from the shoulder – 'pity it wasn't from higher up!'. Within minutes of the last speaker having had his say, the forms are collected, the marks totted and the winners declared. The

chairmen of the winning and losing Tables thank the host Table
for its hospitality. The chairman of the latter thanks everyone
for coming and winds up the proceedings; whereupon the company repairs to the bar, the three Tables mix and members
promise to pay each other reciprocal visits.*

It had not been a serious essay in the difficult art of debating. It
had been a rag – and great fun. It had enabled members of the
three Tables to widen their circle of acquaintanceship. It had
got members to their feet, confidently facing an audience, preparing and putting on an act, which outside Round Table they
would never have had an opportunity of doing. In any event the
dinner setting of most Table meetings was not conducive to
serious discussion; having to get up and speak was an exercise in
means, not ends.

It was another occasion for enlarging and filling in the holes
in the patchwork quilt of fellowship which covered the Area,
along with the Progressive Dinner (elsewhere called the Safari
Supper or Round the Houses), and the Divide and Visit Meeting. With new members coming in every year – first time Tablers and transferees from other Tables – the Progressive Dinner
was a kind of Paul Jones devised to accelerate and ease the process of acquaintanceship. As Rodney Huggins said in his message in the March 1976 issue of *News & Views*, 'Round Table is
the universal introduction overcoming immediately the tedious
barriers of formality and convention'. His Table, Reading Valley Table, subscribed to the cause of Young Acquaintance in
1973 by everyone cycling in relay from Land's End to John
O'Groats.

A Progressive Dinner was less painful. Members were divided into groups of two or three, each of which received a note

---

* There is no claim to this description of a Table meeting in the Home Counties
being 'typical'; atmosphere and procedure varies between one Table and its neighbour ten miles away, between Tables in the North, Tables in the South, Tables
everywhere.

telling them to go to another member's house for the first course of a three-course dinner. Their host would have been warned to prepare Starters for Three, but would have had no idea who was going to turn up. Having eaten their *oeufs florentine* or smoked trout, the three received a telephone call telling them where to go for their main dish – and so did their erstwhile hosts. They ate their game pie or veal cutlets at the Hurleys and then drove to the Burleys for Afters, as instructed on the phone at the Hurleys. Then everyone, wherever they were for their third course, received the same message to go to the Macbeths for coffee – and the whole Table congregated under one roof to review the evening's entertainment, and trust that the aperitives, plonk and brandy they had had while on safari would enable them to reach home without incident.

A Divide and Visit exercise was spread over a longer period. Each Table member received a note on the following lines: 'During the months of February and March could you please arrange to visit Drakeshead Table [another in the Area] with Fred Timson [of his own Table] and invite any of their members to attend our meeting of March 13. There will be a free draw (one ticket a Table) for a bottle of whisky for all Tables attending.'

The Area Debating Contest, the Progressive Dinner, the Divide and Visit Meeting, the Old Boys Night, and countless other sessions of infinite variety devised by Tables north, south, east and west, together with an even greater array of sporting events and overseas visits, all acted to keep members circulating. They gave an excuse for young men to make the acquaintance of others which could lead to lasting friendship. They brought together those who otherwise would spend their lives passing each other in the street as strangers. It was in the fraternal club life of the *Tables* that the movement found its justification; here its spirit was truly located. Louis Marchesi created his Table in Norwich as the setting in which new relationships could be sparked off within the newly created cell; and the 1,208 Tables from Orkney to the Scillies which have been formed between

1927 and 1977 in Britain and Ireland involving 35,000 young men, and fast proliferating Tables overseas – Jamaica no. 1 sponsored by Knaresborough Table came into being in November 1976 – similarly triggered a chain reaction from one Table to another. No one has yet been able to analyse the mix, but the end product is the fast-breeder that confounds all speculation as to what it will do next, the Round Table Movement, poised to bring an exhilarating taste of good-fellowship to greater numbers than ever before in the decades that lie ahead.

Chronological Table of Events

1898   Erminio Gugliemo Luigi (Louis) Marchesi born in Norwich (19 January).

1905   Paul Harris forms a new kind of civic club – Rotary of Chicago.

1910   National Association of Rotary Clubs of America formed.

1911   Rotary spreads to Britain.

1912   NARC re-named International Association of Rotary Clubs.

1914   Outbreak of World War 1.
British Association of Rotary Clubs formed.
Sixteen-year-old Louis Marchesi enrols in British Red Cross.

1915   Henry Giessenbier forms Young Men's Progressive Civic Association in St Louis, USA, later known as Junior Citizens or Jaycees (Junior Chambers of Commerce).
Talbot House Services Club (Toc H) formed at Ypres on western front.

1917   Mervyn Jones forms the International Association of Lions Clubs in Chicago, USA.

1920   Harold Rogers forms Kinsmen Club in Ontario, Canada.

1922   Paul Claiburne forms 20-30 Club in Sacramento, USA.
Active Club formed in Aberdeen, USA.

1925   Louis Marchesi acquires Langford's restaurant in Norwich, whose Smoke Room regulars discuss idea of Round Table in the course of morning coffee sessions with their host.

1926   Coal Miners Strike leads to General Strike (May).
Rotarian Marchesi talks to Norwich Rotary Club on 'Youth and Business' (September); encouraged to form a Young Business and Professional Mens Club, he drafts rules and objects.

1927   British Industries Fair opens in London and Birmingham (21 February).
Prince of Wales speaks at BIF banquet in London and recommends industry to adopt, adapt and improve (21 February).
Meeting in Suckling House, Norwich, to establish a club for the young business and professional men of Norwich (21 February).
Inaugural meeting of The Round Table, an Association of Young Business Men, of Norwich (14 March).

1928   1st annual general meeting of Norwich Round Table club (20 February).
Charlie Smith forms Table no. 2 in Portsmouth.
Rotarian Leonard Hines and Tabler Marchesi address British Rotary AGM at Harrogate on 'The Younger Generation'.

The Central Council of Round Tables of Great Britain and Ireland formed (25 May).

Tables formed in Guildford (no. 3), Southampton (no. 4) and Bournemouth (no. 5).

1929   1st annual conference of National Association of Round Tables at Norwich (3 & 4 April).

Three 'Districts' formed: North; West & Midlands; South.

British Junior Chambers of Commerce formed.

1930   World economic crisis.

Young Business Men's Club formed in Geelong, Australia; later known as Apex Club.

Round Table wives form first 'Ladies Circle'.

1931   With 33 Tables an Area administration is considered.

1932   After five years as Hon. Secretary, Louis Marchesi hands over.

1933   Cyril Marsh joins Round Table.

Area Councils established as an experiment.

1935   100 Tables in year Louis Marchesi becomes President.

1936   First '41 Club' for ex-Tablers formed – in Liverpool.

First Table formed outside Britain – in Copenhagen.

1937   A headquarters office established in London (Ludgate Hill).

C. R. Chambers becomes Organising Secretary.

Louis Marchesi reaches disqualifying age of 40 and is made Founder Honorary Life Member.

1938   'Munich Crisis'; Portsmouth Table contact Anthony Eden, 41-year-old Foreign Secretary.

1939   National headquarters move to 38 Buckingham Palace Road (May).

Clifford Attwell becomes Secretary.

4,600 members in 125 Tables.

On outbreak of World War 2, Cyril Marsh 'runs' Round Table from his home in Merton; Council standing orders suspended.

1940   Age limit of 40 suspended.

1941   Five new Tables formed in Denmark during war.

1943   Internal Reorganisation and Development Committee formed.

1944   Liverpool Table's Reconstruction Report.

1945   York Table's Reconstruction Report.

World Council of Young Men's Service Clubs formed; Round Table support but unable to attend first meeting in Chicago.

End of World War 2; 1,334 members in 90 Tables.

1946   First Dutch Table formed – in Utrecht.

De Nederlandsche Tafelrond formed.

Penang Table formed; & International Round Tables of Asia.

1947   Round Table International (RTI) formed.

133 RTBI Tables; 7 Dutch; 5 Swedish.

1948   Three conferences at Hastings: RTBI, Wo-Co and the first conference of RTI.

Norwich Table no. 1 celebrate their 21st birthday.

Louis Marchesi is 50.

First South African Table formed – in East London.

1949   Number of Areas increased from 18 to 29.

1950   RTI has 250 RTBI Tables, 31 in Denmark, 27 in Holland, 15 in Sweden, 4 in Finland, 3 in Norway, 1 in France, 1 in Belgium.

Children's Holiday Exchange Scheme started.

1951   Vic Collins appointed General Secretary.

330 Tables; 8,600 members.

1952   First German Table formed – in Hamburg.

Table formed in Nairobi – nucleus of Round Tables of East Africa (ARTEA); others in Rhodesia and Malaya.

1953   Silver Jubilee: banquet in London; publication of John Creasey's *Round Table, the First 25 Years*.

Plan to found Chair of Race Relations in Rhodesia.

1954   Louis Marchesi sells Langford's; goes on a tour.

1956   13,700 members in 512 Tables – RTBI is largest unit in both RTI and Wo-Co.

Headquarters move to 15 Park Road.

1958   RTBI financial crisis.

16,000 members in 580 Tables in 39 Areas.

Bournemouth Conference discusses reorganisation.

The Duke of Edinburgh becomes Patron.

1959   RTI has 25,280 members – 1,040 Tables in 21 countries.

1960   Wo-Co get new constitution; RTI wound up.

1962   Capitation fee raised to £1.

1965   The Duke of Edinburgh receives RTBI President and party.

Bognor Conference debates Objects – out of date?

Death of Mrs Louis (Dolly) Marchesi.

1967   40th anniversary luncheon in London; Duke of Edinburgh guest of honour.

27,500 members in 923 Tables.

1968   Death of founder, Louis Marchesi (10 December).

1969   Memorial service for founder in London.

Retirement of Vic Collins, General Secretary; Denis Tizard succeeds.

1,000th RTBI Table formed – at Sandy in Bedford-shire.

1970   British Rotary start 'Rotaract'.

1972   'Rotable' – joint meetings with Rotary.
Press attend annual conference for first time.
Criminal Justice Act creates sentence of 'Community Service'.

1973   Local authorities establish Social Service departments.
Britain joins European Economic Community.
Edward Heath, Prime Minister, speaks to Area 26 dinner.

1974   Duke of Edinburgh attends Pre-Conference Lunch in London.

1975   5,000 attend annual conference at Torbay and consider restructuring National Association.
Capitation fee raised from £2.65 to £3.25.
33,737 members in 1,174 Tables.

1977   GOLDEN JUBILEE YEAR
35,000 members in over 1,200 Tables.
European and Mediterranean Presidents Meeting at Bath.
50th anniversary annual conference at Great Yarmouth (near Norwich).

Appendix A
RTBI Clubs in Golden Jubilee Year
(with Table numbers in chronological order of formation)

1	Norwich	26	Cardiff
2	Portsmouth & Southsea	27	Worthing
3	Guildford	28	Sheffield
4	Southampton	29	City of Manchester
5	Bournemouth	30	Littlehampton
6	Reading	31	Bradford & District
7	Doncaster	32	Eastbourne
8	Liverpool	33	Chesterfield
9	Bristol	34	Middlesbrough
10	Brighton	35	Stockton-on-Tees
11	Stourbridge	36	Hull
12	Poole	37	Lewes & District
13	City of London	38	Maidstone
14	Halifax	39	Leicester
15	Newport, Mon.	40	Horsham
16	Ryde & District	41	Great Yarmouth & District
17	Wolverhampton	42	Bridlington
18	Blackpool	43	Southport
19	Kingston-upon-Thames	44	Birkenhead & District
20	Clapham & District	45	Chatham
21	Hastings	46	Bognor Regis
22	Bromley	47	Wakefield
23	Coventry	48	Hammersmith
24	Rotherham	49	St Helens & District
25	Swindon & District	50	City of Birmingham

51	Leeds	87	Londonderry
52	Ealing	88	Scarborough
53	Belfast	89	Otley & District
54	King's Lynn & District	90	Farnham
55	Rochdale & District	91	Bath & District
56	City of Rochester	92	Northampton
57	Swansea	93	Basingstoke
58	Smethwick	94	Harrow
59	City of Nottingham	95	Haywards Heath
60	Barnsley	96	Stoke-on-Trent & District
61	Acton	97	Catford & Lewisham
62	Wimbledon & District	98	Matlock
63	Winchester & District	99	Darlington & District
64	Woking	100	Aberdeen & District
65	York	101	Bingley
66	Epsom & District	102	Hartlepool
67	Chichester	103	Sunderland
68	Huddersfield	104	Beckenham
69	Retford	105	Inverness
70	Grimsby	106	Southend
71	Walsall	107	Sutton
72	Hornsey	108	Surbiton
73	Camberwell	109	Bury
74	Warrington	110	Weston-super-Mare
75	Gillingham	111	Southgate
76	Chester	112	Watford
77	Dudley	113	Rugby
78	Wigan	114	Dorking
79	Dewsbury	115	Twickenham
80	Carmarthen	116	Kensington
81	Letchworth	117	Brentford & Chiswick
82	Lowestoft & District	118	Sittingbourne & Milton
83	Blackburn	119	Redhill & Reigate
84	Leyton	120	Lincoln
85	Croydon	121	Staines
86	Camberley & District	122	Bedford

123	Exeter	159	Preston
124	Ruislip	160	Lancaster
125	Sutton-in-Ashfield	161	Thornton Cleveleys
126	Derby	162	South Shields
127	Newcastle-upon-Tyne	163	Bootle, Crosby & District
128	Willesden	164	Leamington & District
129	Hinckley	165	Kidderminster
130	Lytham	166	Wallington & Carshalton
131	Richmond (Surrey)	167	Coulsdon & Purley
132	Chelmsford	168	Harrogate
133	New Milton & District	169	Ramsgate & District
134	Scunthorpe	170	Cheltenham
135	Whitehaven	171	Leatherhead
136	Nuneaton	172	Coleraine
137	Walton & Weybridge	173	Weymouth & District
138	Norwood	174	Redcar & District
139	Leigh	175	Dereham & District
140	Taunton	176	Stafford & District
141	Islington	177	Hounslow
142	Glasgow	178	Orpington
143	Dartford & District	179	Alton
144	Oxford	180	Esher
145	Durham City & District	181	Redditch
146	Gloucester	182	Torquay
147	St Albans	183	Sutton Coldfield
148	Woolwich & District	184	Carlisle
149	Sheringham & Cromer	185	Morden & District
150	Hitchin & District	186	Gateshead
151	Wembley	187	Gravesend
152	Hendon	188	Bexhill
153	Keighley	189	Consett & District
154	Worksop	190	Holt & District
155	High Wycombe	191	Bexley
156	Stroud & District	192	Jersey
157	Salisbury	193	City of Edinburgh
158	Luton	194	Fareham & District

195	Royal Tunbridge Wells	231	Guernsey
196	Bolton	232	Ilkley & District
197	Oldham	233	Fleetwood
198	Crewe & Nantwich	234	Canterbury & District
199	Skipton	235	Ashington
200	Perth	236	Holmfirth
201	Sandbach	237	Andover
202	Maidenhead	238	Sowerby Bridge & District
203	Dublin	239	Enfield
204	Burton-on-Trent	240	Ipswich
205	Chelsea	241	Wellingborough
206	Beccles & District	242	Morecambe & Heysham
207	Whitley Bay	243	Paignton
208	Willenhall	244	Hove
209	Solihull	245	Hayes & Southall
210	Ewell & Worcester Park	246	Plymouth
211	Stirling	247	Beverley
212	Ossett & Horbury	248	Uttoxeter & District
213	Workington	249	Bromsgrove
214	Greenwich	250	Lichfield
215	Eltham & District	251	Barrow-in-Furness
216	Walthamstow	252	Gosport
217	Pontefract	253	Barnoldswick & Earby
218	Blyth	254	Finchley
219	Arbroath & District	255	Hornchurch
220	Wallasey	256	Berkhamsted & District
221	Ormskirk & District	257	Worcester
222	Yeovil	258	Sevenoaks
223	Southwold & District	259	Horsforth & District
224	Uxbridge	260	Loughborough
225	Slough	261	Congleton
226	Tynemouth	262	Rushden
227	Newark & District	263	Ripley
228	Kettering	264	West Bromwich
229	Buxton	265	Fakenham & District
230	Batley	266	Skegness

267	Louth	304	Aldershot & District
268	Falkirk	305	Wrexham
269	Folkestone & District	306	Streatham
270	Enniskillen	307	Grantham & District
271	Barnstaple & District	308	Swadlincote & District
272	Shrewsbury	309	Bangor
273	Hemel Hempstead	310	Leighton Buzzard & District
274	Caterham & District	311	Hoylake & West Kirby
275	Wood Green	312	Sleaford & District
276	Wanstead & Woodford	313	Stratford-upon-Avon
277	Windsor & Eton	314	Birmingham Edgbaston
278	Belper	315	Birmingham Handsworth
279	Newton Abbot	316	Birmingham Moseley
280	Chepstow & District	317	Wrekin
281	Colne & District	318	Maghull & District
282	Frome	319	Bridgwater
283	Atherton & Tyldesley	320	Aylesbury
284	Peterborough & District	321	Ilford
285	Ilkeston	322	Hereford
286	Cirencester	323	Dorchester
287	Mexborough	324	Erith & District
289	Bury St Edmunds	325	Cockermouth
290	Sidcup	326	Ashbourne
291	Cambridge	327	Ilfracombe
292	Maryport	328	Bideford
293	Tewkesbury	330	Dundee
294	Hebden Bridge & District	331	North Walsham & District
295	Vale of Evesham	332	Macclesfield
296	Amble & Warkworth	333	Lymington & District
297	Hexham	334	Avalon
298	Ashton-under-Lyne	335	Port Talbot
299	Petersfield	336	Goodmayes
300	Burnley	337	Boston
301	Malvern Hills	338	Welwyn Garden City
302	Armagh	339	Leek & District
303	Morley	340	Brixham

341	Northallerton & District	378	Wombwell & District
342	Sunbury-on-Thames	379	Banbury
343	City of Truro	380	St Austell & District
344	Norbury & Thornton Heath	381	Clevedon & District
345	Romford	382	Barking
346	Bentham & District	383	Halesowen
347	Margate	384	Cleckheaton & District
348	Northwich	385	Brentwood
349	Havant & Emsworth	386	Kendal
350	Tiverton & District	387	Clacton-on-Sea
351	Teignmouth & District	388	Dumfries & District
352	Rhyl & District	389	Alnwick & District
353	Ashford & District	390	Tottenham
354	Barnet & East Barnet	391	Newbury
355	Nelson	392	Keynsham & District
357	Wisbech	393	Edmonton
358	Heanor & Eastwood	394	Wigton
359	Waltham Abbey & Cheshunt	395	Chertsey & Addlestone
360	Richmond (Yorks.) & District	396	Penzance
361	Ballymena	397	Bishop Auckland & District
362	Feltham	398	Kilmarnock
363	Deptford	399	Mold
364	Harwich	400	Dunstable & District
365	Burnham-on-Sea & Highbridge	401	Penrith
366	Grays	402	Chingford
367	Colchester	403	Hampstead
368	Peterlee & District	404	Braintree
369	Forest of Dean	405	Alloa & District
370	Putney	406	Minehead & District
371	Tamworth & District	407	Brierley Hill
372	Pinner	408	Market Drayton
373	Widnes & District	409	Ludlow
374	Stockport & District	410	Huntingdon & District
375	Wednesbury & District	411	Ely & District
376	Llanelli	412	Formby & District
377	Crawley	413	Saltburn & District

414	Chippenham & District	449	Halstead
415	Exmouth & District	450	Selby & District
416	East Ham	451	Brighouse
417	Darwen	452	Chard & District
418	Birmingham Erdington	453	Stevenage & Knebworth
419	Crewkerne & District	454	Elgin
420	Newport, Isle of Wight	455	Harpenden
421	Dagenham	456	Douglas (Isle of Man)
422	Bilston	457	Ripon
423	Shipley & District	458	Falmouth
424	Keswick	459	City of Bangor & District
425	Carnforth & District	460	March
426	Heaton-upon-Tyne	461	Long Eaton
427	Rickmansworth	462	Penge & District
428	Spalding & District	463	Whitby
429	Godalming	464	Hertford & District
430	Ross-on-Wye	465	Eccles & District
431	Newcastle-under-Lyme & District	466	East Grinstead & District
		467	Tenby
432	Forfar & District	468	Crediton & District
433	Mansfield	469	Wallsend
434	Neath	470	Dover & District
435	Swanage	471	Bridgend
436	Felixstowe	472	Newcastle-upon-Tyne Hadrian
437	Mitcham	473	Cheam
438	Hallamshire	474	Oldbury
439	Diss & District	475	Harlow
440	Ulverston	476	Oswestry & District
441	St Neots	477	Watton & District
442	Sale & District	478	Cannock & District
443	Coquetdale	479	Melton Mowbray & District
444	Morpeth	480	Bedlingtonshire
445	Berwick-upon-Tweed	481	Newquay & District
446	Crosshills & District	482	Sidmouth & District
447	Aberdare	483	St Pancras & Finsbury
448	Prescot & District	484	Romsey

557	Heswall	592	Annan & District
558	Saddleworth	593	Newmarket & District
559	Gerrards Cross & The Chalfonts	594	Billericay
560	Birmingham King's Norton	595	Loughton
561	Haverfordwest	596	West Ealing
562	Barnard Castle & District	597	Axe Valley
563	Merthyr Tydfil	598	Brechin & District
564	Abingdon	599	Deal & District
565	Shoreham & Southwick	600	Henley-on-Thames
566	Caernarvon	601	West Bridgford
567	Farnborough, Hants	602	Deeside
568	Gosforth	603	Alsager & District
569	North Cotswold	604	Atherstone
570	Coalville & District	605	Droitwich Spa
571	Stowmarket & District	606	Pudsey
572	Washington	607	Bridport
573	Beeston & District	608	Guisborough & District
574	Linenhall of Belfast	609	Newry
575	Marlow & District	610	Ammanford
576	Towcester & District	611	Stamford & District
577	Bletchley	612	Bridgnorth & District
578	Hucknall	613	Lutterworth & District
579	Hamilton & District	614	Woodbridge
580	Calverley & District	615	Hunstanton & District
581	Ledbury	616	Wilmslow & District
582	Saffron Walden	617	Maldon
583	Weald of Kent	618	Market Harborough
584	Windermere, Ambleside & District	619	Royston & District
		620	Paisley & District
585	Airdrie	621	Chatsworth
586	Llandudno	622	Wearside
587	Kirkcaldy	623	London (West End)
588	Rowley Regis	624	Strabane & District
589	Houghton-le-Spring & District	625	Melbourne
590	Northfleet & District	626	Goole & District
591	Trowbridge	627	Denbigh & District

628	Rossendale	664	York Ebor
629	Westbury-on-Trym	665	Leyland
630	Newton Mearns & District	666	Chigwell
631	Tonbridge	667	Thirsk
632	Altrincham & District	668	Carnoustie & District
633	Welshpool	669	Knutsford & District
634	Swaffham & District	670	East Kilbride & District
635	Fort William	671	Galashiels & District
636	Linlithgow	672	Brigg & District
637	Pembroke	673	Rutland
638	Dursley & District	674	Bramhall & District
639	Milford Haven	675	Rhondda
640	Ardrossan	676	Newtown
641	West Wickham	677	Fraserburgh
642	Norton Radstock	678	Kirkham & Rural Fylde
643	Ringwood & District	679	Sudbury & District
644	Liverpool Childwall	680	Kingsbridge & District
645	Bebington	681	Marlborough & District
646	Montrose & District	682	Crieff
647	Thornbury	683	Billingham
648	Girvan & District	684	Bicester
649	Rugeley & District	685	Leven & District
650	Hull & Humberside	686	Nottingham North
651	Abertillery	687	Wincanton & District
652	Mirfield	688	Lurgan
653	Bishop's Stortford	689	Rayleigh & District
654	Broadstairs	690	Milngavie & Bearsden
655	Wellington	691	Bushey & Oxhey
656	Sheffield Riverdale	692	Addiscombe & Shirley
657	Runcorn & District	693	Colne Valley
658	Elland	694	Buckie & District
659	Mendip	695	Hoddesdon
660	Middlewich & District	696	Redruth
661	Tavistock	697	Seaham
662	Longton & District	698	Potters Bar & Brookman's P
663	Dungannon	699	Wetherby & District

700	Chorleywood	736	Liskeard & Looe
701	Witham	737	Downend
702	Leicester St Martins	738	Tring & District
703	Chapeltown & District	739	Hadleigh & District
704	Barmouth & Dolgellau	740	Driffield
705	Vale of Glamorgan	741	Cowdenbeath & District
706	Epping	742	Market Rasen & District
707	Cardigan & Teifi Valley	743	Sandwich & District
708	Whickham & District	744	Cowal
709	Melksham & Corsham	745	Kingston Hundrede
710	Hyde	746	Alcester
711	Sedgemoor	747	Wickford
712	South Elmsall & District	748	Haverhill
713	Horley & District	749	Plympton & Plymstock
714	Corstorphine	750	Blandford & District
715	City of Salford	751	Musselburgh & District
716	Wymondham & Attleborough	752	Hope Valley
717	Monmouth	753	Thame & District
718	Limavady & District	754	Neston & District
719	Bradford Fairfax	755	Whitstable & District
720	Stanford & Corringham	756	Waterlooville & District
721	Abergavenny & District	757	Heathfield & District
722	Ramsey & Peel	758	Ware & District
723	Prestwich	759	Llangollen
724	Hythe & District	760	Seisdon & District
725	Leominster	761	Elstree & Boreham Wood
726	Blackpool North	762	Sherborne
727	South Molton	763	Barkingside
728	Alfreton	764	Inverurie & District
729	Cumnock & District	765	Lanark & District
730	Grangemouth	766	Dunblane
731	Heckmondwike	767	Devizes & District
732	Whitchurch	768	Dunmow & District
733	Bargoed & District	769	Newton & Ashton
734	Milton Keynes & District	770	Cullompton & District
735	Blairgowrie	771	Camborne

772	Glasgow Queen's Park	807	Kirriemuir & District
773	Worsley & District	808	Middlesbrough (Cleveland)
774	Lisburn	809	Denby Dale & District
775	North Shields	810	Preston Amounderness
776	Isle of Sheppey	811	Haddington & District
777	Sutton Park	812	Knowle & Dorridge
778	Llandeilo & Llandovery	813	Bitterne & Woolston
779	Burgess Hill, Hassocks & District	814	Kinrossshire
		815	Banstead
780	Yarborough	816	Fishguard & District
781	Baldock	817	Bodmin & District
782	Hutton & Shenfield	818	Penarth
783	Warminster & District	819	Portmadoc & District
784	Aylsham & District	820	Kenilworth
785	Bingham & District	821	Welwyn
786	Launceston	822	Peterhead & District
787	Spilsby & District	823	Beaconsfield
788	St Andrews & District	824	Edgware
789	Stranraer & District	825	Buckingham & District
790	Saltash & District	826	Chelmsford Tindal
791	Wallingford & District	827	Llanrwst & District
792	Dalkeith & District	828	Dalton & District
793	Dundalk	829	Cheadle & Gatley
794	Llangefni & District	830	Reading Valley
795	Swansea Valley	831	Wokingham
796	Lymm & District	832	Sawbridgeworth & District
797	Cuffley & District	833	Newton Aycliffe & District
798	Newtownabbey	834	Edinburgh Pentlands
799	Kelso & District	835	Appleby & District
800	Cupar	836	Cumbernauld
801	St Annes-on-Sea	837	Seaford & Newhaven
802	Tower Hamlets	838	Peebles & District
803	Troon	839	Fleet
804	Ilminster	840	Barrhead & District
805	Basildon	841	Holywood
806	Shepperton	842	Colchester Colne

843	Huddersfield Pendragon	879	St Agnes & Perranporth
844	Bramhope	880	Cardiff Castle
845	Isles of Scilly	881	Petts Wood
846	Whittlesey & District	882	Alford
847	Greenock	883	Blackburn Greys
848	Prestwick	884	Broughty Ferry & District
849	Bala & Corwen	885	Pitlochry & District
850	Brownhills & District	886	Mid-Argyll
851	Hagley & District	887	Rutherglen & District
852	Athlone	888	Liverpool Aigburth
853	Cookstown & District	889	Chipping Norton
854	Ipswich Greyfriars	890	Thetford & District
855	Helensburgh & District	891	Galway
856	Huyton	892	Norwich, Wensum & Yare
857	Ringway	893	Tredegar
858	Garforth	894	Cranleigh & District
859	Newent	895	Mildenhall & District
860	Burton Abbey	896	Bourne & District
861	Kidlington	897	Cleeve Hill
862	Midhurst	898	Bude
863	Padiham	899	Queensbury, Shelf & District
864	Motherwell & District	900	Strathaven & District
865	Shaftesbury & Gillingham	901	Pocklington & Market Weighton
866	Huntly & District		
867	Pontypool	902	Kirkby & District
868	Rochdale Roch Valley	903	Wensleydale
869	Flint & Holywell	904	Faversham & District
870	Daventry & District	905	Irvine
871	Glenrothes	906	Brecon
872	Stoke-on-Trent Sutherland	907	Gower
873	Knaresborough	908	Oakengates & District
874	Bridge of Weir & Kilmacolm	909	Leigh-on-Sea
875	Cambridge Granta	910	Urmston & District
876	Princes Risborough	911	Tarporley
877	Brampton, Longtown & Border	912	Wem & District
878	Ruthin & District	913	Cramlington & District

914	Antrim	950	Largs & District
915	Wantage	951	Ryton & District
916	Glossop & District	952	Ponteland
917	Newtownards & District	953	Leith
918	Caerphilly	954	Ellesmere & District
919	Cowes	955	North Berwick & District
920	Rubery	956	Newport-on-Tay (Scotscraig)
921	Egham	957	Portadown
922	Stonehaven & District	958	Newton Stewart & District
923	Easter Ross	959	Stoke-on-Trent Wedgwood
924	Harleston & District	960	Rothwell & District
925	Preston South Ribble	961	South Manchester
926	Dundee Tayside	962	Woodvale & District
927	Downland Eastbourne	963	Wadebridge, Padstow & District
928	Lampeter		
929	Ascot	964	Builth Wells & District
930	Skelmersdale & District	965	Lyme Regis & District
931	Church Stretton & District	966	Longford & District
932	Henfield & Steyning	967	Forres & District
933	Didcot	968	Malling
934	Uckfield & District	969	Blackpool Progress
935	Hull Wyke	970	Portobello & District
936	Pwllheli & District	971	Maesteg
937	Albrighton & District	972	Pontypridd
938	Conwy	973	Shepton Mallet
939	Soke (Peterborough)	974	Wotton-under-Edge & District
940	Frodsham & District	975	Wick & District
941	Kelvin (Glasgow)	976	Aberdeen Deeside
942	Irvine Valley & District	977	Churchdown
943	Abergele & District	978	Ongar
944	Okehampton & District	979	Larbert
945	Storrington & District	980	Crowborough
946	Dun Laoghaire	981	Sandiacre & Stapleford
947	Banff & District	982	Sandhurst & Yateley
948	Garstang & District	983	Risca & District
949	Bishopbriggs & Kirkintilloch	984	Castle Douglas & District

985	Northampton Nene	1019	Warwick & District
986	Ayr Kyle	1020	Clarkston & District
987	Uddingston & Bothwell	1021	Blackwood & District
988	Loanhead & District	1022	Eyemouth & District
989	Horwich-West Houghton & District	1023	Edenbridge
		1024	Birtley
990	North Dublin	1025	Kintyre
991	Irby & Thurstaston	1026	Kilbarchan & District
992	Garnock Valley	1027	Bucksburn & District
993	Sligo & District	1028	City of Wells
994	Faringdon & District	1029	Chew Valley
995	Lapworth & District	1030	York County
996	Shanklin & District	1031	Stourport-on-Severn & District
997	Monifieth & District	1032	Holyhead
998	Derby Merlin	1033	Lucan
999	Darlington Bondgate	1034	Wheathampstead & District
1000	Sandy & District	1035	Hull Wilberforce
1001	Herne Bay	1036	Oldham Medlock Vale
1002	Twyford & District	1037	Brackley & District
1003	Teddington	1038	Malmesbury, Tetbury & District
1004	Buntingford & District		
1005	Headingley	1039	Spennymoor & District
1006	Newcastle-under-Lyme Mainwaring	1040	Gordano Valley
		1041	Penicuik
1007	Wetherby Wharfedale	1042	Coventry Mercia
1008	Llanfyllin & District	1043	Coventry Three Spires
1009	Rye & Rother Valley	1044	Carluke & District
1010	Lagan Valley	1045	Dengie Hundred
1011	Werrington & District	1046	Worcester Elgar
1012	Wroxham & District	1047	Caversham
1013	Southwell & District	1048	Burley-in-Wharfedale & District
1014	Larkhall & District		
1015	Ash & District	1049	Grange-over-Sands
1016	Biggin Hill	1050	Dunbar & District
1017	Holmes Chapel & District	1051	Macclesfield Forest
1018	Ennis & District	1052	Thurso & District

1053	Capel & East Bergholt	1089	Oundle, Thrapston & Distri
1054	Stewarton	1090	The Deepings
1055	Great Missenden & District	1091	Amesbury
1056	Topsham & District	1092	Frinton & Walton
1057	Blane Valley	1093	Byfleet & District
1058	Kilwinning	1094	Penistone
1059	Burnley Calder	1095	Nottingham East
1060	Bishopton & District	1096	Grimsby Clee
1061	Brightlingsea	1097	Weardale
1062	Narberth & Whitland	1098	Crewe & Nantwich Malban
1063	Highworth & Cricklade	1099	Portsdown & District.
1064	Poynton	1100	South Leicester
1065	Stornoway & District	1101	Norwich Castle
1066	Bournemouth North	1102	Bridge of Allan
1067	Bourne End & Flackwell Heath	1103	Upminster & District
1068	Goring & Streatley	1104	Lincoln Minster
1069	Oxford Cherwell	1105	Bearsted
1070	Cheltenham Spa	1106	Wishaw & District
1071	Killingworth & District	1107	Hailsham
1072	Rushen (I. of M.)	1108	Hornsea & District
1073	Ivybridge	1109	Hungerford
1074	Sedgefield & District	1110	Castlederg & District
1075	Maghera & District	1111	Chislehurst
1076	The Langleys	1112	Dartmouth
1077	Kentish Vale	1113	Newcastle & District
1078	Osgoldcross & Elmet		(Co. Down)
1079	Stalham & District	1114	King's Lynn Vancouver
1080	Wilmslow Bollin Valley	1115	Yarm & District
1081	Aberdeen Bon Accord	1116	Boston Fenland
1082	Holbeach & District	1117	Mullingar
1083	Turriff & District	1118	Toddington
1084	Dronfield	1119	Nidderdale
1085	Banchory & District	1120	East Neuk o'Fife
1086	Southampton West	1121	Martock & District
1087	Keith & District	1122	West Forest
1088	Sitlington & District	1123	Birmingham Hall Green

1124	Rother Vale	1160	Shepshed
1125	Orkney	1161	Montgomery & District
1126	Buckley & District	1162	Crook & Willington
1127	Stokesley & District	1163	Llwchwr
1128	Romney Marsh & District	1164	Bo'ness
1129	Calne	1165	Henleaze & District
1130	Speldhurst	1166	Delamere Forest
1131	Arklow & District	1167	Battle
1132	Currie and Balerno	1168	Luton Central
1133	Isle of Skye	1169	Dawlish
1134	Goyt Valley	1170	Stepps & District
1135	Bagshot & District	1171	Brighton Regency
1136	Wythall	1172	Boyle & District
1137	Wylam & District	1173	Cockfosters & Hadley Wood
1138	Perth Strathearn	1174	South Cotswold & Stonehouse
1139	County of Nairn	1175	Tenbury & District
1140	Dingwall	1176	Rugby Webb Ellis
1141	Westerham	1177	Douglasdale
1142	Bromley Ravensbourne	1178	Penkridge & District
1143	Darent Valley	1179	Banbury Cross
1144	Hayle	1180	Burntisland & District
1145	Dunelm	1181	Farnborough (Kent)
1146	Glevum	1182	North Manchester
1147	Avon Valley	1183	Weybridge & Oatlands
1148	Rainford & District	1184	Biddulph
1149	Wendover & District	1185	Eaglesham
1150	Pershore & District	1186	Donaghadee & District
1151	Baildon & District	1187	Bewdley
1152	Basingstoke Alençon	1188	Scarborough Castle
1153	Ellon & District	1189	Nailsea
1154	Bolton-le-Moors	1190	Bradford Idle
1155	Blantyre & District	1191	Duns & District
1156	Shawbury & District	1192	Isle of Bute
1157	Marks Tey & District	1193	Kilsyth & District
1158	Somerton & District	1194	Hamble Valley
1159	Ferndown & District	1195	Nithsdale

Round Table

1196	Tranent & District	1206	Derby Derwent
1197	West Quantocks	1207	South Westmorland
1198	Leatherhead North Down	1208	Aboyne & District
1199	Southport Hesketh	1209	Bromyard
1200	Lichfield District	1210	Isle of Islay
1201	Blessington & District	1211	Westhill & District
1202	Inverkeithing & Dalgety Bay	1212	Millom & District
1203	Mumbles	1213	Alford & District
1204	Ryedale	1214	Bloxwich
1205	Glendale		

Appendix B
Round Table Overseas
Associations

AUSTRIA

BELGIUM

CENTRAL AFRICA

DENMARK

EAST AFRICA

FINLAND

FRANCE

GERMANY

HONG KONG

ICELAND

INDIA

ITALY

JAMAICA

KOREA

LEBANON

LUXEMBOURG

MONACO

MOROCCO

NETHERLANDS

NEW ZEALAND

NORWAY

SOUTHERN AFRICA

SURINAM

SWEDEN

SWITZERLAND

WEST EQUATORIAL AFRICA

ZAMBIA

Countries in which Round Tables Exist but Where There Are No Separate Associations

BOTSWANA	MOZAMBIQUE
BRAZIL	NIGERIA
BURUNDI	REPUBLIC OF SOUTH AFRICA
CONGO	RHODESIA
ETHIOPIA	RWANDA
KENYA	SEYCHELLES
LESOTHO	SWAZILAND
MALAWI	TANZANIA
MALTA	THAILAND
MAURITIUS	UGANDA

Round Tables in Course of Formation

ABU DHABI	GHANA
BAHRAIN	SIERRA LEONE
DUBAI	TEHRAN

Appendix C

Officers of the Round Table 1927-1977

Presidents

1976–77	W. H. R. BURTT	DARLINGTON
1975–76	R. P. HUGGINS	READING VALLEY
1974–75	R. GABRIEL	BARROW-IN-FURNESS
1973–74	R. A. CHAPMAN	CATERHAM
1972–73	J. L. WATTS	WETHERBY
1971–72	C. M. THORPE	SCARBOROUGH
1970–71	R. D. G. STEVENS	HENFIELD AND STEYNING
1969–70	D. H. MASON	SEVENOAKS
1968–69	P. PERRY	GODALMING
1967–68	S. H. MACPHERSON	SWINDON
1966–67	D. M. TATLOW	WOLVERHAMPTON
1965–66	L. D. LAWTON	OLDHAM
1964–65	J. N. GOLDSBROUGH	SUNDERLAND
1963–64	B. S. COKER	GRAYS
1962–63	C. FIRTH	NELSON
1961–62	D. H. BRETHERTON	GLOUCESTER
1960–61	A. R. K. ASHTON	HAMMERSMITH
1959–60	J. A. COOKE	KINGSTON-UPON-THAMES
1958–59	J. P. BUSH	BARNSTAPLE
1957–58	D. A. ELLIOTT	BOURNEMOUTH
1956–57	E. S. BLISS	CARLISLE
1955–56	P. MYERS	WEMBLEY
1954–55	R. McL. HARDY	GUILDFORD
1953–54	G. J. B. THORNE	WOLVERHAMPTON
1952–53	J. WATSON	NORWICH

Round Table

1951–52	J. N. SMALLWOOD	KEIGHLEY
1950–51	I. F. CROMBIE	BRISTOL
1949–50	H. D. PRAAT	WATFORD
1948–49	G. B. WOOLFENDEN	LIVERPOOL
1947–48	F. L. CREW	HASTINGS
1946–47	R. W. H. COVELL	DORKING
1945–46	R. H. BATES	LIVERPOOL
1944–45	L. LILLICRAP	HASTINGS
1938–39	G. GALLIMORE	LEICESTER
1937–38	H. H. NORRIS	GUILDFORD
1936–37	E. M. TATLOW	WOLVERHAMPTON
1935–36	L. MARCHESI	NORWICH
1934–35	E. TAYLOR	DONCASTER
1933–34	A. W. DALLING	BRIGHTON
1932–33	RUTHERFORD LINDSAY	LIVERPOOL
1931–32	B. H. DURRANT	NORWICH
1930–31	K. PASCALL	LONDON
1928–30	J. WEBB	PORTSMOUTH

Honorary Secretaries

1975–77	F. D. PATTISON	WEARDALE
1973–75	W. H. R. BURTT	DARLINGTON
1971–73	C. C. M. EDNEY	BERWICK-UPON-TWEED
1969–71	R. F. BLAKE	WOKING
1968–69	R. D. G. STEVENS	HENFIELD AND STEYNING
1967–68	D. W. USHER	ASHTON-UNDER-LYNE
1964–67	C. K. DRAKE	DEESIDE
1963–64	L. D. LAWTON	OLDHAM
1962–63	J. N. GOLDSBROUGH	SUNDERLAND
1960–62	A. C. PARKHOUSE	NORTHAMPTON
1958–60	D. H. BRETHERTON	GLOUCESTER
1957–58	J. A. COOKE	KINGSTON-UPON-THAMES
1953–57	T. MURRAY	LONDON
1950–53	R. McL. HARDY	GUILDFORD
1948–50	C. W. BERRY	LIVERPOOL

1946–48	G. C. WHITAKER	BRADFORD
1939–46	C. S. MARSH	WIMBLEDON
1938–39	R. H. BATES	LIVERPOOL
1933–38	W. T. BARNARD	BOURNEMOUTH
1929–33	L. MARCHESI	NORWICH

Honorary Treasurers

1976–77	R. J. ANDERSON	SALTBURN
1974–76	R. BANGOR-JONES	LIVERPOOL CHILDWALL
1972–74	H. M. M. JOHNSTON	FALKIRK
1971–72	R. A. CHAPMAN	CATERHAM
1970–71	F. COLLINS	BERKHAMPSTEAD
1968–70	J. E. THOMPSON	BROMLEY
1966–68	J. D. BAKER	WALSALL
1963–66	D. W. USHER	ASHTON-UNDER-LYNE
1961–63	F. I. W. MOFFAT	FALKIRK
1960–61	B. S. COKER	GRAYS
1958–60	T. G. MASON	BECKENHAM
1956–58	R. PALFREYMAN	HEANOR
1952–56	C. M. CRAPPER	LONDON
1951–52	W. J. R. JUDKINS	CHATHAM
1949–51	C. K. SANDERS	WARRINGTON
1946–49	J. ALLEN	OXFORD
1945–46	S. LANE	BROMLEY
1939–45	F. L. CREW	HASTINGS
1936–39	J. H. ARCHER	FARNHAM
1935–36	W. J. PALMER	POOLE
1933–35	W. T. BARNARD.	BOURNEMOUTH
1929–33	W. G. QUINTON	NORWICH

Honorary Editors

1975–77	B. le MARQUAND	JERSEY
1974–75	J. JACKSON	SWADLINCOTE
1972–74	R. JAMES	CANNOCK
1971–72	C. W. BALDWIN	CHATHAM

1970–71	J. D. BELL	BROADSTAIRS
1968–70	D. A. ATHERTON	HATFIELD
1966–68	D. MASON	SEVENOAKS
1964–66	M. J. E. HARRISON	STRATFORD-UPON-AVON
1962–64	D. M. TATLOW	WOLVERHAMPTON
1961–62	J. N. GOLDSBROUGH	SUNDERLAND
1960–61	C. FIRTH	NELSON
1957–60	C. J. GEORGE	BRIGHTON
1955–57	C. TIPLER	GRANTHAM
1953–55	A. C. THORN	DARTFORD
1948–53	D. L. THORN	ROCHESTER
1946–48	H. COTTON	OXFORD
1938–45	H. M. RILEY	WOLVERHAMPTON
1936–38	C. A. RAMSDEN	HALIFAX
1933–36	B. D. WHITEAKER	WOLVERHAMPTON
1929–33	L. MARCHESI	NORWICH

Appendix D
RTBI Annual Conference Locations,
1927–1977

1977	GREAT YARMOUTH	1956	SCARBOROUGH
1976	BLACKPOOL	1955	TORQUAY
1975	TORBAY	1954	BRIGHTON
1974	BOURNEMOUTH	1953	BLACKPOOL
1973	BLACKPOOL	1952	BOURNEMOUTH
1972	BIRMINGHAM	1951	GREAT YARMOUTH
1971	BRIGHTON	1950	WESTON-SUPER-MARE
1970	EDINBURGH	1949	SOUTHPORT
1969	LONDON	1948	HASTINGS
1968	PWLLHELI	1947	HARROGATE
1967	BLACKPOOL	1939	SOUTHAMPTON
1966	BOURNEMOUTH	1938	CARDIFF
1965	BOGNOR REGIS	1937	SCARBOROUGH
1964	DOUGLAS (I. of M.)	1936	LONDON
1963	BRIGHTON	1935	HASTINGS
1962	SCARBOROUGH	1934	LIVERPOOL
1961	BLACKPOOL	1933	BRIGHTON
1960	EASTBOURNE	1932	BOURNEMOUTH
1959	ABERDEEN	1931	BLACKPOOL
1958	BOURNEMOUTH	1930	PORTSMOUTH
1957	HASTINGS	1929	NORWICH

Appendix E
The World Council of Young Men's Service Clubs (WOCO)

Wo-Co is a federation of the following young men's clubs: Active 20/30 International in USA and Central America; Apex clubs in Australia, South-East Asia, Papua, New Guinea, Sri Lanka; Kinsmen clubs in Canada; Round Table clubs in Austria, Belgium, Brazil, Central Africa, Denmark, East Africa, Finland, France, Germany, Great Britain and Ireland, Hong Kong, Iceland, India, Italy, Korea, Lebanon, Luxembourg, Monaco, Morocco, Netherlands, New Zealand, Nigeria, Norway, Southern Africa, Surinam, Sweden, Switzerland, West Equatorial Africa, Zambia. The JECC Clubs of Japan is an associate member.

The ideals and objects of Wo-Co are five-fold:

1. Concern for others
   Concern for others expressed by service projects large and small, internationally and locally, club and national projects to help the young, the sick, the handicapped, the old, the permanently disabled, the homeless, the victims of natural disasters such as earthquake and flood. All receive individual and collective support.

2. Worldwide fellowship
   To break through the barriers of nationalistic attitudes; to break down prejudices born through lack of first-hand knowledge, through contact, travel and meaningful discussion.

3. Promotion of tolerance, peace and understanding
   To have courage to seek to promote human dignity, tolerance, peace throughout the world regardless of colour, political or religious beliefs.

4. Cultivating high ideals

By cultivating the highest ideals in business, professional and civic traditions, demonstrating responsible and positive citizenship.

5. Improving the quality of life

To improve the quality of life through universal promotion of the above objectives and continued expansion of membership.

In its own information booklet issued in 1973 Wo-Co gave this answer to the question 'What is World Council?':

World Council is not a secret organisation nor is it a junior version of Rotary International. It is a universal federation of young men whose ideals are fellowship and service to others. These same ideals, born out of man's need for friendship, fellowship and understanding, have spread, been accepted and acclaimed in six continents by young men from business and professional backgrounds, representing many vocations and the widest range of religious and political beliefs, regardless of colour and creed.

Wo-Co has a strength of almost 100,000 young men *with each member* intent on attaining a high level of citizenship individually and the collective benefits which collective efforts can achieve.

Fellowship, Service, Understanding – this, in a few words, is World Council.

Bibliography

Kenneth Adams, *Exploring the Business Ethic*, London, St George's House Windsor Castle, 1971

Dr W. G. S. Adams, 'Voluntary Social Service in the 20th Century', *Voluntary Social Services Handbook*, London: National Council of Social Service, 1948

A. P. Cooper, *A fine city, Norwich*, Norwich: Norwich Publicity Association, 1970

John Creasey, *Round Table, The First Twenty-five Years*, London: National Association of Round Tables Great Britain and Ireland, 1953

C. R. Hewitt, *Towards My Neighbour, The social influence of the Rotary Club movement in Great Britain and Ireland*, London: Longmans, 1950

Maurice Horspool, *Scarborough 88, the Story of Scarborough Round Table 1934 to 1968*, Scarborough, 1968

Roy Lewis and Angus Maude, *The English Middle Classes*, London: Phoenix House, 1949

Kenneth Lindsay, 'Early Days of PEP – a Fragment of History', *Contemporary Review*, February 1973, vol. 222, no. 1285

R. S. Love and V. M. Branson, *Apex, The First Twenty-five Years*, Adelaide, 1955

Robert S. Lynd and Helen Merrell Lynd, *Middletown, A Study in American Culture*, New York: Harcourt Brace, 1929; London: Constable, 1929

Bibliography

Milner Riley and Arthur Johnson, *Wolverhampton Round Table no 17, the first 40 years history 1929/69*, Wolverhampton, 1969

Jean M. Robinson, *Circle, the Story of NALC*, Keighley: NALC, 1974

A Rotarian, *The Meaning of Rotary*, London: Percy Lund Humphries, 1927

Robert Tyre, *The Cross and the Square, the Kinsmen Story 1920–70*, Association of Kinsmen Clubs, 1970

Index

293

Index

Index

Index

Index

Index